Society for Arabian Studies Monographs No. 9

Series editors D. Kennet & St J. Simpson

Ports and Political Power in the *Periplus*: Complex Societies and Maritime Trade on the Indian Ocean in the First Century AD

Eivind Heldaas Seland

BAR International Series 2102
2010

Published in 2016 by
BAR Publishing, Oxford

BAR International Series 2102

Society for Arabian Studies Monographs 9
Ports and Political Power in the Periplus*: Complex Societies and Maritime Trade on the Indian Ocean in the First Century AD*

ISBN 978 1 4073 0578 3

© E H Seland and the Publisher 2010

The author's moral rights under the 1988 UK Copyright,
Designs and Patents Act are hereby expressly asserted.

All rights reserved. No part of this work may be copied, reproduced, stored,
sold, distributed, scanned, saved in any form of digital format or transmitted
in any form digitally, without the written permission of the Publisher.

BAR Publishing is the trading name of British Archaeological Reports (Oxford) Ltd.
British Archaeological Reports was first incorporated in 1974 to publish the BAR
Series, International and British. In 1992 Hadrian Books Ltd became part of the BAR
group. This volume was originally published by Archaeopress in conjunction with
British Archaeological Reports (Oxford) Ltd / Hadrian Books Ltd, the Series principal
publisher, in 2010. This present volume is published by BAR Publishing, 2016.

Printed in England

PUBLISHING

BAR titles are available from:

	BAR Publishing
	122 Banbury Rd, Oxford, OX2 7BP, UK
EMAIL	info@barpublishing.com
PHONE	+44 (0)1865 310431
FAX	+44 (0)1865 316916
	www.barpublishing.com

Society for Arabian Studies Monograph Series

Series editors: D. Kennet & St J. Simpson

The *Society for Arabian Studies Monograph Series* was launched in 2004 with the intention of encouraging the publication of peer-reviewed monographs on the archaeology, early history, ethnography, epigraphy and numismatics of the Arabian Peninsula and related matters. Creating a specific monograph series within the *British Archaeological Reports International Series* is intended to allow libraries, institutions and individuals to keep abreast of work that is specifically related to their areas of research. Whilst research and conference volumes in the series will all be peer-reviewed according to normal academic procedures, the decision was taken to allow the publication of doctoral theses, field reports, catalogues and other data-rich work without peer review where this will permit the publication of information that, for one reason or another, might not otherwise be made available.

Already published:

BAR –S1248, 2004 Sasanian and Islamic Pottery from Ras al-Khaimah *Classification, chronology and analysis of trade in the Western Indian Ocean* by Derek Kennet with a contribution by Regina Krahl. Society for Arabian Studies Monographs No. 1. ISBN 1 84171 608 1.

BAR –S1269, 2004 Trade and Travel in the Red Sea Region *Proceedings of Red Sea Project I held in the British Museum October 2002* edited by Paul Lunde and Alexandra Porter. Society for Arabian Studies Monographs No. 2. ISBN 1 84171 622 7.

BAR –S1395, 2005 People of the Red Sea *Proceedings of Red Sea Project II held in the British Museum October 2004* edited by Janet C.M. Starkey. Society for Arabian Studies Monographs No. 3. ISBN 1 84171 833 5.

BAR –S1456, 2005 The Tihamah Coastal Plain of South-West Arabia in its Regional Context c. 6000 BC – AD 600 by Nadia Durrani. Society for Arabian Studies Monographs No. 4. ISBN 1 84171 894 7.

BAR –S1661, 2007 Natural Resources and Cultural Connections of the Red Sea *Proceedings of Red Sea Project III held in the British Museum October 2006* edited by Janet Starkey, Paul Starkey and Tony Wilkinson. Society for Arabian Studies Monographs No. 5. ISBN 9781407300979

BAR –S1776, 2008 La Péninsule d'Oman de la fin de l'Age du Fer au début de la période sassanide (250 av. – 350 ap. JC) by Michel Mouton. Society for Arabian Studies Monographs No. 6. ISBN 978 1 4073 0264 5

BAR –S1826, 2008 Intercultural Relations between South and Southwest Asia *Studies in commemoration of E.C.L. During Caspers (1934-1996)* edited by Eric Olijdam and Richard H. Spoor. Society for Arabian Studies Monograph No. 7. ISBN 978 1 4073 0312 3

BAR –S2052, 2009 Connected Hinterlands *Proceedings of Red Sea Project IV held at the University of Southampton September 2008* edited by Lucy Blue, John Cooper, Ross Thomas and Julian Whitewright. Society for Arabian Studies Monographs No. 8. ISBN 978 1 4073 0631

Potential contributors

Please contact the editors in the first instance:

Dr Derek Kennet: Department of Archaeology, Durham University, South Road, Durham, England DH1 3LE
Derek.Kennet@durham.ac.uk

Dr St John Simpson: Department of the Middle East, The British Museum, London, England WC1B 3DG
ssimpson@thebritishmuseum.ac.uk

Summary

In the centuries around the turn of our era, long distance trade based on the monsoon winds connected all coasts of the western Indian Ocean. Ships from India, Arabia, Egypt, East Africa and Mesopotamia conveyed luxuries such as silk, spices and slaves, but also subsistence goods including grain and inexpensive textiles between coasts separated by thousands of kilometres of water. In the same period the first complex societies emerged in parts of Africa and Southern India. In other regions existing states reorganised or were replaced or marginalised by new polities. This study aims at exploring the significance of maritime commerce to societies on the Indian Ocean rim, by examining how rulers adjusted their policy in order to control and profit from trade. The point of departure is the anonymous Greek first century AD *Periplus of the Erythraean Sea*. This is a guide to navigation and trade on the Indian Ocean, covering the coasts of the Red Sea, Gulf of Aden, East Africa and India. The unknown author, who to a large extent relied on personal experience, included not only sailing directions, but also a wealth of information on local products, markets and political conditions.

Chapter 1 introduces the subject and the setting. Chapter 2 discusses how to measure the impact of trade on complex societies. Chapter 3 deals with the content and reliability of the *Periplus*. Chapters 4 through 8 survey the situation along the coasts of Arabia, Africa and western / southern India in detail, and argue that rulers and states utilised a range of policies in order to profit from the monsoon trade: Trade was centralised to one port in each kingdom, where it could be taxed and controlled. Rulers established restrictions or monopolies on the production, export and import of certain products or trade in general, and states invested heavily in infrastructure and military / administrative infrastructure to secure income from maritime trade.

The survey of trade and rulers reveals that societies on the Indian Ocean rim pursued targeted policies in order attract, facilitate and control maritime trade. Moreover, the eight polities discussed in the study show significant similarities with regard to the organisation of commercial activities. Most commodities traded in the Indian Ocean commerce originated in peripheral inland regions. All long-distance trade took place from one designated port of trade at the coast. Political centres were situated in agricultural areas inland, and were well positioned to control the flow of imported goods from the coast and exports from the countryside. Secondary centres of population and agriculture also existed, but these had access to the coast and the maritime trade only by way of the political centre. While climatic and topographical conditions influenced this situation, it is argued that the similarities between the different policies are sufficient to create a descriptive model of the relationship between maritime, long-distance trade and the early states on the Indian Ocean rim (chapter 10). This enables comparison across time and space, and constitutes a case for the significance of long-distance trade as an agent of change: one common impulse, maritime trade, spurred similar responses in different parts of a interregional system, supporting a rare case of interdependence in the ancient world.

Table of contents

Summary i
Table of contents iii
List of tables, maps and figures v
Acknowledgements vii

CHAPTER 1: THE CIRCUMNAVIGATION OF THE RED SEA 1
    Inland elites and maritime trade 1
    A cosmopolitan world in postcolonial context 2
    Classical history, colonial historiography, postcolonial criticism 3
    Scope 4

CHAPTER 2: TRADE AND THE INDIAN OCEAN STATE 7
    THE STATE AND THE ROLE OF TRADE 9
    RESEARCH STRATEGY 10

CHAPTER 3: THE *PERIPLUS MARIS ERYTHRAEI* 13
    TEXTUAL TRADITION, TEXTS AND TRANSLATIONS 13
    CONTENTS, AUTHOR, NATURE 14
    RELIABILITY 15

CHAPTER 4: SOUTHERN ARABIA 17
    SABA-HIMYAR 18
        Ports of Saba-Himyar 19
        Okêlis 19
        Eudaimôn Arabia 19
        Muza, myrrh and the maritime trade of Saba-Himyar 22
        A king and his vassal 25
        Saba-Himyar – the picture of government control 26
    HADRAMAWT 26
        Kanê – the market of Hadramawt 26
        Frankincense, frankincense production and frankincense ports 27
        Moscha Limên / Khor Rori / Sumhuram 29
        Hadramawt – the picture of government control 31

CHAPTER 5: THE AFRICAN COAST 33
    AKSUM – THE KINGDOM OF ZÔSKALÊS 34
        Trade at Adulis 36
        Zôskalês 38
        Aksum – the picture of government control 38
    THE "FAR-SIDE PORTS" – ALONG THE COAST OF THE SOMALI PENINSULA 39
        Avalitês 39
        Malaô and Mundu 39
        Mosyllon, the Spice Market and Opônê 40
        A detour into the cassia yielding regions 40
        Far-side Ports: trade and the state with no state 41
    RHAPTA AND THE EAST AFRICAN COAST 42
        Trade at Rhapta 43
        Rhapta: trade and the state with no state II 44
    DIOSCURIDÊS / SOCOTRA 44
        Dioscuridês: trade and the state with no state III 45

THE AFRICAN COAST - CONCLUSIONS	46
CHAPTER 6: FROM THE INDUS TO THE KONKAN	**47**
PORTS AND KINGDOMS	48
TRADE AT BARBARIKON / MINNAGAR	49
Trade and the state in Skythia	*50*
ARIAKÊ AND BARYGAZA	51
Royal involvement in trade at Barygaza	*54*
Networks meeting at Barygaza	*55*
SKYTHIA AND ARIAKÊ – THE PICTURE OF GOVERNMENT CONTROL	56
CHAPTER 7: THE MALABAR AND SOUTHERN INDIA	**57**
SOUTHERN PORTS AND KINGDOMS	57
THE *PERIPLUS* ON TRADE IN THE TAMIL KINGDOMS	59
THE ECOLOGY AND ECONOMY OF SOUTHERN INDIA	62
THE IMPACT OF TRADE	63
ROMAN COINS IN SOUTHERN INDIA	64
THE MALABAR AND SOUTHERN INDIA – THE PICTURE OF GOVERNMENT CONTROL	66
CHAPTER 8: INDIAN, PARTHIAN AND ARABIAN NETWORKS IN THE *PERIPLUS*	**67**
CHAPTER 9: SEPARATE SOCIETIES, SIMILAR STRUCTURES	**71**
SPATIAL ORGANISATION	71
Aksum	*71*
Saba-Himyar	*71*
Hadramawt	*72*
Skythia	*72*
Ariakê	*72*
Chera, Pandya, Chola	*73*
Conclusions: historical geography and infrastructure	*73*
Test case: areas outside state control	*74*
TRADE AND RULERS – STRATEGIES AND ATTITUDES	74
Centralisation	*74*
Administration	*76*
Expansion	*77*
KEY RESOURCES – IMPORTS AND EXPORTS	77
Imports	*77*
Exports	*78*
Test case: areas outside state control	*79*
TRADING DIASPORAS	79
SEPARATE STATES, SIMILAR STRUCTURES: CONCLUSIONS	80
CHAPTER 10: COMPLEX SOCIETIES AND MARITIME TRADE IN THE *PERIPLUS*	**83**
CONCLUDING REMARKS	85
BIBLIOGRAPHY	**87**
SOURCES	87
SECONDARY LITERATURE	89

List of tables, maps and figures

Table 1: Contents and reliability of the *Periplus* 15
Table 2: Quality of imports to Barygaza - past and present 52
Table 3: Regions reflected in Tamil love-poetry (adapted after K. Zvelebil) 62
Table 4: Rule of emperors mentioned in Chapter 7 64
Table 5: Indian, Arabian and Parthian maritime contacts in in the *Periplus* 68
Table 6: Terms denoting ports in the Periplus 75
Table 7: Terms denoting centres in the *Periplus* 84

Fig. 1: Map of the Indian Ocean at the time of the *Periplus* viii
Fig. 2: Map of Southern Arabia at the time of the *Periplus* 17
Fig. 3: The African coast at the time of the *Periplus* 33
Fig. 4: Map of India at the time of the *Periplus* 47
Fig. 5: Map of Southern India at the time of the *Periplus* 57
Fig. 6: Map of Indian, Parthian and Arabian trade routes in the Graeco-Roman sources 67
Fig. 7: Aksum: spatial-economic organisation 71
Fig. 8: Southern Arabia: spatial-economic organisation 72
Fig. 9: Skythia and Ariakê: spatial-economic organisation 73
Fig. 10: Tamil South India: spatial-economic organisation 73
Fig. 11: The Indian Ocean state and the monsoon trade 85

Cover illustration

Codex Palatinus Graecus 398: 41r, the page of the manuscript of the *Periplus* describing the Aksumite kingdom and the port of Adulis. Photo courtesy of Heidelberg University Library.

Acknowledgements

This monograph is a revised version of a thesis accepted for the PhD degree at the University of Bergen, Norway, 2006. I am much indebted to the editors of the Society for Arabian Studies Monographs, Dr. Derek Kennet and Dr. St John Simpson for their initiative, editorial efforts, comments and constructive criticism in the process of turning the thesis into a book. I am also grateful for the invaluable advice I have received along this road from Professor Vincent Gabrielsen, Dr. Sunil Gupta and Associate Professor Ingvar Mæhle, who served on the doctoral committee, and from the referee of this monograph in the present series.

My gratitude goes to the Norwegian Research Council for funding the PhD research, to Professor Jørgen Christian Meyer, who supervised the work, Professor Emeritus Richard Holton Pierce for extensive additional advice and tutoring, and the many friends and colleagues in Bergen and elsewhere, who contributed with their input, encouragement, practical help, hospitality or by sharing their work.

Finally, my greatest thanks go to my wife and our daughters, for their steadfast support and enthusiasm.

Fig. 1: Map of the Indian Ocean at the time of the *Periplus*

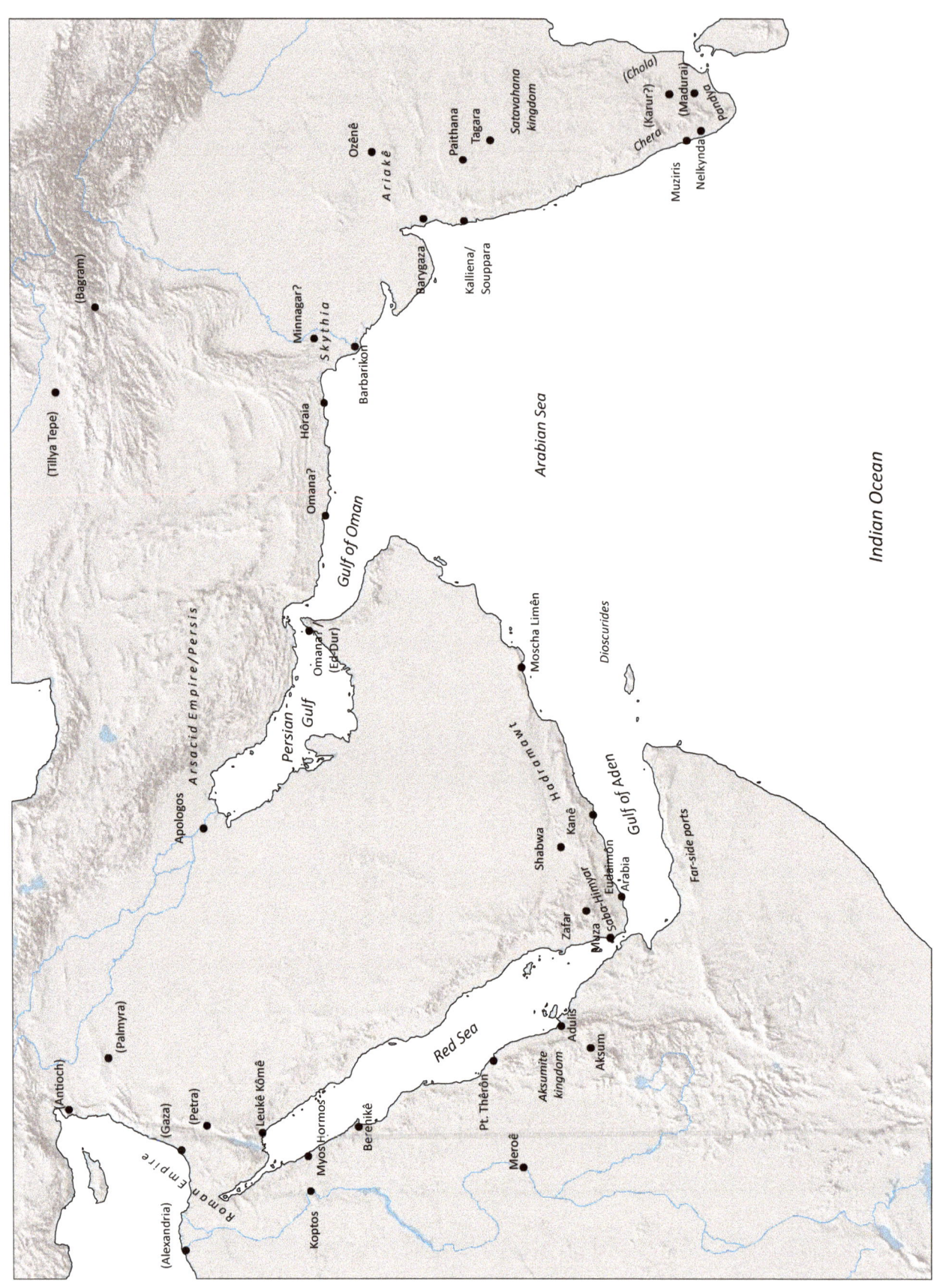

Chapter 1: The Circumnavigation of the Red Sea

In the mid first century AD, a merchant or sea-captain had his knowledge of the Red Sea and Indian Ocean committed to papyrus. A Byzantine scribe copied the Greek text to parchment in the early tenth century, and thus the report has survived in the work known to us as the *Periplus Maris Erythraei*, or "The Circumnavigation of the Red Sea". In those days this referred to the oceans known to us as the Red Sea, Gulf of Aden, Arabian Sea, Persian Gulf, Gulf of Oman and Bay of Bengal. Large parts of the anonymous document seems to be based on personal experience or firsthand accounts, marking it as unique in the corpus of surviving Graeco-Roman literature and among other sources from the Indian Ocean before Islam. The 66 brief chapters outline how to sail, what to sell, what to buy and who rules where along the coasts from Egypt to the Malay Peninsula. *En route*, the text provides an outsiders perspective on a number of aspects of exchange, production and political organisation in the societies on the Indian Ocean rim.

The backdrop for this practical handbook was the trade based on the monsoon winds, which had developed over the preceding centuries, connecting all shores of the western Indian Ocean. Ships from India, Africa, Arabia, and Mesopotamia hugged the coasts, or set sail straight across the ocean helped by the monsoon winds. The monsoons blow steadily from the southwest in the summer and from the northeast in the winter, facilitating passage from most ports and back again in the course of less than a year. Among the cargoes carried were horses, spices, textiles, metals, aromatics, ivory, silk, wine, slaves and grain.

In the same period, some of the regions participating in this maritime exchange experienced an increase in social complexity, and came to organise or reorganise their societies as what we call states. Arguably this was the case with the Chera, Pandya and Chola kingdoms formed in Southern India, which emerged among the more than a hundred dynasties known to modern scholars, to establish a three-state structure that remained stable for centuries. The kings of Aksum, controlling areas in modern Ethiopia and Eritrea, rose from seemingly unexceptional origins and established the first centralised polity in that region in more than 300 years. In areas that already had long traditions of statecraft, old kingdoms were overrun or marginalised by new or expanding polities. In Southern Arabia the kingdoms of Qataban, Main and Saba lost importance to and were eventually vanquished by other inland polities – Hadramawt and Himyar. In Northwestern India, the Sakas, a nomadic people from Central Asia, established two kingdoms called Skythia and Ariakê in Greek geographical literature, on the foundations of Alexander's Hellenistic successor-states and the Indian kingdoms formed after the collapse of the Maurya Empire. The Sakas in turn, would be ousted by Indo-Parthians and Kushans. In yet other regions, the Horn of Africa and the coast of East Africa, less complex levels of societal organisation were retained throughout the pre-Islamic period. Using the *Periplus Maris Erythraei* as its point of departure, the aim of this study is to investigate the relationship between the parallel processes of the developing monsoon trade and the emergence or reorganisation of complex societies on the Indian Ocean rim. The empirical objects are the historical polities of Aksum, Saba-Himyar, Hadramawt, Skythia, Ariakê, Chera, Pandya and Chola, while other regions on the Indian Ocean rim, are used as contrasting test cases.

Inland elites and maritime trade

These early polities in the western Indian Ocean were not primarily coastal. They all had access to the sea, but in most regions the littoral plains were unable to sustain large, sedentary populations. In Arabia and on the Red Sea coast of Africa this was due to lack of precipitation. In western India arable land was relatively scarce outside narrow river valleys. More attractive areas for agriculture were available on high ground inland, where political centres would not only be able to centralise the necessary agricultural surplus, but could also act as mediators between coastal populations and marginal areas like forests, mountains and areas outside the state, from which many commercially interesting products originated. With the notable exception of the lower Indus, the western Indian Ocean lacked major, navigable, perennial rivers. As power centres were situated inland and often in the highlands, overland caravan routes were the best alternative for regional exchange in most regions, while the rugged, hot and in many cases very dry coasts combined with the regularity of the monsoon system made maritime transport an attractive option for long-distance trade.

The start of the monsoon trade is lost in prehistory, but coastal and transoceanic networks were established already in the Bronze Age with the Pharaonic Red Sea expeditions to the elusive country of Punt and the trade between Mesopotamia and the Harappan cities.[1] In 332 BC Alexander the Great conquered Egypt from the Achaemenids, two years later Mesopotamia was added to his empire, and the northern coasts of the Red Sea and Persian Gulf became a part of the Hellenistic world. Gradually, the newcomers learned to master this novel seascape by adopting the patterns of already existing Indian Ocean networks.[2]

---

[1] Ray 1998: 11ff.; Ray 2003: 82ff, 103ff.
[2] Tchernia 1997: 250ff.

In 30 BC, Egypt was annexed by the Roman Empire, and with its connections on the Red Sea and Indian Ocean it became a part of an integrated Mediterranean economy. This coincided with the start of a prolonged period of political unity and stability in the Mediterranean, arguably fostering an increase in trade and a measure of economic growth, per capita as well as absolutely.[3] While imperial authorities appear to have taken little interest in the eastern trade except as a source of revenue,[4] their empire nevertheless constituted a significant new agent in the Indian Ocean trading system. The Roman world had a population at this time conservatively estimated by modern scholars at around 60 millions.[5] In terms of numbers, many were wealthy, in terms of proportions; most of them lived near subsistence level. All of them, however, had a potential interest in commodities from the Indian Ocean region, whether expensive silk garments for the super-rich or grains of pepper or frankincense for cooking, medical or religious use. Such commodities were expensive if measured by weight, but affordable to many or most if sold by the grain. To a large extent, this demand was paid for with a supply of prestige products, which local elites in the Indian Ocean region were able to utilise in political process within regional political structures.

A cosmopolitan world in postcolonial context

In the wake of Edward Said's *Orientalism* (1978), which constituted a fundamental critique of western literary and academic constructions the East, and Martin Bernal's *Black Athena* (1981), strongly criticising the ethnocentrism of classical studies, several works have shown how Graeco-Roman authors' descriptions of remote regions, including India and the Indian Ocean, must be considered literary constructions of "the other" rather than factual accounts.[6] It is important to maintain, however, that this does not apply equally to all Graeco-Roman literature or to all parts of Graeco-Roman accounts of India. As Grant Parker points out in *The Making of Roman India* (2008), several Roman geographic texts also incorporate information from merchants and travellers who had personal experience from the Indian Ocean Region, and the *Periplus* remains an exception to the general rule, being one of the very few non-literary texts in the classical tradition.[7]

The Indian Ocean world described by the *Periplus* was cosmopolitan in the truest sense of the word. The seasonality of the monsoon trade made it necessary for traders and seamen to spend prolonged periods of time away from home. A ship sailing to Egypt from an Indian port in January would arrive in February / March and return in July – September / October, stopping on its way in Arabia or Africa in order to replenish its water supplies. Monsoon travel was perhaps predictable, but not without risk, and shipwreck, piracy and slave trade would cause many people to end up in places far from home. As any process of cross-cultural trade in the pre-modern world, the ancient monsoon trade was characterised by lack of information, lack of security, asymmetrical power relations and high transaction costs. The customary institutional approach to these challenges was to deal through settlements of merchants on foreign ground, so-called trading-diasporas.[8] In the Indian Ocean at the time of the *Periplus,* we encounter a variety of such communities, which interacted not only with local authorities and merchants, but also with each other. In a setting like this, labels of nationality or ethnicity, whether ancient or modern, bear little weight. The *Periplus* itself, for instance, based on the language it was written in, is arguably a Greek work, but it was composed in the postclassical *Koinê* variety of that language, which was widely used in the eastern Mediterranean and parts of the Near East, by people of different ethnical and cultural backgrounds. The work can also be characterised as Roman, as it originated within the Roman Empire and relates to that political context, but it has Egypt as its point of view when approaching its subject, the Red Sea and Indian Ocean world. Judging from its contents, the unknown author spent considerable parts of his life in African, Arabian and Indian ports, but if his career as a captain or merchant was even moderately successful, chances are that he would spend as much as possible of his time in Egypt somewhere else than the hot and arid Red Sea coast.

Richard Hingley has convincingly argued that British imperial discourse was shaped by the 19th and early 20th century perception of the Roman Empire, and that the modern perception of that empire, including the study of ancient history and Roman archaeology, was in turn influenced by modern imperial discourse.[9] Himanshu P. Ray has shown how this legacy came to shape colonial archaeology on the Indian subcontinent.[10] The colonial origin of and influence on other regional archaeologies of the Indian Ocean seaboard are also clear. This study draws upon past scholarship in the tradition criticised by Hingley and Ray. In light of this, it might be useful to clarify that the many labels like Arabian, Aksumite, Indian, Roman etc., which are used in this study, are intended simply as geographical terms and are not meant to carry ethnic, national or other connotations. As Steven E. Sidebotham has pointed out, most traders on the Indian Ocean were probably Egyptian, Greek, Nabataean, Palmyrene, South Arabian and Indian;[11] we might safely add East African and Parthian as well. Still, Egypt was a part of the Roman Empire and "Roman" does remain a

---

[3] Hopkins 2002; Saller 2002.
[4] Sidebotham 1986: 176f.; Young 2001: esp. 73f., 89.
[5] Hopkins (2002: 198, 210f.)
[6] See Romm 1992 and Cartledge 2002 on the subject in general. Karttunen 1989; Whittaker 1998 and Parker 2008 on India and the Indian Ocean in particular.
[7] Parker 2008: 2f., 74ff., 118ff.171ff.

[8] Curtin 1996, esp. 1ff; 60ff., 96ff.
[9] Hingley 2000.
[10] Ray 2007, esp. 211f.
[11] Sidebotham 1986: 176.

convenient and accurate shorthand for ships that sailed out of the ports of that empire.

Classical history, colonial historiography, postcolonial criticism

Modern interest in the ancient monsoon trade and the Indian Ocean reaches back to the age of the early modern European expansion. Rulers, navigators and scientists found use for the then recently rediscovered Graeco-Roman texts on geography and navigation, which they hoped could help them in their own quest for domination of African and Asian waters. This resulted in a number of printed editions and translations of the *Periplus* and other geographical treatises.[12] That these texts were read for their surmised practical value is, for example, attested by the Italian translation of the *Periplus* by the Venetian scholar Giovanni Battista Ramusio, who included the ancient geographical work along with descriptions of the great discoveries of his own age in the first volume of his famous *Navigationes et Viaggi* from 1550. 17th century traveller Pietro Della Valle made reference to the *Periplus* in the description of his crossing from Surat to Basra in March 1623.[13] 150 years later, the Danish traveller Carsten Niebuhr still referred to the *Periplus* in his account of the crossing from Mocha in Yemen to Bombay in August – September 1763.[14]

The more scholarly interest in the history of the region started in the early 19th century, represented by William Vincent's annotated paraphrase of the *Periplus* and of the account of the voyage of Nearchus, Alexander the Great's admiral, from the Indus to the Persian Gulf, published in the years 1797-1805.[15] Several influential editions of the *Periplus* followed over the next century.[16] These spurred scores of books and articles on the ancient monsoon trade or aspects thereof in the period up to World War II. Theodor Mommsen's passages on Arabia, Africa and India in volume V of his monumental *Römische Geschichte* (1885),[17] can only impress the modern reader for their analytical sharpness and broad perspective, especially as they appeared in a work where they must have been of peripheral interest to the main subject matter. E.H. Warmington's *The Commerce between the Roman Empire and India* (1928) should be noted for its regional approach rather than a focus on one of the geographical areas bordering the Indian Ocean. This is a full history of the pre-Islamic monsoon trade, which also touched upon Indian, African and Arabian navigation. Nevertheless, the work has a clear emphasis on Roman trade combined with a tendency to see other actors in the trade as passive hosts and recipients, something that should perhaps be ascribed to its origin during the heyday of British imperialism.

While the large finds of Roman coins in Southern India had long been known, archaeology only entered the Indian Ocean study in earnest with the discovery of considerable amounts of "Roman" material (some of which has later been shown to be of Mesopotamian origin)[18] at the site of Arikamedu near Pondicherry in Southern India in the mid 1940s.[19] Mortimer Wheeler's *Rome Beyond the Imperial Frontiers* (1954) was to a large extent based on his own work at Arikamedu and elsewhere in India and Pakistan. Although Wheeler himself was aware of the problems with equating the presence of Mediterranean artefacts with the presence of Mediterranean traders,[20] and although he attempted to see the monsoon trade from an Indian point of view,[21] his work represents perhaps the culmination of Indian Ocean history as *Roman* history.[22]

George F. Hourani's *Arab Seafaring* (1951) concentrated on Arabian participation in the monsoon trade, but largely in the Islamic period. J. Innes Miller's *The Spice Trade of the Roman Empire* (1969), despite the title of the work, contributed to downplaying the Mediterranean role in the monsoon trade as it focused on other networks as suppliers in the spice trade. Manfred Raschke's *New Studies in Roman Commerce with the East* (1978) was a critical survey of 20th century research on Indian Ocean and so-called Silk Road trade. Raschke warned that too heavy reliance on the archaeological record was apt to give a biased picture of the balance and extent of ancient trade between Orient and Occident: few eastern artefacts, e.g. textiles and spices, have survived in western soil,[23] and western finds in eastern contexts report little or nothing about how or through whom they arrived.[24] Raschke unveiled a number of lofty constructions based on meagre sources, but arguably ended up in a minimalist trap with this hypercritical approach. He was unwilling to accept significant non-Roman participation in the Indian Ocean commerce except in coastal and regional exchange,[25] thus effectively reducing the pre-Islamic Indian Ocean trade to a Roman network of the first two or three centuries AD.[26] This view of commerce as a one-sided affair is not only incompatible with the available source material, but also undermines our understanding

---

[12] See Schoff 1995: 17ff. on early editions of the *Periplus*.
[13] Valle 1665: 5.
[14] Niebuhr 1774: vol. 1, 452.
[15] Vincent 1998.
[16] Müller 1855; Fabricius 1883 (critical editions); Schoff 1995 (translation and commentary, first published 1912).
[17] Mommsen 1904: 596ff.

[18] Tomber 2007.
[19] Wheeler, Gosh and Deva 1946.
[20] Wheeler 1955: 206f.
[21] Wheeler 1955: 158ff.
[22] See also Ferguson 1978; Raschke 1978; Dihle 1984 and Puskas 1987 in this tradition; Ray 2007 on colonial archaeology in India.
[23] Raschke 1978: 677f. This balance has improved after Raschke's days with the excavations of several port sites. Examples include non-Roman pottery sherds from Khor Rori in Oman (Sedov and Benvenuti 2002: 192ff.) and Berenikê in Roman Egypt, (Begley and Tomber 1999). At Berenikê botanical remains of a range of eastern imports have also been identified, Wendrich *et al.* 2003: 62ff.; Cappers 2006. See Parker 2004 for textiles.
[24] Raschke 1978: 677.
[25] Raschke 1978: 645.
[26] Raschke 1978: 678f.

of trade as a possible agent of cultural change. Two aspects of Raschke's work, however, have earned it lasting credit: his 75 page article was followed by more than 600 pages of notes, bibliography, maps and indices, making it an important source of bibliographical and historiographical information on the ancient Indian Ocean and overland trade, and his critique of the modernist tradition in ancient economic history indirectly opened the way for new studies of regional networks and subsistence trade.

From the 1980s onwards, history and archaeology have joined in a series of studies that emphasise the diverse nature of and participation in the Indian Ocean networks.[27] Excavations of coastal sites provide the material context of the meeting places of maritime trade.[28] Archaeological histories of Southern Arabia,[29] Aksum[30] and India[31] have replaced outdated or colonial studies and clarify the chronology and background of political and economic development. At the same time Indian Ocean archaeology is emerging as a field distinct from the regional archaeologies of the Indian Ocean countries,[32] and a series of interdisciplinary conferences have shed light on both ends and both sides of the Red Sea as zones of interaction.[33] New studies of the written sources have given insight into how the various commercial networks operated,[34] while research from a Mediterranean point of view has continued to increase our understanding of the Roman role in the trade.[35] Roberta Tomber's *Indo–Roman Trade from Pots to Pepper* (2008) surveys this recent research and brings together the different traditions in a way that will serve as a firm base for future studies in the field.

Himanshu P. Ray has over the last decades repeatedly demonstrated the potential of a multidisciplinary approach, combined with an outspoken regional focus on Indian Ocean history.[36] Ray combines Graeco-Roman sources with Indian literature, archaeology, marine archaeology and ethnoarchaeology. The picture emerging from her work is that of an Indian Ocean system reaching back to the Bronze Age and originating in coastal and regional exchange.[37] Ray writes Indian Ocean history in the *longue-durée*. In that perspective, the Mediterranean presence on the Indian Ocean stage is an episode of passing significance.[38] While her perspective is diametrically opposite from that of Raschke, the implications of their work arguably overlap: Raschke saw the Romans as the only interesting actors in long-distance trade,[39] but also claimed that the contact with the Mediterranean had little or no effect on the Indian Ocean societies it touched.[40] Ray disagrees with Raschke on the dominant role of Mediterranean traders, but also holds long-distance trade with the Mediterranean to be of secondary importance and interest to more stable internal and regional structures when interpreting the historical dynamics of the Indian Ocean.[41] This study takes a third stand, namely that the monsoon trade *was* important, that the different monsoon networks resembled each other closely, and that the impact of trade with the Mediterranean on Indian Ocean economy and political structure *was* significant. Moreover, that this was not through some western dynamic inspiration on a never-changing East, as a historian like Warmington, working in the colonial period, could claim,[42] but because the monsoon trade provided local elites around the Indian Ocean with the tools they needed in order to succeed in their regional struggles for power.

Scope

The key issue, then, pursued throughout this book, is the relationship between the states on the Indian Ocean rim, represented by their rulers, and the long-distance maritime exchange networks as they appear in the *Periplus*. The historiographical tradition provides the point of departure, but leaves open important problems in terms of trade and political power. How did rulers relate to trade? How could the development of complex societies benefit from trade? Vice versa, did trade benefit from the existence of centralised power? In other words, do our sources enable us to establish the importance of trade for the formation, existence or organization of complex societies on the Indian Ocean rim, thus explaining a similar development in regions separated by vast stretches of water?

Most new research on the Indian Ocean in antiquity stems from archaeology. This is a work of history, and it is essentially an analysis of the Red Sea and Indian Ocean world as it appears in the *Periplus*. This leads to omissions. The Kushans and Andhras / Satavahanas of India, the Parthian / Arsacid Empire of Mesopotamia, Persia and the Persian Gulf, and the early kingdoms of Sri Lanka are for instance barely mentioned, as they hardly figure in the *Periplus*. This does not imply that

---

[27] Begley and De Puma (eds.) 1991; Boussac and Salles (eds.) 1995; 2005. Reade (ed.) 1996; De Romanis and Tchernia (eds.) 1997; Ray and Salles (eds.) 1998; Ray (ed.) 1999; Gupta 2002; Peacock, Williams and James (eds.) 2007 ; Seland (ed.) 2007; Tomber 2008.
[28] Prominently Qana in Yemen (Sedov 1992; 1998; 2007), Arikamedu in India (Begley 1983; Begley *et al.* 1996), Berenikê in Egypt (Sidebotham and Wendrich 1999; Wendrich *et al.* 2003), Myos Hormos in Egypt (Peacock and Blue 2006), Adulis in Eritrea (Peacock *et al.* 2004; Peacock and Blue 2007), Khor Rori in Oman (Avanzini 2002) and Kamrej in India (Gupta *et al.* 2004).
[29] Schippmann 2001; De Maigret 2002.
[30] Munro-Hay 1991; Phillipson 1998; Finneran 2007.
[31] Champakalakshmi 1999; Chakrabarti 2001; Olivelle (ed.) 2006.
[32] In this respect the launching of the annual *Journal of Indian Ocean Archaeology* in 2004 is perhaps of special significance along with works like Ray 1998; 2003 and Tomber 2008, which all combine detail with overview.
[33] Lunde & Porter (eds.) 2004; Starkey (ed.) 2005; Starkey, Starkey & Wilkinson (eds.) 2007; Blue *et. al.* (eds.) 2009.
[34] E.g. Frezouls 1984; Salles 1995; 1996; De Romanis 1997a; 1997b; Parker 2002; Seland 2005a; 2005b.
[35] Sidebotham 1986; Young 2001.
[36] Ray 1986; 1998; Ray 2003.

[37] Ray 1998: 2, 12ff.; 2003: 82ff.
[38] Ray 1998: 5ff., 50f.; 2003: 165ff., 181f.
[39] Raschke 1978: 645.
[40] Raschke 1978: 679.
[41] Ray 1995; 1998: 5f., 48ff.; 2003: 161f.
[42] Warmington 1995: 1.

their role in Indian Ocean history is not acknowledged. Similarly, other literary sources and the large and growing archaeological database of the Indian Ocean rim are utilised here to provide and fill out the context for the snapshot provided by *Periplus*, rather than for their own sake, for the account of the *Periplus* is and remains a snapshot. It gives a broad view of the Red Sea-Indian Ocean world at one point in history, providing the same kind of information for a series of different communities. This is also its great merit. What it lacks in detail and diachronity is made up for by its suitability for comparison and for the study of interdependence: how different parts of a system relate to each other.

In the next chapter state definitions, theories of the origin of the state and the place of trade in the development of complex societies are discussed in order to arrive at a theoretical point of departure for the subsequent empirical discussion. It concludes with an outline for a research strategy on how to measure the impact of trade on state development, based on the fragmentary and partly static source material at hand. Chapter 3 goes into details on the main source for this study and what we can expect to learn from it.

In Chapters 4 through 7 the relationship between trade and political power is explored, dealing with the coasts of Arabia, Africa, Northwest India and South India respectively. These chapters follow the narrative flow of the *Periplus* with one important divergence: Arabia is treated before Africa in order to supply the political and historical background for the Arabian diaspora encountered on the African coasts. Chapter 8 looks briefly at Indian, Parthian and Arabian trading networks as they are depicted in the *Periplus*. In Chapter 9, empirical finds are compared and discussed thematically in the light of the research strategy outlined in Chapter 2. The study ends with the introduction of a model of trade and the Indian Ocean state as seen in the *Periplus*.

Chapter 2: Trade and the Indian Ocean state

What is the state, or more to the point: what can be called a state in an Indian Ocean context? How can we measure the impact of trade on the development, existence or policy of complex or state societies in an Indian Ocean setting? This chapter surveys the theoretical tradition on the formation of complex societies, with emphasis on the potential of Max Weber's model of the patrimonial state as a point of departure for the study of trade and the state. Weber's patrimonial state is seen in connection with Karl Polanyi's methodological approach to pre-modern trade. The aim is not to give an exhaustive account of theoretical problems connected to the broader subjects of the ancient economy and its relation to the origin of the complex societies, but to supply the analytical tools needed to approach the available source material for the different first-century Indian Ocean kingdoms.

The most influential modern state definition was coined by Max Weber in 1919 in his lecture *Politik als Beruf*. To Weber, three characteristics of the modern state were fundamental: its territorial control, its monopoly on the use of legitimate force within this territory and the legitimacy of the state itself, justifying its existence, its territoriality and its use of force.[43] As Weber was well aware, few pre-modern political organisations lived up to these demands.[44] Ancient polities seldom had strictly defined territorial boundaries and seem often to have been established by the relationship between rulers and subjects as much as by their territory. In the *Periplus* we encounter rulers and polities such as "Malichus, king of the Nabataeans",[45] "Charibaêl, legitimate king of two peoples, the Homerite and the one lying next to it, called the Sabaean"[46] and – "the kingdom of Eleazos, the frankincense-bearing land."[47] While the latter example does connect the ruler to a territory, the others emphasise groups of subjects. The point is not that ancient rulers did not care about territories as they most certainly did, but to keep in mind that "state" is a modern term, with varying relevance to historical societies. As better options are lacking, the term is widely used for a range of pre-modern political organisations, although its demarcation is and has been subject to controversy.[48]

Starting with Friedrich Engels in the late 19th century, a lengthy historical and anthropological tradition has tried to explain the nature and origin of the first complex societies. Engels focused on social stratification due to differential access to key resources as the prime mover in the process in state formation,[49] an approach which had considerable influence in the 20th century, not least due to the Morton Fried,[50] whose work can be said to represent a modern and mature version of Engel's theories on state formation, although without the constraints of orthodox Marxism. Another school of thought, starting with Robert Lowie, was rooted in the much older philosophical notion of the social contract. Lowie held that voluntary co-operation in order to meet desirable ends over time resulted in the social stratification, which is generally seen as a hallmark of statehood.[51] Gordon Childe and particularly Karl Wittfogel believed the development and management of irrigation to be of prime importance,[52] and Elman Service focused on the existence of charismatic and resourceful leaders who achieved key positions in re-distributional networks.[53]

These approaches, however, had one common weakness: they claimed universal validity. Critics were able to find ample examples of societies that appeared to follow different patterns of development, and of societies that seemingly met the prerequisites for statehood, but where states never developed. The failure to find universal, mono-causal explanations to the origin of the state caused subsequent research to take a different approach. In place of the search for prime movers, comparative studies were conducted with the aim of finding characteristics common to early states, and the existence of various roads to statehood was accepted. Henri Claessen, Peter Skalnik and Ronald Cohen led the way in this work,[54] but one unsolvable problem remained: what one chooses to call a state will inevitably depend on which definition one applies.

In an article on the formation of the ancient Kingdom of Israel, David Master has questioned the relevance of this evolutionary tradition to the study of ancient Near Eastern societies.[55] Master claimed that the focus on a teleological band-tribe-chiefdom-state development prevalent in the theoretical tradition reduces historical research on these societies to subjective exercises of categorisation.

Master's answer was to blow the dust off Max Weber's work.[56] While Weber heavily influenced how we view the modern state, his thoughts on the ancient state have

---

[43] Weber 1992: 157ff.
[44] Weber 1992: 158f.
[45] *Periplus* 19:6.29, (πρὸς) Μαλίχαν, βασιλέα Ναβαταίων.
[46] *Periplus* 23:7.27-28, Χαριβαήλ, ἔνθεσμος βασιλεὺς ἐθνῶν δύο, τοῦ τε Ὁμηρίτου καὶ τοῦ παρακειμένου λεγομένου Σαβαίτου.
[47] *Periplus* 27:9.4-5, βασιλείας Ἐλεάζου, χώρας Λιβανωτοφόρου.
[48] See Fried 1967; Claessen and Skalnik 1978 and Marcus and Feinman 1998 for different approaches to terminology and definitions.

[49] Engels 1970.
[50] Fried 1967.
[51] Lowie 1962.
[52] Childe 1950; Wittfogel 1959.
[53] Service 1975.
[54] Claessen and Skalnik 1978; Cohen and Service 1978.
[55] Master 2001: 123ff.
[56] Master 2001: 128ff.

largely been overshadowed by the traditions following and opposing Engels. In Weber's view, the main difference in terms of organisation between modern and pre-modern societies was the emphasis of modern society on authority resting on rational norms: according to the norm, office is held by those qualified for it and their authority is limited to their area of qualification.[57] This is the bureaucratic way of organising society. According to Weber, ancient society was, in contrast to this, founded on tradition and personal association, rather than on rational norms as we see them.[58]

Here Weber drew on the model of the so-called *oikos-economy* introduced in the second half of the 19th century, first by K. Rodbertus[59] but later revised and developed by Karl Bücher,[60] who was to spur the first round of the huge and not very enlightening modernism - primitivism controversy within the academic discipline of ancient history.[61] According to Bücher, the basic unit of ancient society was the *oikos* or household. A single adult male acted as the sole ruler and legal representative of such households, which included not only children and wives but also slaves, workers and other dependants. In the closed household economy all production was aimed at consumption within the household. In its pure form, exchange did not take place. There was no upper limit to the size of an *oikos*. Each household saw to its own needs, not only in agricultural produce, but also in tools, metal, clothing and the like. The state is simply seen as a large household, where a sole king or emperor or a body of citizens like a city council, fills the position of the "housefather".[62]

Weber, who adopted the main aspects of this analysis,[63] held that ties of loyalty within such households could be both strong and flexible to the extent that its members accepted tradition and respected their master. Clusters of such households could and would frequently organise on the model of a single household, and when this happened, the combined economic strength of the households would be at the disposal of their common leader(s). The model is also applicable on a state level, where the result would be what Weber called *Patrimonialherrschaft* – the patrimonial state. In this kind of society, the ruler would have certain obligations to his subjects and his power would be constrained by tradition, still he would in theory control the productive capacity and surplus of the entire population.[64]

Weber's *Idealtypus* of the patrimonial state would face the same problems as other theories of social evolution if put to test on the large and diverse empirical material. It would certainly be not only possible but also quite easy to find aspects of first century Indian Ocean societies, which do not fit with Weber's model. But the model of the patrimonial state is not valid or invalid as such, just more or less relevant to the problems and data at hand, and it has the merit of being highly relevant in one important respect: it focuses on rulers rather than on institutions as the representatives of dynamic societies. Weber's view of the state underlines the continuity from the big-man role in archaic society as described for instance by Elman Service,[65] to the role of the king or other rulers in complex societies. The ruler carries with him his portfolio of functions into early state society, including the re-distributional role to which trade was potentially important.

Regarding the polities around the Indian Ocean in the ancient period, there is little doubt that at some point of time they did eventually reach a level of societal complexity which can reasonably be described as statehood according to most definitions of early or archaic states proposed in the evolutionary tradition. At what time these societies took the step from "tribal-" to "state" society is interesting in itself, and it could perhaps be determined even from the fragmentary source material we have at hand. Still, the answer would inevitably depend on what state-definition is applied and would remain open to debate. Weber's approach frees us from this problem. Rather than a set of pre-defined stages it underlines complex society as a dynamic process where different factors have the potential to play different roles in different situations and at different times.

The apparent impossibility of creating a state-definition valid for ancient society in general and the Weberian view of the state as a continuous process rather than a set of stages do not, however, free us from the problem of describing the state as we encounter it on the Indian Ocean rim in the ancient period. In *The Ground Plans of Archaic States*, Kent V. Flannery argued that the existence of settlement hierarchies of at least four levels as reflected by differences in size and nature of archaeological sites, has proved a successful criterion for identifying states archaeologically.[66] Flannery in turn drew on the work of Henry T. Wright and Gregory A. Johnsen, who focused on the existence of hierarchies of administrative centres as the hallmark of complexity in their work on south-western Iran.[67] Only limited archaeological data of this kind is available for the Indian Ocean rim, but the consistent use of terms denoting rulers

---

[57] Weber 1964: 1034ff.
[58] Weber 1964: 739ff.
[59] Rodbertus 1865.
[60] Bücher 1979.
[61] "Primitivists", later often called "substantivists" in the parallel debate in the social sciences in order to avoid chronological connotations, held that the economic sector of ancient society was embedded in the larger social context, and could therefore not be analysed using the concepts of modern economic science. Modernists or formalists, on the other hand believed that the basic difference between ancient and modern economy was of scale rather than of nature, and that such analytical concepts were thus well adapted to all economies ancient and modern.
[62] Bücher 1979: 103ff.
[63] Weber 2006: 327ff.

[64] Weber 1964: 745ff.
[65] Service 1975: esp. 291ff.
[66] Flannery 1998: 15ff.
[67] Wright and Johnson 1975.

and centres in the *Periplus* provides us with a literary alternative. Although they did not use the terminology, the ancients had their own conception of the difference between complex and less complex societies, and the author of our main source, the anonymous Greek merchant's handbook *Periplus Maris Erythraei*, operates with a consistent hierarchy between "king" – *basileus* and "chief" – *tyrannos*. While we do not know what criteria, if any, our author used to determine which polities were ruled by kings and which by chiefs, we cannot ignore that his choice of the terms represented a distinction that very much resembles our need for a separation between states and non-states. Moreover, he identifies several levels of centres in the societies he describes: in polities where he knows where the king lives, he is said to live in a *mêtropolis*,[68] a "capital". Other important centres are called "cities" – *poleis*. One of them, Sauê in Southern Arabia was the seat of a *tyrannos* who seems to have acted as a vassal ruler for the *basileus* of the kingdom of Saba-Himyar.[69] Another *polis*, Ozênê, was a former seat of royal residence in western India,[70] which had by the time of the *Periplus* come under control of a different *mêtropolis*. Market towns on the coast are called "ports of trade" – *emporia*. Other coastal centres are labelled "villages" – *kômai* and "harbours" – *hormoi*.[71] The author of the *Periplus* was an outsider. He probably had only limited and incomplete knowledge of the political hierarchies in the societies he described. This, however, is amended by his external perspective, which provides us with a consistent terminology covering the whole region in question, and which we could not hope to get by way of archaeology or by combining indigenous sources.

Inspired by Wright / Johnson and Flannery's approach to the problem of identifying the early state, this allows us to derive a set of minimum criteria shared by all societies around the Indian Ocean ruled by kings (*basileis*), and not shared by those ruled by chiefs (*tyrannoi*). Following the *Periplus*, we arrive at the following state-definition valid for the empirical setting of first century Indian Ocean:

> The state is a political organisation controlling a territory (not necessarily continuous) with a hierarchy consisting of at least two levels of centres united under a ruler or a body of rulers, exercising control over secondary centres from a primary centre.

The state and the role of trade

Having thus defined the state it is time to turn our attention to trade. In order to appreciate the role of trade for the state the first choice should be to go by way of the state itself. Weber's approach outlined above allows us to focus on how *rulers* related to trade, which is exactly what our sources can tell us about. Is it possible to show that participation in maritime exchange was vital to the rulers of the states around the Indian Ocean? If so, the importance of maritime trade to the states themselves has also been established. The most interesting actors in this context are not the merchants, but the rulers. The critical question is not *who* conducted the trade or *how* they did it, but *what function did it serve?*

The means to answer that question was proposed in 1957 by professor in economic history at the Columbia University, Hungarian born Karl Polanyi. Together with Harry W. Pearson and anthropologist Conrad Arensberg he headed a research project on the origins of economic institutions. The result of their joint work, the book *Trade and Markets in the Early Empires*[72] was to change the way we interpret ancient economic history. Polanyi's main point was that a market economy where prices fluctuate according to supply and demand, is not and never has been a universal phenomenon, but first and foremost an 18th century and later European. Through a series of empirical studies they bridged the gap between theory and empirical data, and they showed the irrelevance (in their opinion) of modern economic theory to the study of historical societies, because these (in their view) lacked the institution that is the very subject of economic theory, viz. the price-making market. As people in pre-modern societies had no concept of economy in the modern sense, the lack of this institution in Polanyi's opinion made the study of "primitive" economic life independent of other aspects of society impossible. Economic actions were guided by social relationships, or to use their own words: "The facts of the economy were originally embedded in situations that were not in themselves of economic nature, neither the ends nor the needs being primarily material".[73]

Polanyi and his co-workers were concerned with the role of the economy in ancient society, rather than with the origin of the ancient state. They supplied the framework needed to make use of anthropological data and theory in the analysis of the economy of ancient societies. The tools they provided came from anthropological rather than economic theory and were the concepts of *reciprocity, redistribution and exchange*. Reciprocity, often called gift-exchange, is the mutual exchange of goods or services of comparable value between individuals or groups on the same social level in order to strengthen, establish or maintain social ties. Redistribution describes the collection and distribution of goods through a centre, e.g. a temple or a ruler, and exchange means the process of goods changing hand by impersonal transactions in a market, whether by sale or by barter.[74]

---

[68] This information is unavailable for two kingdoms, Chera and Pandya in Southern India, where the author of the *Periplus* knows only that the kings "reside in the interior", *Periplus* 55:18.11-12, (οἱ βασιλεῖς) ἐν τῇ μεσογαίῳ κατοικοῦσιν.
[69] *Periplus* 22-23.
[70] *Periplus* 48.
[71] Ch. 10, pp. 83ff. deals with this hierarchy in detail.

[72] Polanyi, Arensberg, and Pearson 1957.
[73] Polanyi, Arensberg, and Pearson 1957: 242.
[74] Polanyi, Arensberg, and Pearson 1957: 250ff.

With this analytical toolbox, Polanyi made the importance of trade to ancient societies easier to approach. Not only do the terms of "reciprocity" and "redistribution" bridge the gap between economic and social ties, making them two sides to the same story, they also lend meaning to the political logic of archaic society as we find it expressed in a multitude of sources and inscriptions, ranging from Norse sagas to Tamil poems, perhaps best expressed in the Roman saying *do ut des* – "I give, that you may give".[75]

Polanyi defined trade as the "relatively peaceful way of acquiring goods which are not available on the spot," the word "peaceful" underlining its two-sidedness and separating it from piracy, hunts etc.[76] By adopting Polanyi's rather wide definition it should be possible to avoid the trenches of the century-old and still flourishing debate about the nature of the ancient economy that started with the introduction of Bücher's *oikos*-theory. The questions of how trade was organised, how much it contributed to the economic output of ancient states and whether it followed the rules of modern economic science or not *do* remain interesting. Nevertheless, the vital aspect is that goods changed hand, and within Polanyi's framework, rulers and states could perfectly well engage in trade. Reciprocity and exchange would be the two possible ways of conducting this trade, whereas reciprocity and redistribution explain the need of rulers to engage in trade and their potential for mobilising resources to that end.

Polanyi and his colleagues drew a picture of typical ancient states as inland/river based, sceptical or even fearful of trade[77] and primarily concerned with consumption[78] rather than production. Polanyi's view of pre-modern society drew heavy and substantial criticism,[79] but as with Weber, it is not his description of history, but his analytical tools that remain interesting decades after they were introduced. Exactly in this focus by early states and rulers on *consumption* and as Moses Finley would later emphasise, on *status*,[80] lies the key to understand the relative importance of trade to these societies. Trade, regardless whether it was conducted through reciprocal gift-giving, barter or market-exchange, was the best possible source of prestige goods needed for the conspicuous consumption,[81] redistribution and further gift exchange vital to the social structure of the participating societies and instrumental in the competition between elites described by Colin Renfrew as "peer polity interaction".[82] The exchange or redistribution of prestige goods was a way of forming relationships to allies and subjects in these societies. In the empirical context of the Indian Ocean in the ancient period, such goods included wine, slaves and tableware imported especially for the local ruler. Such commodities were not necessarily numerous, but that does not mean that they were unimportant.

Research strategy

It is time to return to the Indian Ocean. This study surveys the importance of trade for the kingdoms of Saba-Himyar, Hadramawt, Skythia, Ariakê, Aksum, Chera, Pandya and Chola. The latter four of these polities were relative newcomers as we enter the history of the Indian Ocean in the first century AD. The other four had roots centuries back in time, either indirectly as secondary states taking over the areas of earlier states by conquest, or as independent polities of their own. By the first century, however, these established states all seem to have undergone recent organisational changes that could coincide with external factors, for instance trade. The discussion above made it clear that we cannot hope to identify trade as the single cause of the emergence of statehood in these areas. Still, the states around the Indian Ocean seem to reveal remarkable similarities despite the fact that they were separated by thousands of kilometres of water. When setting out to explain a parallel development in areas separated by such formidable distances and barriers, it is crucial to identify which potential agents of change they have in common. On the Indian Ocean rim around the turn of our era, long-distance maritime trade stands out.

Any research strategy must be developed in dialogue with the available source material, and a critical problem in the study of the importance of trade for the emerging state is the nature and scarcity of the sources. Our sources provide glimpses of the situation in one or several regions at specific point of times. These glimpses can to some degree be compared to show change over time, but the reconstruction of a development for the whole region remains hazardous. It might be possible to suggest, but it will probably be impossible to conclude, that trade was a critical factor in the process of increased complexity in these societies. What it will be possible to measure, however, is *the significance of trade* for these polities at the time of our sources.

How, then, can one study the significance of trade for the state? As the monsoon trade in the Indian Ocean is the common background the societies are seen against, their attitude to maritime trade and their economic organisation and development in matters related to this trade seem attractive indicators of the relative importance of trade. The underlying assumption is that if it can be established that a) rulers took active measures to participate in and/or profit from trade, and that b) the rulers who succeeded in getting their share of the monsoon trade were the rulers who succeeded in establishing or maintaining power, the importance of trade for the existence and development of these societies has been established. Four variables shed light on this:

---

[75] Known through Justinian's *Digesta* 19.5.5.
[76] Polanyi, Arensberg, and Pearson 1957: 257f.
[77] Polanyi, Arensberg, and Pearson 1957: 38ff.
[78] Polanyi, Arensberg, and Pearson 1957: 258f.
[79] E.g. Cook 1966; Firth 1972: 468ff.
[80] Finley 1992: 51ff.
[81] Veblen 1957: 68ff.
[82] Renfrew 1986.

• **Spatial organisation – historical geography and infrastructure:** A society is more than its institutions. In an economic context, its geography and infrastructure is just as, or maybe even more, interesting. Where did trade routes run? Where were the main centres of habitation, production and commerce situated, and how did these relate to each other and to the political centre? The economic layout of the kingdoms as shown by settlement, production and exchange patterns can indicate to what extent the political centre controlled production, import and export of key commodities.

• **Trade and rulers – strategies and attitudes:** Rulers adopted different strategies in order to profit from trade. Perhaps the most straightforward solution was piracy directed against traders passing their coasts. Another possibility was to demand gifts from visiting traders in return for protection and the right to trade, whereas a third solution was to guarantee safety of trade by law and to levy set taxes in return. The two latter strategies both enabled rulers to take active part in the trade if they wished to, but did they? To the extent that rulers participated in the trade, did they maintain monopolies on certain goods or even on foreign trade in general?

• **Key resources – imports and exports:** It is vital to establish the key products of the monsoon trade, their provenance and function. Certain imports, such as wine in South India, seem to have had a political function in the receiving societies. Similarly, aromatics were extensively used for religious, medical, cosmetic and funerary purposes across the ancient world. It is crucial to identify such goods and their function. They represent powerful incentives to engage in trade, and are potential instruments of social stratification in the participating polities. The question of exports is of equal importance, because it tells us why the area was commercially interesting to outsiders. Outside demand for local products constitutes a stimulus to participate in maritime exchange, and control of key exports was of the greatest importance if rulers were to acquire the goods they desired themselves.

• **Trading diasporas:** Our sources attest the presence of groups of merchants settled on foreign soil around the Indian Ocean. Such diasporas are highly interesting as they constitute not only possible agents of change, but also an institutional framework for trade in areas with no centralised power.

These four variables serve as the backdrop for a discussion of the coasts of Arabia, Africa and India, as they are described in our main source, the *Periplus Maris Erythraei*, with normative, diachronic and archaeological views supplied by other available sources. In Chapter 9 we shall return to the variables outlined here and compare the results in order to establish whether similarities outweigh differences in the way the states on the Indian Ocean rim related to maritime trade.

Chapter 3: The *Periplus Maris Erythraei*

The empirical point of departure for this study is the anonymous Greek work labelled *Periplous tês Erythras Thalassês* – "The circumnavigation of the Red Sea", commonly referred to by the Latin name ascribed to it after its renaissance rediscovery,[83] *Periplus Maris Erythraei*. This short text is written in the Greek *Koinê* variety, the *lingua franca* of the eastern Mediterranean and Near East in the first century AD. The *Periplus* contains a description of ports, countries, peoples, navigation and commercial activity on the Red Sea and Indian Ocean rim.

A longstanding debate about the date of the *Periplus* seems to have reached a conclusion. Over the last century, scholars have attributed the work to different periods between the early first and the early third century AD.[84] The dating has for the most part been based on the rulers mentioned by the author of the *Periplus* in his descriptions of African, Arabian and Indian kingdoms. Aksumite, Nabataean, South Arabian and Saka chronology are all insecure. Kings of different generations frequently had the same name, and the rendering of non-Greek names in the *Periplus* is often less than accurate, so the controversy persisted for nearly 100 years. Advocates of later dates have tried to show that some chapters of the work are later interpolations, or that the *Periplus* was a handbook in continuous use and updated over several centuries.[85] The notion of the *Periplus* being a compilation of different texts has not been shared by any of the editors of the text, and separate studies of Nabatean,[86] Indian[87] and Arabian[88] chronology now point towards a mid first century date. This, however, refers to *the information* contained in the work. We should bear in mind that the *Periplus* probably builds on years of practical experience, and that the author's data on different parts of the Indian Ocean are likely to be of different dates.

Textual tradition, texts and translations

There are two extant manuscripts of the *Periplus*. One is from the 15th century and now in the collections of the British Library (add. 19391). It is reported to be a copy of the other manuscript,[89] *Codex Palatinus Graecus 398*, fols. 40v-54v, in the Heidelberg University Library. The latter manuscript was written in the tenth century[90] in minuscule hand. Most of it is well preserved, but important passages are corrupt, and it incorporates lacunae from the manuscript it was copied from, marked by the scribe with open spaces in the text. The manuscript was brought to Rome during the Thirty Years War, and was only returned to Heidelberg in 1816.[91]

In the Heidelberg manuscript, the text is ascribed to a certain Arrianos,[92] long believed to be identical with the famous second century historian of Alexander the Great, a friend of the Emperor Hadrian and author of the small geographical report *Periplus Pontus Euxini* – "The circumnavigation of the Black Sea". Neither contents, date nor style of our work, however, agree with the life and confirmed works of Arrian, and already in the 16th century, editors suspected the attribution to be wrong.[93] Possibly the scribe attributed the text to Arrian because it is placed just after his probably authentic *Periplus Pontus Euxini* in the Heidelberg codex.[94] The actual author of our *Periplus* remains unknown.

The *Periplus* also has a long history as a printed text. The first edition was published in 1533, and with its errors served as the basis of further editions and translations until the manuscript was returned from its Roman exile. A number of editions with translations into Latin, Italian, German and English were published over the following three centuries.[95]

The modern textual tradition starts with the return of the manuscript to Heidelberg. Critical editions with parallel Greek text and translations were published in Latin by Karl Müller[96] and in German by B. Fabricius.[97] These remain important because they served as the basis for Wilfred Schoff's 1912 translation, which was published without the Greek text. Fabricius was rather liberal in his emendations. Schoff employed Müller's Greek text, but accepted most of Fabricus' changes without further comment.[98] Schoff's publication was the only modern

---

[83] The Latin name seems to go back to the 1577 edition / translation by Wilhelm Stuck, cf. Schoff 1995: 18.
[84] For a summary of the debate see Dihle 1965, who also thoroughly rejects attempts of redating the *Periplus* to the late second or early third century.
[85] E.g. Palmer 1947: 140; Wissmann 1976: 434.
[86] Casson 1989: 6f.
[87] Fussman 1991.
[88] Robin 1997. Robin only concludes that the text should be ascribed to the first century AD, but places the reigns of the kings mentioned in the *Periplus* to ca 50 AD.
[89] Casson 1989: 5. See also Mathew 1975: 147ff. for a more positive evaluation of the British Library manuscript than other commentators.
[90] Fabricius 1883: 3.
[91] See Fabricius 1883: 1ff. and Frisk 1927: 25ff. on manuscript and manuscript tradition.
[92] CPG 398: 40v.
[93] Cf. Fabricius 1883: 22.
[94] See discussion in Fabricius 1883: 22f.
[95] Listed in Wilfred Schoffs introduction to his 1912 translation, Schoff 1995: 17ff.
[96] Müller 1855.
[97] Fabricius 1883.
[98] Schoff 1995: 41.

translation available in English until 1980, and has been the basis of much of the 20th century literature on the Indian Ocean trade. In this way the emendations of Fabricius, which were in some cases quite speculative,[99] made their way into the research literature. Schoff's edition has its important merits, particularly the historical part of his commentary, which incorporates the considerable 19th century research to an extent un-echoed by later scholars. Still, the lack of a Greek text and Schoff's reliance on Fabricius' emendations makes his translation useless for scientific purposes without both Müller's and Fabricius' editions at hand.

The Swedish philologist Hjalmar Frisk felt that none of the 19th century text-editions satisfied modern philological standards[100] and that neither Müller nor Fabricus had the proper appreciation and knowledge of *Koinê*.[101] On Fabricius he also passed a graver sentence: in his desire to present an easy and elegant text, Frisk felt that Fabricius had treated the manuscript tradition arbitrarily.[102] In 1927 he published a critical edition of the Greek text,[103] which has been the basis of subsequent editions, on which this study has been based. In addition to Schoff's translation, G.W.B. Huntingford's 1980 translation[104] and particularly Lionel Casson's 1989 parallel text edition have been employed.[105] The latter included a reprint of Frisk's text with some corrections reflecting philological research after 1927. Casson's edition is the most recent and best documented version available, and his translations are used in all citations of longer passages. Single words in Greek have been transliterated in the main text, while Greek letters have been maintained in the notes. Unless otherwise stated, Greek text quoted is based on Casson's revised reprint of Frisk's text. Following Casson,[106] references to specific passages or single words in the Greek text are given to **section:page.line** in Frisk's edition.

Contents, author, nature

The *Periplus* is a practical handbook of trade and navigation on the Indian Ocean and the Red Sea. In 66 brief chapters, it first describes the coast of Africa from Egypt's Red Sea ports southwards to the unidentified port of Rhapta in East Africa. Then the description starts from the north again with the eastern shore of the Red Sea, continues along the southern coast of the Arabian Peninsula and the Persian Gulf, down the coasts of modern Iran, Pakistan and India and along the coasts of the Bay of Bengal.

Along the way we get information on what to buy and what to sell at the different ports. We are often told who rules the region described, what gifts should be brought to the local king or chief, and how visiting foreigners are perceived by the local inhabitants. The sailing directions are sketchier, but some distances are given, as are the best times to set out to different ports, basic information on how to make use of the monsoon for the haul across the open sea from Arabia or Africa to India and information about how to deal with difficult tides when approaching the Indian port of Barygaza in the Gulf of Khambhat.

Almost nothing is known about the anonymous author of the *Periplus*. The only thing we can be fairly certain about is that he was resident in Egypt, as he always names the months with their Egyptian equivalent along with the Roman name.[107] Lionel Casson also points out that in one passage he refers to "the trees we have in Egypt".[108] Most commentators hold that our unknown author was a merchant or a sea captain or perhaps both.[109] No reader can doubt that he was not only a practical man, but also had considerable firsthand knowledge of his subject.

While we do not know what the author called his work, it shares the Greek title and genre ascribed to it in the manuscript – *periplous*, "circumnavigation", with a number of other ancient works, several of them known only through references in other ancient texts.[110] The other preserved *periploi* are little more than lists of ports with the distances between them. They are the maritime version of the Latin *itineraria*, descriptions of roads and routes with lists of road stations and towns with the distances between them. These texts probably served a dual purpose as information for bureaucrats and travellers and as sources for ancient mapmakers. Our *Periplus* has aspects of this, although the book would be of little use to a mapmaker, as the author is far from consistent in his listing of distances and directions. What makes the *Periplus* especially interesting is, however, the wealth of political, commercial and ethnographic information it provides. Its commercial aspect is unparalleled in the preserved sources. Its political and ethnographic content resembles that of the ancient historians and geographers more than it does the other *periploi*, but it diverges from such works in three vital respects: it is almost devoid of information of a supernatural or mythical character; it describes the present rather than the past, and it is to a large, albeit uncertain, extent based on firsthand knowledge.

An intriguing question is the purpose of the *Periplus*. Why did our unknown author choose to share his knowledge of people and places in the Indian Ocean, and

---

[99] Frisk 1927: 25f.
[100] Frisk 1927: 25f.
[101] Frisk 1927: 25f.
[102] Frisk 1927: 25.
[103] Frisk 1927.
[104] Huntingford 1980.
[105] Casson 1989.
[106] Casson 1989: xvii.

[107] *Periplus* 6:3.6, 14:5.8, 24:8.12, 39:13.13, 49:16.32, 56:18.29, cf. Casson 1989: 8.
[108] Casson 1989: 7; *Periplus* 29:9.27, ἡμῖν ἐν Αἰγύπτῳ δένδρων. Huntingford finds this less convincing (1980: 7).
[109] E.g. Huntingford 1980; Casson 1989: 8; Schoff 1995: 15f.
[110] See Huntingford 1980: 5f. for a list.

who was his intended audience? The author keeps strictly to his subject matter. In no place does he reveal whom he wrote for or to what purpose.

The text has been seen as some kind of report, either to the head of a merchant house in Alexandria[111] or to the Roman authorities in Egypt, as an administrative report on the Indian Ocean trade.[112] Both options are possible, but in the form the work has come down to us, neither can be confirmed. The notion of a handbook is perhaps most attractive,[113] considering the combined practical and descriptive nature of the *Periplus*. If we ask ourselves who would be interested in a practical guide to the Indian Ocean, the evident answers would be other merchants, captains and investors, but on the other hand these were potential competitors and should have been able to learn by personal experience. In the end the question of the purpose, however intriguing, is less important than the fact that the wonderful little work exists.

Reliability

If the mid first century date now commonly accepted is correct, it is justifiable to consider the *Periplus* a firsthand source to first century trade in the Indian Ocean. Even if the text is unlikely to be a compilation, it can be analysed in clearly identifiable parts. The primary division is between two main sailing routes: the first is the journey along the African coast to Rhapta in East Africa, the second is the route along the Arabian coast, across to India and along both Indian coasts.[114] It seems clear that the author did not travel the entire length of both journeys himself, but different opinions exist on which parts he only knew from hearsay.

It is generally agreed that the author never visited the Persian Gulf himself, an area from which he has only very vague ideas of geography and commerce.[115] Likewise, he probably never set foot on the island of Socotra. His knowledge of the island leaves much to be desired, and he can report that it is placed under guard by merchants who had farmed the trading rights of the island from the king of Hadramawt,[116] thus preventing people like him from visiting.

The sections on Africa south of Cape Guardafui and India east of Cape Comorin have also been subject to debate. Lionel Casson tended towards considering these parts as firsthand accounts in his commentary to the 1989 edition.[117] Earlier commentators doubted this, because of the summary treatment these areas receive in the *Periplus*, and the text's increasingly diminishing reliability regarding ports and distances.[118]

Below, the different sections of the *Periplus* are tabulated with their position in the text and a proposal as to whether they should be considered firsthand reports or are based on what the author learned from other travellers or from the people he met in the ports he actually visited. The division is based on two criteria, the first proposed by Jørgen Christian Meyer.[119] He pointed out that the *Periplus* gives no list of Egyptian exports to the ports on the Indian east coast, and interpreted this as a sign that these ports were of no commercial interest to the Romans and that the author thus never visited these parts. This distinction seems applicable to most of the text and strengthens the traditional view about which parts can be considered firsthand reports. The second distinction is between regions for which the *Periplus* provides departure times from Egypt, and regions about which the work remains silent in such matters. The idea is that the author would provide such information wherever he had access to it, that is he would report about ports where he or his colleagues went regularly. The two variables correlate nicely and draw a clear distinction between firsthand reports and hearsay in the *Periplus*.[120] The demarcation is not absolute, we cannot expect that the author personally set foot in all ports, even in areas he had personal experience with. Nevertheless, his knowledge about such ports is likely to have been better than about ports in regions he never visited at all.

Table 1: Contents and reliability of the *Periplus*

Ports:	Chapters:	Main route described:	Reliability:
Myos Hormos - Opônê	1-14	Egypt - Horn of Africa	Firsthand
East Africa - Rhapta	15-18	Arabia - East Africa	Secondhand
Leukê Kômê - Kanê	19-28	Egypt - Arabia	Firsthand
Socotra and Moscha	29-32	Internal Hadramawt	Secondhand
Parthian ports	33-37	Persian Gulf - India	Secondhand
Barbarikon - Barygaza	38-49	Egypt - India	Firsthand
Akabaru - Tyndis	50-54	Coastal	Secondhand
Muziris - Nelkynda	54-57	Egypt - India	Firsthand
Balita - Sôptama	58-60	Coastal	Secondhand
Kamara - Ganges / Chrysê	61-63	Costal / India - S.E. Asia	Secondhand

---

[111] Mathew 1975: 153f.
[112] Mathew 1975: 153f.
[113] Casson 1989: 8.
[114] Frezouls 1984.
[115] See esp. Salles 1995.
[116] *Periplus* 31.
[117] Casson 1989: 8 and notes 14 and 17 p. 8.

[118] Fabricius 1883: 28; Schoff 1995: 16, 234. Vincent 1998: vol 1, 519ff. even labelled the part of the *Periplus* describing the Indian coast east of Cape Comorin "the sequel".
[119] Meyer 2007.
[120] Imports are listed for several ports probably not visited by merchant from Egypt, e.g. the Parthian ports of Apologos and Omana (*Periplus* 36), but in these cases the imports are invariably labelled Indian or Arabian. The only possible exception is Rhapta (*Periplus* 16), but these imports seem to be from Muza in Arabia rather than from Egypt.

Chapter 4: Southern Arabia

Fig. 2: Map of Southern Arabia at the time of the *Periplus*

Southern Arabia, the *Arabia Felix* of the Romans, *Eudaimôn Arabia* of the Greeks,[121] already had long traditions of statecraft by the turn of our era.[122] In the highlands of modern Yemen a civilisation based on limited areas of dry-farming and large scale irrigation evolved in the first millennium BC. The main geographical features of the south-western corner of the peninsula are a narrow coastal plain from which tall mountains rise steeply. The mountain range scrapes the monsoon clouds coming in from the Indian Ocean, providing comparably plentiful rainfall on the highland plateau of central Yemen,[123] enabling some measure of dry farming and the highest population densities in all of Arabia.[124] The country then descends northwards and eastwards towards the large sandy desert called Rub al-Khali – "the Empty Quarter". These mountain slopes and valleys provided opportunities for water harvesting, irrigation and thus agriculture.[125] Further east, the large inland valley of Wadi Hadramawt offered the same opportunities.[126]

The kingdoms of Southern Arabia had been involved in trade with the Mediterranean for centuries before the time of the *Periplus*. Caravans brought myrrh and frankincense northwards from present day Yemen and Oman to the Nabataeans in modern Saudi Arabia and Jordan, who transhipped the aromatics to the Mediterranean by way of the port of Gaza in Judea.[127]

---

[121] Meaning "Arabia the Happy" or Arabia the Blessed". See Retsö 2000 on the use and possible origin of these names in the Greek and Roman world.
[122] Schippmann 2001: 31ff.; De Maigret 2002: 163ff, 195ff, 198ff.
[123] Schippmann 2001: 5.
[124] Wilkinson 2002: 103.
[125] Wilkinson 2002: 106f.
[126] Sedov 1996: 69, 86; Schippmann 2001: 7; De Maigret 2002: 17f.
[127] Pliny (12.64) describes the route to Gaza. Strabo (16.4.4) describes the route from Southern Arabia to Aelana in the Gulf of Aqaba, and from there onwards to Gaza (16.2.30). Strabo (16.2.20) also contains a reference to merchants from Arabia Felix being pestered by bandits as far north as the vicinity of Damascus, and reports an otherwise

SOUTHERN ARABIA

The geography of the Arabian Peninsula made it possible to control the trade. Desert areas, wells, mountain passes and fortresses narrowed the choice of routes so that the aromatics had to pass through a chain of kingdoms and cities on their way to the Mediterranean.[128] The system must have relied on relatively stable relations between the South Arabian kingdoms. The suppliers of myrrh and frankincense depended on safe passage through other kingdoms, which in their turn had to be careful not to stop the flow of trade from which they profited with excessive taxes or harassment.

A maritime route probably also led from Southern Arabia to the Nabataean Red Sea port of Leukê Kômê.[129] The Greek geographer Strabo reports that large Nabataean caravans from that port went to their capital at Petra.[130] Still, circumstances point towards the Red Sea trade gaining real momentum as an artery of commerce at the expense of the caravan trade only with the incorporation of Egypt in the Roman Empire in 30 BC, which drew the Arabian trade in aromatics into the monsoon system and diminished the importance of the old caravan routes. Strabo describes the development like this:

> "When Gallus was prefect of Egypt, (…) I learned that as many as one hundred and twenty vessels were sailing from Myos Hormos to India, whereas formerly, under the Ptolemies, only a few ventured to undertake the voyage and to carry on traffic in Indian merchandise."[131]

> "In earlier times, at least, not so many as twenty vessels would dare to traverse the Arabian Gulf far enough to get a peep outside the straits, but at the present time even large fleets are despatched as far as India and the extremities of Aethiopia."[132]

Strabo had travelled through Egypt together with his friend Aelius Gallus who held the office of prefect there, probably during the years 27-25 BC.[133] Strabo does not seem to have visited the Red Sea ports himself, and must have relied on the accounts of others. He might also have been stressing the benefits of the recent Roman takeover of Egypt and the achievements made under the administration of his friend, who must have been hard pressed after his failed military adventure in Arabia. Even if the increase in trade might be exaggerated, Strabo's account does seem to reflect a substantial and real change in the patterns of trade in light of later sources, which describe trade between Southern Arabia and the Roman Empire as primarily maritime. By the time of the *Periplus*, the mid first century AD, any changes in Southern Arabia due to the shift from caravan to maritime trade and direct trade between Egypt and India described by Strabo would have had time to have effect.

In 13 brief chapters, the *Periplus* (20-32) gives us a description of the coast of Southern Arabia beyond Leukê Kômê, "White Village", the last Nabataean port on the Red Sea, to the beginning of Parthian controlled territory, east of Moscha Limên on the coast of modern Oman. We learn of two kingdoms, six ports of differing functions, two kings, the vassal of one of them and three inland cities. Contrasted with what we know of South Arabian history from other sources, the *Periplus* supplies the ideal background for studying government involvement in ancient trade and the significance of trade for the States of Arabia Felix.

Saba-Himyar

The first South Arabian kingdom mentioned in the *Periplus* is the kingdom of the Homerites and the Sabaeans. We are informed that the "legitimate king"[134] Charibaêl ruled both nations from his inland residence in the *mêtropolis* of Saphar.[135] Moreover, a vassal ruler, a *tyrannos*, of the province of Mapharitis lived in the city of Sauê.[136] His name was Cholaibos. The Homerites and Sabaeans had access to at least three ports on the Red Sea and the Indian Ocean: the busy market town of Muza, Okêlis, at that time little more than a watering station,[137] and the once important, but at the time of the *Periplus*, insignificant town of Eudaimôn Arabia.[138]

The 'kingdom of the Homerites and the Sabaeans' refers to a union between the South Arabian tribes of Saba and Himyar. The kingdom of Saba is the most ancient and well-attested kingdom of Southern Arabia. The names of their kings are known back to the eight century BC, when they were mentioned in Late-Assyrian records.[139]

---

unknown 40 day haul from Hadramawt across or around the Rub al-Khali to Gerrha on the Persian Gulf (16.4.4).
[128] Bowen 1958: 36ff.
[129] Probably identical with Aynunah in modern Saudi Arabia, see Casson 1989: 143f. also for other suggestions as to where this port was situated.
[130] Strabo 16.4.23.
[131] Strabo 2.5.12, transl. Jones 2001: vol. I., 455, ὅτε γοῦν Γάλλος ἐπῆρχε τῆς Αἰγύπτου, (...) ἱστοροῦμεν ὅτι καὶ ἑκατὸν καὶ εἴκοσι νῆες πλέοιεν ἐκ Μυὸς ὅρμου πρὸς τὴν Ἰνδικήν, πρότερον ἐπὶ τῶν Πτολεμαϊκῶν Βασιλέων ὀλίγων παντάπασι θαρρούντων πλεῖν καὶ τὸν Ἰνδικὸν ἐμπορεύεσθαι φόρτον.
[132] Strabo 17.1.13, transl. Jones 2001: vol VIII, 53, πρότερον μέν γε οὐδ' εἴκοσι πλοῖα ἐθάρρει τὸν Ἀράβιον κ ὅλπον διαπερᾶν, ὥστε ἔξω τ ῶν στενῶν ὑπερκύπτειν, νῦν δὲ καὶ στόλοι μεγάλοι στέλλονται μέχρι τῆς Ἰνδικῆς καὶ τῶν ἄκρων τῶν Αἰθιοπικῶν.
[133] Some doubt exists as to exactly when Gallus held office in Egypt and exactly when the campaign took place, see Jameson 1968: 77ff.

[134] *Periplus* 23:7.28, ἔνθεσμος βασιλεύς.
[135] *Periplus* 23.
[136] *Periplus* 22:7.24-26. Sauê is identified with a site some 22 kilometers south of modern Taizz, Robin 1997: 50.
[137] *Periplus* 25.
[138] *Periplus* 26.
[139] See Doe 1971: 74ff. for a summary of the history of Saba, and for a more recent version, De Maigret 2002: 198ff. See Schippmann 2001: 35ff. and De Maigret 2002: 163ff. on the controversial issue of South Arabian chronology. The Old Testament reports the queen of Sheba's visit to King Solomon in Jerusalem already in the 10th century BC. (1. Kings, 10). Biblical chronology is, however, not unproblematic, see Groom 1981: 38ff. for a summary of Biblical mentions of South Arabia. Groom (p. 40) places 1. Kings "some time after the sacking of Jerusalem and the fall of the Monarchy in about 586 BC".

The Sabaeans established their capital at Marib, where the mountains of western Yemen meet the desert. Here they could control the main caravan routes northwards while the mountains provided possibilities for water harvesting and irrigation farming. Saba played a leading part in the history of the region throughout the earliest and longest part of the pre-Islamic period.

The Himyarites were originally one of several tribes in the southwest corner of Arabia. Through a series of wars during the first century BC and the first two centuries AD, they marginalised their former lieges, the kings of Qataban,[140] and in time they came to subdue their Sabaean neighbours as well.[141] Struggling for supremacy with their eastern neighbours in Hadramawt, and interrupted by Aksumite interference on the Red Sea coast, the Himyarites would eventually assume Saba's role as the leading South Arabian kingdom and rule most of Southern Arabia for long periods of time until the Sasanian Empire took over around 570. At the time of the *Periplus*, they had established themselves as *de facto* rulers of the southwestern part of the peninsula, while the kings of Hadramawt ruled the eastern part of modern Yemen. From their inland base in Wadi Bayhan, the kings of Qataban still remained in power,[142] but now cut of from the coast.

The capital of the Himyarites was Zafar (*Periplus*: Saphar),[143] in the mountains near present day Yarim. Contrary to what some scholars have held,[144] inscriptions discovered over the last decades seem to indicate that they still paid allegiance to the king of Saba in the first century of our era.[145] This fits well with the double title given Charibaêl in the *Periplus* – 'King of two nations, the Homerites and (...) the Sabaeans',[146] but less well with the *Periplus*' report that Saphar, not Marib, was the capital of the kingdom. Charibaêl was probably identical with a certain Karibil Watar Yuhanim I, belonging to the Sabaean dynasty from Marib.[147] Here we can leave aside the question of who had the upper hand in the relationship between Saba and Himyar in the first century. It suffices to say that the unified kingdom controlled the *Arabian* coastline on both sides of Bab al-Mandeb, the straits separating the Red Sea from the Gulf of Aden and Arabia from Africa.

Ports of Saba-Himyar

The *Periplus* mentions three ports on the coast of Saba-Himyar: Muza,[148] Okêlis[149] and Eudaimôn Arabia.[150]

Muza a still unidentified site near, near modern Mokha, was the main outlet of maritime trade from the kingdom. Okêlis, situated at the Bab al-Mandeb, was a port of clearly secondary importance, as was Eudaimôn Arabia, probably underlying the site of modern Aden.[151] The *Periplus* places all these ports within the Kingdom of Charibaêl, but there ends their similarity.

Okêlis

Saving Muza for later (p. 22, below), Okêlis was the next port reached when sailing down the Arabian side of the Red Sea. It is described in the *Periplus* as "not so much a port of trade as a harbour, watering station, and the first place to put in for those sailing on".[152] We are then informed that Okêlis belonged to the same province as Muza,[153] and a glance at the map confirms that even if little more than a village, it must have been a convenient spot to control the traffic through and across the strait.

Okêlis is also mentioned in one of the sections of the *Periplus* dealing with the African coast.[154] We learn there that the inhabitants of the African side, the *Barbaroi*, sometimes came across the straits on rafts to Okêlis and Muza with such goods as aromatics, myrrh, ivory and tortoise shell. So some amount of trade was conducted at Okêlis, even if not with merchants coming from Egypt like the author of the *Periplus*. Still, the port had some significance outside the purely local trade. While the *Periplus* describes it as "the first place to put in for those sailing on," Pliny, writing few decades later, could confirm where they were heading;[155] Okêlis was the first stop on the voyage from Egypt to India. The situation at or very near the straits must have made it a convenient place to wait for the right wind to head from the Red Sea and into the Gulf of Aden and the Indian Ocean.

Eudaimôn Arabia

Sailing on, anyone following the description of the *Periplus* would reach the village (*kômê*) Eudaimôn ("prosperous", "happy" or "blessed") Arabia. The author of the *Periplus* gives us three important pieces of information about this port: it used to be an important city earlier, when ships from India and Egypt met there, it belonged to Charibaêl's kingdom; and it had been attacked not long before the time of *Periplus*:

> "Eudaimôn Arabia, a village on the coast belonging to the same kingdom, Charibaêl's. (...) a full-fledged city in earlier days, was called Eudaimôn when, since vessels from India did not go on to Egypt and those from Egypt did not dare sail to the places further on but came only this far,

---

[140] De Maigret 2002: 221, 235ff.
[141] De Maigret 2002: 243f.
[142] Schippmann 2001: 60.
[143] *Periplus* 23.
[144] Doe 1971: 78f. and Schippmann 2001: 58, 60 represent the traditional view.
[145] De Maigret 2002: 235ff.
[146] *Periplus* 23:7.24, βασιλεὺς ἐθνῶν δύο, τοῦ τε Ὁμηρίτου καὶ τοῦ (...) Σαβαίτου.
[147] De Maigret 2002: 235.
[148] *Periplus* 21-24.
[149] *Periplus* 25.

[150] *Periplus* 26.
[151] See Casson 1989: 147f. and 157ff. or Huntingford 1980: 100ff. for the location of these three ports.
[152] *Periplus* 25, transl. Casson 1989: 65, ο ὐχ οὕτως ἐμπόριον ὡς ὅρμος καὶ ὕδρευμα καὶ πρώτη καταγωγὴ τοῖς ἔσω διαίρουσιν.
[153] *Periplus* 25.
[154] *Periplus* 7.
[155] Pliny 6.104.

it used to receive the cargoes of both, just as Alexandria receives cargoes from overseas as well as from Egypt. And now, not long before our time, Caesar destroyed it."[156]

The account of the *Periplus* here seems to support the report of Strabo, that the patterns of the monsoon trade had changed in the period after the Roman takeover in Egypt.[157] It would, however, be too easy to ascribe the decline of Eudaimôn Arabia to a change in trading patterns between Egypt and India alone. Arabia had plenty of products to offer for visiting traders herself. She was quite able to carry on a profitable trade in aromatics with both India and Egypt, even without acting as intermediary between the two.

The *Periplus*, however, also informs us that a certain Caesar had attacked the town "not long before our time",[158] and this must have been the blow that finally reduced Eudaimôn Arabia from an important market for Arabian goods to the mere watering station and safe harbour it was at the time of the *Periplus*. But who was this Caesar? The question has puzzled translators, commentators and historians alike for more than a century.[159] The manuscript reading is sound in this spot, using the term *kaisar*,[160] but if there is one thing we can be fairly certain about, it is that he was not a Roman emperor, neither in person, nor by proxy.

We know of only one Roman military expedition to these parts of Arabia; the misadventure of Strabo's friend Aelius Gallus some 70 years before the *Periplus* was written. Gallus's route is fairly well known through the account of Strabo.[161] There is no indication in the text of Strabo that Gallus ever reached the Gulf of Aden or the city of Eudaimôn Arabia. The failure of Aelius Gallus' Arabian expedition must have served as a firm discouragement to those harbouring thoughts of further adventures. Pliny, writing in the years before ca 70 AD, should be better informed than we are. He states about Arabia, that "Only Aelius Gallus of the equestrian order has carried Roman arms into this region until now".[162] As long as a mid first century date for the *Periplus* remains the most likely option, it thus seems safe to rule out that a Roman attack on Aden ever took place before that time.[163] In the *Periplus*, Charibaêl, king of Saba-Himyar and of Eudaimôn Arabia is introduced as a friend of the emperors,[164] and we are left in the dark as to why the Romans would want to attack his port.

Soldiers from the *Legio III Cyrenaica* were stationed as far south as Hegra / Mada'in Saleh in Saudia Arabia after the detachment of the legion to the province of Arabia during the reign of Hadrian (117-138),[165] and a recently

---

[156] *Periplus* 26, transl. adapted from. Casson 1989: 65, Εὐδαίμων Ἀραβία, κώμη παραθαλάσσιος, βασιλείας τ ἧς α ὑτῆς Χαριβαήλ, (...) πρότερον οὖσα πόλις, ὅτε, μήπω ἀπὸ τῆς Ἰνδικῆς εἰς τὴν Αἴγυπτον ἐρχομένων μηδὲ ἀπὸ Αἰγύπτου τολμώντων εἰς τοὺς ἔσω τόπους διαίρειν ἀλλ᾽ ἄχρι ταύτης παραγινομένων, τοὺς παρὰ ἀμφοτέρων φ όρτους ἀπεδέχετο, ὥσπερ Ἀλεξάνδρεια καὶ τὰ ἔξωθεν καὶ τῶν ἀπὸ τῆς Α ἰγύπτου φερομένων ἀποδέχεται. Νῦν δὲ οὐ πρὸ πολλοῦ τῶν ἡμετέρων χρόνων Καῖσαρ αὐτὴν κατεστρέψατο. I have followed the translation of Casson with one exception: Casson's rendering of κατεστρέψατο, the aorist middle of καταστρέφω by "sacked" is not unproblematic. Lidell, Scott and Jones (1996: 915a), give the translation "subject to oneself, subdue" of the middle voice, which suggests a more permanent action than "sack". This sense was the one adopted by Fabricius (1883: 65), who translated κατεστρέψατο with "unterworfen". Huntingford (1980: 35) and Schoff (1995: 32), both chose "destroyed", which has the same temporal implications as "sacked" – the city has been successfully attacked, but the attackers have left after plundering (sacking) or destroying the place. The Lidell, Scott and Jones / Fabricius option on the other hand implies that the Romans occupied the city for some time or that it was in some way incorporated into the empire. This agrees badly with the information given earlier in *Periplus* 26, namely that Eudaimôn Arabia belonged to the kingdom of Saba-Himyar, ruled by king Charibaêl, who, in *Periplus* 23:7.29-30, is said to be the friend of the emperors. I have chosen to maintain the temporal implications of Casson's reading, but to follow Huntingford and Schoff and translate κατεστρέψατο as "destroyed". Hjalmar Frisk, who prepared our only modern, critical edition of the text, commented that the author of the *Periplus* on a number on occasions where he uses a verb more than once, employs both the middle voice and the active, but that there is no discernable difference in meaning due to this (1927: 59f.). Thus we cannot from the use of the middle voice alone rule out other meanings of κατεστρέψατο than "subdue" or "subject to oneself". In texts roughly contemporary with the *Periplus*, Καταστρέφω seems to have the broader meaning of "destroy". See Bauer 1988: 852 and Josephus, *bell.* 1.199, who refers to the walls of Jerusalem as κατεστραμμένα, which can hardly be taken to mean anything else than "destroyed" or "ruined". Polybius (23.11.2), although significantly earlier, uses the word in the sense "ruin" or "destroy" with regard to livelihood, offspring and importantly also cities: καὶ βίον καὶ τέκνα καὶ πόλεις ἄρδην καταστραφότας.

[157] Finds of local pottery, "rouletted ware" seemingly inspired by Mediterranean forms at the site of Arikamedu on the east coast of India have been used to push back the contacts between Egypt and South India at least as far as the second century BC (Begley 1983: 469ff.; 1988). The supposed western inspiration and early date for this rouletted ware is, however, disputed, see Sedov 1992: 127; Mac Dowall 1998: 79ff., and even if it should attest such early contacts, its presence is not necessarily a result of direct trade. The description in the *Periplus* of Eudaimôn Arabia as a former meeting point for Indian and Egyptian traders seems to indicate just the opposite.

[158] *Periplus* 26:8.31-32, Νῦν δὲ οὐ πρὸ πολλοῦ τῶν ἡμετέρων χρόνων Καῖσαρ αὐτὴν κατεστρέψατο - "now, not long before our time, Caesar destroyed it". Cf. note 156, above.
[159] See Casson 1989: 160 for a short summary of different views on the issue. Raschke (1978: 647 and notes 908-915) give an extensive bibliography. Nigel Groom (1995: 183f.) is the most recent advocate of a long standing theory originally proposed by Mordtmann (1890: 180) that the author of the *Periplus* knew about Aelius Gallus' expedition to the region of Arabia Eudaimôn, the Greek name for the whole of Southern Arabia, Latin: *Arabia Felix*, and confused it with Arabia Eudaimôn - the city, mistakenly believing that Romans had indeed sacked the place. This could explain the use of the term *kaisar* in the *Periplus*. Still, as we know quite much about the route of Gallus expedition from Strabo (16.4.22-23), see also Wissmann 1976: 313ff., this misconception on behalf of the author of the *Periplus* would just confirm that no Roman emperor ever attacked Eudaimôn Arabia (the city). If the city had indeed been attacked, this must presumably have been by an Arabian ruler.
[160] CPG 398: 45v, 14.
[161] Strabo 16.2.22-24.
[162] Pliny 6.160, *Romana arma solus in eam terram adhuc intulit Aelius Gallus ex equestri ordine.*
[163] An opinion also held by Wellesley (1954) although he argues along different lines.
[164] *Periplus* 23:7.29-30. As has long been noted, (Schoff 1995: 115), our anonymous author here describes his ruler with the term αὐτοκράτωρ, not Καῖσαρ, which has been taken as an indication that the term Καῖσαρ in *Periplus* 26 does not refer to the Roman emperor.
[165] Bowersock 1971: 230, 232f.

published Latin inscription from the Farasan islands attests a Roman military presence in the southern Red Sea during the reign of Antoninus Pius.[166] Together with Gallus' expedition, the inscriptions show imperial Roman interest in the Hejaz and in Southern Arabia, and military capability to intervene in the region. They refer, however, to Roman activities separated by almost two centuries and report nothing about the state of affairs at the time of the *Periplus*.

Schoff conveniently solved the problem by simply replacing the Caesar with Charibaêl, king of the Sabaeans and the Homerites,[167] perhaps ascribing the reference to Caesar to an understandable error of a scribe who substituted an unknown name with a name he knew well when he copied the manuscript. L. Casson left the question of the Caesar open,[168] whereas G.W.B. Huntingford kept the name "Caesar", in his translation from 1980, but concluded in the commentary that it probably refers to some local ruler.[169] Schoff's reasoning about why the passage cannot refer to a Roman emperor remains sound, but he jumped to conclusions when involving Charibaêl. Even if it does seem probable that an Arabian ruler was behind the attack on Eudaimôn Arabia rather than a Roman, and it is very possible that he was a Himyarite ruler as Charibaêl was, we simply do not know who attacked Eudaimôn Arabia,[170] if the city was indeed ever attacked.

Even if an attack on Eudaimôn Arabia did take place, and even if an Arabian ruler was responsible rather than a Roman Caesar, the use of the term *Kaisar* in the *Periplus* calls for an explanation. There is one such explanation that leaves the text of the *Periplus* and the account of Strabo intact. It could seem that the author of the *Periplus* was simply deceived when he ascribed the attack on Eudaimôn Arabia, whether real or not, to Caesar, and that the deceiver was none else than Caesar Augustus himself. In the end it all comes down to a confusion of terms:

Eudaimôn Arabia – "Arabia the Happy" or "Arabia the Blessed", was not only the name of a village that had once been a city. The conventional use of the name in Greek sources is as a label for the entire Arabian Peninsula south of an imaginary line from the Gulf of Aqaba in Jordan to modern Kuwait. This is also how the name is used by Strabo,[171] our source to the expedition of Aelius Gallus.

A brief comparison with the *Periplus* reveals an important difference. In the *Periplus* this conventional use of the name is unknown. "Eudaimôn Arabia" refers to a seashore village only. The rest of Arabia is referred to simply as "Arabia" and by the names of the peoples and their rulers in the following manner: "Malichus, king of the Nabataeans",[172] "Charibaêl, legitimate king of two nations, the Homerite and the one lying next to it, called the Sabaean",[173] and finally "the kingdom of Eleazos, the frankincense-bearing land".[174] It seems thus, perhaps not entirely surprising, that there was a difference in terminology between the merchants trading on the Red Sea and Indian Ocean by the mid first century AD and the literary elite of the Roman Empire, represented by Strabo. To the latter, "Eudaimôn Arabia" referred to an almost unknown land of riches; to the former it was simply a seashore village in Southern Arabia with a prosperous past. But where does Augustus enter the picture?

In section 5.26 of Augustus' political will, the inscription known as *Res Gestae Divi Augusti*, "the Acts of the Divine Augustus", we can read the following narrative, first in F.W. Shipley's translation of the Latin texts, then in its Latin original, and finally in the ancient Greek translation that accompanied the Latin text as it is attested to us:

"On my order and under my auspices two armies were led, at almost the same time, into Ethiopia and into Arabia which is called the "Happy," and very large forces of the enemy of both races were cut to pieces in battle and many towns were captured. Ethiopia was penetrated as far as the town of Nabata, which is next to Meroë. In Arabia the army advanced into the territories of the Sabaei to the town of Mariba."

"Meo iussú et auspicio ducti sunt (duo) exercitús eódem fere tempore in Aethiopiam et in Ar(a)biam, qua appel(latur) eudaemón, (maxim)aeque hos(t)ium gentís utr(iu)sque cop(iae) caesae sunt in acie et (c)om(plur)a oppida capta. In Aethiopiam usque ad oppidum Nabata pervent(um) est, cuí proxima est Meroé. In Arabiam usque ín fines Sabaeorum pro(cess)it exerc(it)us ad oppidum Mariba."

"Ἐμῆι ἐπιταγῆι καὶ οἰωνοῖς α ἰσίοις δύο στρατεύματα ἐπέβη Α ἰθιοπίαι καὶ Ἀραβίαι τ ῆι

---

[166] Phillips, Villeneuve, and Facey 2004.
[167] Schoff 1995: 115.
[168] Casson 1989: 160.
[169] Huntingford 1980: 35, 10.
[170] Groom (1995: 182ff.) denies that Charibaêl / Karibil Watar could have been responsible. Groom argues that that use of the words "now, not long before our time" / Ν ῦν δὲ οὐ πρὸ πολλοῦ τῶν ἡμετέρων χρόνων in the *Periplus* (26:8.31-32), must be taken to mean at least 20 years earlier (p. 184). Groom then compares certain differences between the accounts of India in Pliny and in the *Periplus*, which he takes to support the dating of Fussman (1991) to ca 40 - 45 AD as the best available for the *Periplus*. Robin (1997: 58) states that Karibil Watar probably ascended the throne between 40 and 50, which means that he cannot have been behind the attack if Groom is right that "not long before our time" must mean at least 20 years. The problem with Grooms' conclusion is, however, that even if a mid first century date for the *Periplus* seems the most plausible, it is quite safe to assume that what was meant by "not long before our time" will remain open to speculation.

[171] Retsö 2000.
[172] *Periplus* 19:6.29, (πρὸς) Μαλίχαν, βασιλέα Ναβαταίων.
[173] *Periplus* 23:7.27-28, Χαριβαήλ, ἔνθεσμος βασιλεὺς ἐθνῶν δύο, τοῦ τε Ὁμηρίτου καὶ τοῦ παρακειμένου λεγομένου Σαβαίτου.
[174] *Periplus* 27:9.4-5, βασιλείας Ἐλεάζου, χώρας Λιβανωτοφόρου.

εὐδαίμονι καλουμένηι, μεγάλας τε τῶν πολεμίων δυνάμεις κατέκοψεν ἐν παρατάξει καὶ πλείστας πόλεις δοριαλώτους ἔλαβεν καὶ προέβη ἐν Αἰθιοπίαι μέχρι πόλεως Ναβάτης, ἥτις ἐστὶν ἔγγιστα Μερόη, ἐν Ἀραβίαι δ ὲ μέχρι πόλεως Μαρίβας."[175]

According to Suetonius,[176] the *Res Gestae* was commissioned by Augustus as a monument commemorating his life and achievements, to be published on bronze tablets in front of his mausoleum on the Tiber. The original long lost, the text is known to us through a copy in the temple of the Divine Augustus in the provincial city of Ancyra – modern Ankara in Turkey. The inscription in Ancyra also contained a translation into Greek on one of the outer walls of the temple, making the important text legible to a large public around the eastern Mediterranean. Fragments of the inscription have been found in Apollonia and Antioch in modern Turkey. This makes it likely that copies were displayed in a number of cities across the Roman world, including Egypt, a province belonging to the imperial household, and the likely home of the author of the *Periplus*.

So presumably our unknown author will have had opportunity to read the inscription commemorating the campaigns of Augustus, and he will have read it in Greek. The inscription as cited above makes two statements about Arabia, firstly that an army was led "into Arabia which is called the Happy (*in Arabiam, qua appellatur eudaemón*) ... and many towns were captured". The text clearly implies a country or geographical region rather than a city or a village. Secondly we learn that, "and in Arabia the army advanced into the territories of the Sabaei to the town of Mariba" (*in Arabiam usque in fines Sabaeorum processit exercitus ad oppidum Mariba*). In the Greek translation of the inscription "Arabia which is called the Happy" is rendered *Arabiai têi eudaimoni kaloumenêi*. This, however, resembles the name that was familiar to the author of the *Periplus* as the name of a village, not that of a country. In the second statement Arabia is simply called "Arabia" without any epithet both in the Greek and in the Latin version, and this was the name under which the author of the *Periplus* knew the Arabian Peninsula with *all* its kingdoms.

Thus we have to consider the possibility that the author of the *Periplus* read the two passages on Arabia in the *Res Gestae* as referring to two different Arabias. A reasonable interpretation of the inscription as he must have understood it would be that a Roman army had landed in *the village* of Eudaimôn Arabia and pressed northwards from there through the land of the Sabaeans towards Mariba, a town unknown to him, in *the country* of Arabia, capturing many towns on their way. This would explain the report of a Roman attack on Aden in the *Periplus*, without compromising the manuscript reading or Strabo's account of Gallus' expedition.

If we accept that the change of trading patterns described in the *Periplus* and in Strabo was not alone sufficient to reduce Eudaimôn Arabia to the state that the author of the *Periplus* found it in, we still have to maintain that an attack on the city did take place, even if the author of the *Periplus* was mistaken in ascribing it to a Roman emperor. But why would Charibaêl or another Arabian king want to attack Eudaimôn Arabia? It is tempting to see the event in connection with the gradual conquest of the Qatabanian kingdom by its rivals, Saba-Himyar and Hadramawt, in the two centuries around the turn of our era. Strabo indicates that the Qatabanians had controlled the entire southwest corner of Arabia, and hence the Red Sea trade until the rise of Himyar.[177] In light of the account of the city's glorious past in the *Periplus*, the destruction of Eudaimôn Arabia, the logical outlet of maritime trade from Qataban, would have been a harsh blow to their position.

The main overland route from Eudaimôn Arabia probably led to Wadi Bayhan, the heartland of the Qatabanian kingdom and their capital at Timna,[178] not to the political centres of Saba-Himyar at Sauê and Saphar. Saba-Himyar kept Eudaimôn Arabia open as a harbour and a watering post after its destruction, but they did not need it as a market. They already had one to supply their court with imported goods and to serve as an outlet for their most important export, myrrh: Muza was not only closer to the capitals at Zafar and Marib, but also less dependent on the monsoon because it was situated on the Red Sea coast. Eudaimôn Arabia was more vulnerable to the rival kingdoms of Qataban and Hadramawt, so by keeping trade away from that port, the king of Saba-Himyar would not only deprive his rivals of their shares of the maritime trade, but would also make sure that *their* trade had to pass through *his* hands. Meanwhile, his own trade was both safer and closer at Muza.

Muza, myrrh and the maritime trade of Saba-Himyar

The port of Muza is described as a busy harbour with a long list of imports and exports.[179] We get to know that the town carried on trade with the Indian port of Barygaza, with the African coast and with Egypt, and that local merchants and ship owners were numerous.

Although some import took place at Okêlis,[180] Muza was the port, which linked the kingdom of Saba-Himyar with the monsoon networks. Given this special position, the list of exports and imports at Muza provided in the description of the port in the *Periplus* should supply us with a good picture of the maritime trade of Saba-Himyar as a whole:

> "Merchandise for which it offers a market are: purple cloth, fine and ordinary quality; Arab

---

[175] Ed. and translation Shipley 1924: 388ff.
[176] Aug. 101.
[177] Strabo 16.4.2. This has been debated among modern scholars, See De Maigret (2002: 219) in favour and Beeston (1978) against.
[178] Bowen 1958: 36ff.
[179] *Periplus* 21-24.
[180] *Periplus* 7.

sleeved clothing, either with no adornment or with the common adornment or with checks or interwoven with gold thread; saffron; *cyperus*;[181] cloth; *abollai*;[182] blankets, in limited number, with no adornments as well as with traditional local adornments; girdles with shaded stripes; unguent, moderate amount; money, considerable amount; wine and grain, limited quantity because the region produces wheat in moderate quantity and wine in greater. To the king and the governor are given: Horses and pack mules; goldware; embossed silverware; expensive clothing; copperware. Its exports consist of local products – myrrh, the select grade and *stactê*,[183] the Abeirian and Minaean; white marble – as well as all the aforementioned merchandise from Adulis across the water".[184]

The *Periplus* describes several flows of trade meeting at Muza: with the Nabataean kingdom and the port of Leukê Komê,[185] with the African coast of the Red Sea – "Adulis across the water" and the coast of East Africa,[186] between Arabia and Africa,[187] and finally the trade with Egypt, in which the author of the *Periplus* took part himself. At Muza, these networks intersected with each other and with coastal and inland networks within Southern Arabia.

The author of the *Periplus* uses the term *emporion nomimon*[188] for Muza and for two other ports – Adulis[189] on the coast of modern Eritrea and the Parthian port of Apologos.[190] Lionel Casson translated this as "a legally limited port of trade",[191] and interpreted the *emporion nomimon* as a term denoting a port where the local ruler held a monopoly on trade, and that this meant that all trade had to pass through the king's representatives.[192] The description of Muza in the *Periplus* does not support this view:

> "The whole place teems with Arabs – shipowners or charterers and sailors – and is astir with commercial activity. For they share in the trade across the water and with Barygaza, using their own outfits".[193]

Firstly we get to know that numerous "shipowning and seafaring people" (*nauklêrikoi anthrôpoi kai nautikoi*) of Arabian origin frequented the port. Nothing in the text indicates that these shipowners were in government service. That the port literally "moves" (*kinetai*) with commerce hardly rings of administered trade. The passage even states that these people engaged in trade with India and Africa using "their own equipments" (*idioi exartismoi*).

The lists of commodities traded at Muza[194] give the impression of a varied import, and a more restricted export. Imported goods represent a wide range in quality and price. This is evident for example in the case of clothing, about which the author of the *Periplus* gives detailed information as to what kinds could be sold. One example is the "Arab sleeved clothing" in four varieties: "either with no adornment or with the common adornment or with checks or interwoven with gold thread".[195] Different qualities of clothing tell us that there were different kinds of buyers at the market in Muza. While the clothing interwoven with gold thread would be for the rich, it was not necessarily exclusively for the king and his entourage.

While there is no explicit mention of a royal monopoly at Muza or the two other *emporia nomima*, descriptions of trade at other ports do contain such references. At the Hadrami port of Moscha Limên we learn that trade was conducted through royal agents and only with royal permission.[196] At Barbarikon at the mouth of the Indus, "all cargoes are brought up the river to the king at the metropolis".[197] As the author of the *Periplus* was obviously aware of such regulations and considered them important enough to mention in his descriptions of other ports, it is curious that he gives no such information at Muza, at Adulis and at Apologos, the two other *emporia nomima,* if the term did in fact imply a royal monopoly of trade.

A further indication that there was no royal monopoly of trade at Muza is the telling fact that the description of the harbour in the *Periplus* contains a separate list of imports for the king.[198] Any monopoly in existence should be for these goods, not the others mentioned without any clauses.

---

[181] A plant product used for medicine and perfume (Casson 1989: 153).
[182] Cloaks (Casson 1989: 111).
[183] Myrrh oil (Casson 1989: 155).
[184] *Periplus* 24, transl. Casson 1989: 65, Φορτία δὲ εἰς αὐτὴν προχωρεῖ πορφύρα διάφορος καὶ χυδαία καὶ ἱματισμὸς Ἀραβικὸς χειριδωτός, ὅ τε ἁπλοῦς καὶ ὁ κοινὸς καὶ σκοτουλᾶτος καὶ διάχρυσος, καὶ κρόκος καὶ κύπερος καὶ ὀθόνιον καὶ ἀβόλλαι καὶ λώδικες οὐ πολλαί, ἁπλοῖ τε καὶ ἐντόπιοι, ζῶναι σκιωταὶ καὶ μύρον μέτριον καὶ χρῆμα ἱκανόν, οἶνός τε καὶ σῖτος οὐ πολύς· φέρει γὰρ καὶ ἡ χώρα πυρὸν μετρίως καὶ οἶνον πλείονα. Τῷ τε βασιλεῖ καὶ τῷ τυράννῳ δίδονται ἵπποι τε καὶ ἡμίονοι νωτηγοὶ καὶ χρυσώματα καὶ τορ[ν]ευτὰ ἀργυρώματα κ αὶ ἱματισμὸς πολυτελὴς καὶ χαλκουργήματα. Ἐξάγεται δὲ ἐξ αὐτῆς, ἐντόπια μ έν, σμύρνα ἐκλεκτὴ καὶ στακτή, Ἀβειρ<αία καὶ> Μιναία, λύγδος καὶ τὰ ἀπὸ τῆς πέραν Ἀδουλι προειρημένα φορτία πάντα.
[185] This trade between Leukê Komê and Arabia is not mentioned in the description of Muza, but is attested in *Periplus* 19.
[186] *Periplus* 7, 8 and 16.
[187] *Periplus* 21.
[188] *Periplus* 21:7.19.
[189] *Periplus* 4:1.20.
[190] *Periplus* 35:11.32.
[191] Casson 1989: 63.
[192] Casson 1989: 274ff.

[193] *Periplus* 21, transl. Casson 1989: 63, Τ ὸ μὲν ὅλον Ἀράβων, ναυκληρικῶν ἀνθρώπων καὶ ναυτικῶν, πλεονάζον [δὲ] καὶ τοῖς ἀπὸ ἐμπορίας πράγμασι κινεῖται· συγχρῶνται γὰρ τῇ τοῦ πέραν ἐργασίᾳ καὶ Βαρυγάζων ἰδίοις ἐξαρτισμοῖς.
[194] *Periplus* 24, cited p. 22, above.
[195] *Periplus* 24:8.2-3, transl. Casson 1989: 65, ἱματισμὸς Ἀραβικὸς χειριδωτός, ὅ τε ἁπλοῦς καὶ ὁ κοινὸς καὶ σκοτουλᾶτος καὶ διάχρυσος.
[196] *Periplus* 32.
[197] *Periplus* 39:13.5-6, τ ὰ δὲ φορτία πάντα ε ἰς τ ὴν μητρόπολιν ἀναφέρεται διὰ τοῦ ποταμοῦ τῷ Βασιλεῖ.
[198] *Periplus* 24, cited p. 22, above.

From a South Arabian setting, the so-called *Mercantile code of Qataban* (RES 4337) offers evidence for the kind of regulations of trade, which might have characterised a port recognised by visiting traders as an *emporion nomimon*. The code was inscribed on a stela displayed in the market place of Timna, the capital of the Qatabanian kingdom. Although it predates the *Periplus*[199] and deals with overland trade, it still provides a comparative view of how South Arabian rulers sought to regulate trade.

A.F.L. Beeston points out two general principles in his commentary to the code, the first being to centralise trade at Timna in order to facilitate taxation, the second to regulate the rights of Qatabanian and other merchants and the relationship between them.[200] Alessandra Avanzini stresses the effort to concentrate trade at the market square and to bestow privileges on Qatabanian citizens vis-à-vis others.[201] Beeston suggested that the motive for these regulations was fiscal.[202] While transactions carried out on the market place were easy to monitor and tax, transactions conducted in the countryside would be hard to control. In this respect the internal commerce of Qataban echoes the maritime exchange of Saba-Himyar described in the *Periplus*: all trade was centralised to one market. Centralisation of trade at Timna might also have had a second aspect connected not only with taxation, but also with supply. If all trade was to take place at Timna, the resources of the kingdom would be concentrated at the capital. This would provide the population of the largest city of the kingdom with goods needed for daily subsistence. It would also centralise the surplus of Qataban's export goods, most importantly myrrh, at the capital where it would be available for export or sale to foreign merchants.

While no direct comparison is possible, RES 4337 is an example of how South Arabian kings took active interest in trade, which resembles the labelling of certain ports as *nomimos* – "customary", "lawful", "legitimate". In conclusion, the term surely implies some sort of regulation, but hardly a monopoly. As Alain Bresson has argued, it is not necessarily a legal term, but might simply indicate a port where trade was conducted in a safe, orderly and lawful manner.[203] At Muza the king was certainly an important participant in the trade, but he was not the only one. Casson's theory of a royal monopoly on trade based on Muza classified as an *emporion nomimon* seems hard to maintain.

Nevertheless, the separate list of imports for the king at Muza and at most other ports of trade serving as commercial outlets of Indian Ocean states point towards a slightly different kind of restriction on trade: a regulation on certain kinds of import.

The *Periplus* reports that certain goods – horses, mules, expensive clothing, gold, silver and copperware – were "given" (*didontai*) to the king and to his vassal, the *tyrannos*,[204] by visiting merchants. It is easy to agree with Casson that this can hardly be understood as gifts in the sense that these goods were handed over free, just to ensure the goodwill of the authorities.[205] We have no other evidence that such lavish gifts were normal or required in the monsoon trade or that traders could afford to just give it away. A more attractive interpretation is that such goods must have belonged to a separate sphere of trade, the trade in Muza's chief export: myrrh.

Myrrh was certainly the most important commodity supplied by the kingdom of Saba-Himyar in their trade with the Mediterranean, and perhaps also in their Indian trade. Myrrh could potentially be cultivated or harvested in large parts of their kingdom and on the territory of their neighbours and rivals in Qataban.[206] A monopoly on the production of myrrh would thus have been hard to maintain. Nevertheless it would be possible to control and tax the trade, but how?

There were two main possibilities for the exportation of myrrh: the land and the sea routes. The ancient land routes leading through the desert to the Nabataean Kingdom in what is now northern Saudi Arabia and Jordan went through narrow passes, fortified cities and outposts controlling water supplies.[207] Trade could easily be taxed in such places. By restricting the sea trade to one single port, Muza, the same could be achieved with the maritime trade. Eudaimôn Arabia had a better harbour and was perhaps closer to the main myrrh growing areas than Muza, but it was further away from the king's power base at Zafar, and closer to the kingdoms of Hadramawt and Qataban, the other important South Arabian kingdoms of the time. Muza might have been considered a safer choice. Whatever the actual reasons were, the effect was that even though myrrh was produced throughout the kingdom and imported from the African side in small quantities at Okêlis,[208] it was exported from one place only: Muza.

All trade in myrrh was thus under the surveillance of the king's representatives, and we must assume that the trade was taxed in some way. Pliny states in his *Natural History*, certainly without firsthand knowledge and probably with reference to the first century BC, that the Qatabanians used to levy a 25% tax in kind on the myrrh

---

[199] The law was passed during the rule of King Shahr Hillal II. This provides a date of ca 110 BC according to a tentative chronology by K.A. Kitchen (1994: 74ff.; 2000: 542). A. Avanzini, however, places RES 4337 within the earlier and wider timeframe of the fifth through third centuries BC.
[200] Beeston 1959: 13.
[201] Avanzini 2004: 285.
[202] Beeston 1959: 13.
[203] Bresson 1993: 193ff. See ibid.: 191ff. for an extensive discussion of the term.
[204] *Periplus* 24:8.7, Τῷ τὲ βασιλεῖ καὶ τῷ τυράννῳ δίδονται.
[205] Casson (1989: 154).
[206] See Van Beek 1958: 143ff., 150f., 152 (map). Groom (1981: 96ff.) provides an in-depth study and argues against Van Beek's views on some points.
[207] Bowen 1958: 36ff.
[208] *Periplus* 7.

production.²⁰⁹ What the kings of Saba-Himyar charged we do not know, but as taxes on production would probably be in kind rather than in coin,²¹⁰ they would easily make the state the single largest possessor of myrrh, as the income would far exceed the needs of the royal household. To this should be added any aromatics produced on royal land or harvested by the state itself. The kingdom of Saba-Himyar would thus have had a healthy surplus of myrrh available for export from Muza.

On the import side, tableware made from precious metals as that mentioned on the list of goods for the king at Muza, was a favourite royal import in all areas bordering the Mediterranean cultures. Roman wine bowls have been found in elite graves in Gaul and as far away as Scandinavia. The northern neighbours of the states of Southern Arabia, the Nabataeans, were famous at the time, for their golden and silver vessels.²¹¹ The need for these expensive articles was based on the seemingly almost universal and tradition of communal drinking as a way to form and strengthen social ties within the elites of archaic societies.²¹² The *Periplus* can inform us that the South Arabians produced wine themselves,²¹³ so even though wine could be a politically important commodity, a monopoly on its import would be of little use to the king. Gold and silver tableware for use during symposia would, however, have been an appropriate way of showing off his wealth, splendour and power to his followers.²¹⁴ It was the ideal gift to allies and vassals, and in this way it must have held higher prestige and value than ordinary coins or bullion. The prestige would, however, only last thus far: if such vessels became commonplace, they would lose much of their function, thus it was sensible for the king to wish to restrict and control their import.

This is the appropriate background for the list of goods for the king and with reference to which the use of the term "given" in the *Periplus* should be viewed. The king's household used tableware in gold, silver and copper. Pack mules were vital for the internal infrastructure of an inland kingdom where the terrain rendered wheeled transport impossible. Horses were suitable both for military purposes and for royal displays of splendour. These goods should not be seen simply as bribes to ensure the goodwill of the authorities and the right to trade in safety, but as a list of some of the goods demanded by the king in exchange for his large share of the myrrh export. In Muza, trade probably had to commence on the terms dictated by the king, but this does not necessarily mean that royal agents were the only Arabian traders at the port. Again, a parallel might be found in the *Mercantile code of Qataban*, which states that "the king of Qataban in person has authority over all transactions and goods that pass over his territory".²¹⁵

What we witness at Muza is thus not a royal monopoly on trade, but rather two separate spheres of exchange, the king being the only buyer of some prestige goods and a major, but not the only, supplier of the key export.

A king and his vassal

The king of Saba-Himyar was obviously a man of some importance and influence in the maritime trade, but how did he control the trade, or did he? While the *Periplus* left us in the dark about the nature of Charibaêl's double title, the source reveals another interesting piece of information about the political layout of first century Southern Arabia. We learn that the kingdom of Saba-Himyar was divided into smaller entities – *chôrai*, "territories",²¹⁶ and that one of them was called Mapharitis.²¹⁷ The vassal ruler in control of Muza was a chief (*tyrannos*), named Cholaibos, resident in the city of Sauê, three days from Muza.²¹⁸ He is mentioned alongside the king in the list of special imports.²¹⁹ This tells us that he had access to the same imported goods as the king, and it also implies that he acted not only on behalf of the king, but also next to the king.

The *tyrannos* of Mapharitis is not only mentioned in the *Periplus* in the description of the kingdom of Saba-Himyar. He also figures together with his liege in the description of the port of Rhapta on the coast of East Africa,²²⁰ or Azania as the Greeks and Romans called the sub-Saharan part of the continent. We shall return to this region in the next chapter. For now it suffices to state that the area around Rhapta was under the rule or administration of the *tyrannos* of Mapharitis, who evidently had control over trade and large land areas, in Arabia as well as overseas.

As A.F.L Beeston has argued, kingship in South Arabia did not mean absolute power or solitary rule, and

---

²⁰⁹ Pliny 12.68, *regi tamen Gebbanitarum quartas partes eius pendunt*.
²¹⁰ This certainly seems to be the case in the passage of Pliny. Pliny also reports that frankincense was taxed by measure in Hadramawt. (12.63). The name seems to imply that "the fourth" (*tetartê*), a tax levied on eastern imports in the Roman Empire was also collected in kind. The *tetartê* is attested at Leukê Kômê (*Periplus* 19), Alexandria (P. Vindob. G40822) and possibly at Antioch, as an inscription from Palmyra (Inv. X.29) mentions a member of the council in Antioch as collector of the "fourth".
²¹¹ See Vickers 1994 both on the use of these vessels in the Nabatean kingdom and on their export to such areas as Gaul, Carthage and India.
²¹² On communal drinking as a political institution, see Qviller 2004. Cf. Wells 1980: 65f. and esp. 95ff. who examines the potential political impact of wine import to early Iron Age Northwestern Europe. See Wells 1980 also on the significance of imported luxuries in general.
²¹³ *Periplus* 24.
²¹⁴ See Veblen (1957: 68ff.), who argued that such conspicuous consumption is a universal phenomenon among elites and would-be elites in modern and historical societies alike.

²¹⁵ Res 4337c 11-14, transl. Avanzini 2004: 290.
²¹⁶ *Periplus* 22:7.25. Casson (1989: 63) prefers "province" with a corresponding translation of τύραννος with "governor", this would reflect a system akin to the Roman with territories of administrative nature and an appointment of representatives on lower administrative levels by those on higher, which the source does not warrant.
²¹⁷ *Periplus* 22:7:25: Μαφαρ<ί>τιδος λεγομένης χ ώρας, "The place/country/land/territory known as Mapharitis".
²¹⁸ *Periplus* 22.
²¹⁹ *Periplus* 24.
²²⁰ *Periplus* 16.

kingdoms remained confederations of tribes under a common ruler.[221] Cholaibos might have been the ruler of one of these tribes. Nevertheless, the emphasis on Charibaêl's title and legitimate claim to his kingdom in the *Periplus*,[222] together with the information that the merchants of Muza paid tribute to him for their privileges in Rhapta,[223] leaves us with little doubt about who was in charge. Aside from realities of political power, the reason might have been Charibaêl's control of the bulk of the myrrh grown inland, without which Muza and its governor would be of little interest in the Indian Ocean and Red Sea trade.

Saba-Himyar – the picture of government control

In conclusion, the kingdom of Saba-Himyar as described in the *Periplus* stands out as an example of ruler effort and success in taking advantage of the maritime trade on the Red Sea and Indian Ocean. A king based in the inland city of Zafar exercised control of the trade in collaboration with a vassal ruler in the town of Sauê closer to the coast. These inland elites excluded the two other possible coastal markets of Okêlis and Eudaimôn Arabia from the maritime trade with India and the Roman Empire. The rationale behind this was probably to control all export from the kingdom, but also to control the influx of certain prestige imports. In this way the king could not only maximise his income from custom dues, but also sell the surplus of myrrh collected as tax or from his own estates, unafraid of competition, control or influence prices, supply and terms of trade, monopolise some key imports, and even ensure that trade in myrrh grown in the rivalling kingdom of Qataban would have to pass through Himyarite or Sabaean markets.

To the extent that that the *Periplus* reveals any economic policy on behalf of the king of Saba-Himyar, it bears the heading "control" and it seems to be ruled by two main motives: the fiscal and consumption needs of the state represented by its ruler.

Hadramawt

A traveller heading eastwards from Eudaimôn Arabia at the time of the *Periplus* would soon reach the other important kingdom of Southern Arabia at the time, Hadramawt, or "the Frankincense-bearing land" as it is called in the *Periplus* after its chief export.[224] The identification of the Frankincense-bearing land with the kingdom of Hadramawt is certain. While the political landscape of the southwestern corner of the Arabian Peninsula changed with the rise, decline and sometimes resurgence of the states of Saba, Awsan, Main, Qataban, and Himyar, the kingdom of Hadramawt stayed in control of the eastern part of modern Yemen and southern part of modern Oman until it was conquered by Himyar in the late third century.

The *Periplus* reveals that the country was governed from an inland *mêtropolis* of Saubatha, where king Eleazos reigned.[225] The country's most important coastal settlement was the *emporion*, port of trade, of Kanê (Qana),[226] but we also learn of a harbour, *limên*, and a fortress at Syagros[227] and the "designated harbour", *hormos apodedeigmenos*, of Moscha Limên (Khor Rori).[228] In addition to his mainland possessions, Eleazos controlled the island of Dioscuridês, modern Socotra, due east of Cape Guardafui on the Horn of Africa, but at the time of the *Periplus*, the island had been rented out to merchants and was under guard.[229] Socotra will be discussed in Chapter 5, dealing with the African coast.

Commentators agree that Saubatha is to be identified with Shabwa, the once famous, but long since abandoned capital of Hadramawt. Pliny wrote in his *Natural History* that the main city of the Hadramis (*Atramitae*), which he called "Sabota", boasted no less than 60 temples,[230] but archaeological remains cannot confirm this report today. Shabwa was situated at the entrance of Wadi Hadramawt, where seasonal rains provided water and silt for irrigation and cultivation. French archaeologists excavating the site of the ancient city in the 1980s noted that the walled city was situated not only on fertile soil and made extensive use of irrigation, but also on the crossing of trade routes leading to Timna (Qataban), Marib (Saba) and the port of Kanê.[231] King Eleazos of *Periplus* has been identified as one of several kings of Hadramawt carrying the name Il'azz.[232]

Kanê – the market of Hadramawt

Kanê was the main outlet of maritime trade on the coast of the Frankincense-bearing land. The emporium has been identified with ruins situated below the cliff of Husn al-Ghurab,[233] about 300 km east of Aden, and well situated for overland communication with Shabwa.[234] According to a modern navigation handbook, the *Red Sea and Gulf of Aden Pilot*, the bay formed by Husn al-Ghurab, "a black square shaped hill (...) with steep sides, and some ancient ruins on its summit", provides anchorage for "small vessels with local knowledge" during the southwest monsoon,[235] which must have been the time of year when merchants from Egypt called there. Russian–Yemeni excavations at the site have shown that in the port's first documented period of existence in the first and second century AD, the settlement consisted of a fortification on top of the hill of Husn al-Ghurab and

---

[221] Beeston 1972.
[222] *Periplus* 23.
[223] *Periplus* 16.
[224] *Periplus* 27:9.4-5, χώρα Λιβανωτοφόρος.
[225] *Periplus* 27.
[226] *Periplus* 27-28.
[227] *Periplus* 30.
[228] *Periplus* 32.
[229] *Periplus* 31.
[230] Pliny 6.155.
[231] Breton 1991: 419.
[232] Doe 1971: 100.
[233] Doe 1961: 182.
[234] See Ingrams 1945 for his description of the journey between the two places, Ingrams noted that the path was walled off in certain places to keep caravans from selecting alternate routes, but the antiquity of these precautions is uncertain (1945: 175).
[235] Hydrographer of the Navy 1967: 406, 408.

large warehouses for frankincense on the beach below.[236] Sherds of amphorae and tableware show contact with the Mediterranean and Iran and probably trade in wine.[237] The finds are consistent with the report of the *Periplus*, and Peacock, Williams and James have shown that a large percentage of basalt stones found at Egyptian Red Sea ports probably stems from Qana, reflecting the need for additional ballast for ships carrying relatively light-weight frankincense to Egypt.[238] Alexander V. Sedov who was in charge of the excavations concluded that the development of Kanê as a harbour coincided with the start of the monsoon trade with the Mediterranean.[239] The limited area of the first settlement at Qana and its partly defensive, partly commercial nature points towards a site founded with the intention of participating in maritime trade. The ruins of Husn al-Ghurab could well be the material remains of a royal initiative to adept to new commercial conditions fostered by increased importance of maritime trade over land routes.

As was the case with Muza, the *Periplus* supplies detailed lists of imports and exports at Kanê:

> "Its imports from Egypt are: wheat, limited quantity, and wine, just as to Muza; also as to Muza, Arab clothing, either with common adornment or no adornment or of printed fabric, in rather large quantities; copper; tin; coral; storax;[240] and the rest of the items that go to Muza. Also, for the king, embossed silverware and money, rather large quantities, plus horses and statuary and fine-quality clothing with no adornment. It exports local wares, namely frankincense and aloe; the rest of its exports are through its connections with other ports of trade".[241]

The textually attested imports are very much the same as at Muza. One difference is, however, worth notice: at Muza, money was mentioned as a general import, at Kanê it is placed among the goods reserved for the king,[242] which could indicate that the king of Hadramawt wanted to control the influx of foreign money. The excavations at Kanê and Khor Rori have yielded considerable amounts of South Arabian coins, and at Khor Rori a possible mint has been identified,[243] indicating coin circulation at Hadrami ports.

Like Muza, Kanê was not only a port of call for Roman merchants, but also the node of an Arabian network.[244] The *Periplus* mentions connections with Barygaza, Skythia, Omana and "the Kingdom of Persis" (the Parthian Empire).[245] Barygaza and Skythia were in India. Omana is not securely identified,[246] but is reported in the *Periplus* to be a port under Parthian influence.[247] In the archaeological record, this eastern dimension of Qana's trade is well attested only from the second century AD onwards,[248] but this does not mean that it was not important at the time of the *Periplus*. It also seems likely that merchants from Hadramawt were the ones who had acquired the rights to trade with Dioscuridês / Socotra,[249] as the *Periplus* indirectly reveals that merchants from Muza and India who traded with the island earlier had been excluded by the mid first century.[250] In addition we learn that some trade or transport by sea existed along the Arabian coast between the ports in Hadramawt.[251]

The author of the *Periplus* was mainly concerned with the trade with Egypt, so we are largely left in the dark concerning exactly what products Kanê dealt with in this trade with other ports. Some hints are available in the lists of the exports from those ports, but these cannot be trusted to be complete for products not relevant to the author of the *Periplus* are likely to have been left out.

Frankincense, frankincense production and frankincense ports

The main export of Kanê and Hadramawt was the aromatic resin called frankincense. However, frankincense trees (*boswellia sacra*) in significant numbers do not grow near Kanê, nor in the vicinity of the capital of Shabwa, and the commodity seems to have been harvested and collected through a network of routes and settlements along the coast.

Our sources for the distribution and production of frankincense in ancient times are twofold. We have the reports of Greek and Roman writers, but unfortunately most of them were not very trustworthy on the subject. None of them, except the unknown author of the *Periplus*, ever visited Southern Arabia themselves; nor do

---

[236] Sedov 1992: 120f.; Sedov 2007: 90ff.
[237] Sedov 1992: 118ff.
[238] Peacock, Williams and James 2007: 59ff.
[239] Sedov 1998: 23f.
[240] An aromatic resin (Casson 1989: 163f.).
[241] *Periplus* 28, excerpt, transl. Casson (1989: 67), Εἰσάγεται δὲ εἰς αὐτὴν ἀπ' Αἰγύπτου μὲν ὁμοίως πυρὸς ὀλίγος καὶ οἶνος ὥσπερ καὶ εἰς Μούζα, ἱματισμὸς Ἀραβικός, [καὶ] ὁμοίως καὶ κοινὸς καὶ ἁπλοῦς καὶ ὁ νόθος περισσότερος, καὶ χαλκὸς καὶ κασσίτερος καὶ κοράλλιον καὶ στύραξ καὶ τὰ λοιπὰ ὅσα εἰς Μούζα· τὰ πλείονα δὲ ἀργυρώματα τετορευμένα καὶ χρήματα τῷ βασιλεῖ, ἵπποι τε καὶ ἀνδριάντες καὶ ἱματισμὸς διάφορος ἁπλοῦς. Ἐξάγεται δὲ ἐξ αὐτῆς ἐντόπια μὲν φορτία, λίβανος καὶ ἀλόη, τὰ δὲ λοιπὰ κατὰ μετοχὴν τῶν ἄλλων ἐμπορίων.
[242] The Greek text (28:9.17) reads χρήματα – the plural of "money", cf. Lidell, Scott and Jones 1996: 2004f. Casson (1989: 255f.) maintained this reading, but points out that it is tempting to emend it to χρυσώματα – "wrought gold, goldware", as it appears next to ἀργυρώματα – "silverware", which are both listed as imports to Muza. Fabricius (1883: 66 n. 1) carried the emendation through, as is also reflected in Schoff's transation, Schoff (1995: 33). While the emendation does seem plausible "money" is also a plausible import to Kanê. Indeed, if this commodity were missing from the list, Kanê, would be the only port serving as an outlet of royal trade that did not import the commodity, in view of that, there is no reason to overrule a sound manuscript reading here (CPG 398: 46r, 5). See also pp. 37f., 40, 53ff., 64ff. and notes 637 and 683 on the import of money top other ports.
[243] Albright 1982: 32f.
[244] See ch. 8, pp. 67ff.
[245] *Periplus* 27.
[246] Casson 1989: 180f.
[247] *Periplus* 27:9.12, 33:11.12, 36:12.4-5, 38:12.29.
[248] Sedov 2007: 104.
[249] See also ch. 5, p. 44.
[250] *Periplus* 30-31.
[251] *Periplus* 32.

we have any indication that the latter ever ventured inland from the ports he described. The most important use of frankincense, like myrrh, was religious and it is understandable that the knowledge of its origin and production became mixed with myth.[252]

Archaeology has as yet yielded few results on this particular subject, so the other important source remains the distribution of the frankincense tree as it is today, and as reported by travellers to Southern Arabia from the 18th century onwards.[253] Frankincense is a demanding species in terms of climate, and its distribution was and remains limited. In modern times, the Dhofar region of Oman is the only part of the Arabian Peninsula, from which frankincense has been exported.[254] Nigel Groom has, however, pointed out the demand must have been much greater in antiquity, due to religious needs and the lack of good substitutes.[255] Based on available reports, he expands the frankincense growing area somewhat to include the area westwards to the start of Wadi Hadramawt at modern Sayhut,[256] but that still leaves us more than 300 kilometers east of ancient Kanê. Frankincense of economic value also grows in some parts of northern Somalia, on the island of Socotra; and scattered species have been reported elsewhere in Southern Arabia.[257]

Passages 29-32 in the *Periplus* at first seem to support Groom's view that in the first century, the distribution of frankincense harvested for sale was somewhat wider than it is today. The report of frankincense production is contained in the section describing a coastline called Sachalitês, a bay between Kanê and the next port to the east, Syagros.[258] Dhofar, the modern frankincense yielding region is, however, probably the region called the bay of Omana in the *Periplus*,[259] further east between Syagros and the port of Moscha. Even if this indicates a slightly wider distribution of the aromatic in the ancient period, it also means that the author of *Periplus* was either somewhat mistaken or at least very vague in his assumptions.

The author of the *Periplus* never visited the frankincense-producing districts himself. He assures us that they were "terribly unhealthy, harmful to those sailing by and absolutely fatal to those working there."[260] That he lived to report such stories should be enough to establish that he never went there personally; otherwise he would either have perished under such terrible conditions or would have discovered that they were in fact rumours, like so many others surrounding the origin of frankincense in the ancient world.[261]

Nevertheless he reports two military strongholds of the king of Hadramawt on the coast east of Kanê. Situated on a headland called Syagros ("wild boar"), was a fortress facing east, overlooking the coast and a deep bay called Omana in the *Periplus*.[262] Below the fortress were a harbour and a warehouse where frankincense was collected. The description is short and to the point. As far as we can tell, Syagros was a not a port of trade visited by foreign merchants, but just what the text says, a military stronghold and a collection point for the frankincense produced nearby.[263]

Following the coast eastwards, the next port of call was Moscha Limên – *limên* means "harbour". In the *Periplus* the port is described as "a designated harbour for loading the Sachalite frankincense".[264] A possible site was identified by Mabel and J.T Bent, travelling in the area in 1890, and their assumptions have since been supported by archaeological excavations: Moscha Limên was probably the settlement that would become the site known as Khor Rori in modern Oman.[265]

"Sachalitês" is the toponym used by the author of the *Periplus* for what he reports to be the frankincense-producing shoreline after Kanê.[266] He has, however,

---

[252] On the sacred use of aromatics and spices in the ancient world, see Detienne 1977 and Groom 1981.
[253] Van Beek (1958: 141ff, and map p. 152) has compared the Graeco-Roman sources and the modern distribution of frankincense and myrrh. He provides a description and a map of the relevant areas of distribution. See also Singer (2007: 7-10), who to a large extent supports Van Beeks finds.
[254] Van Beek 1958: 141.
[255] Groom 1981: 109ff. and map p. 99.
[256] Groom 1981: 109ff.
[257] Van Beek 1958: 142.
[258] *Periplus* 29.
[259] *Periplus* 32.
[260] *Periplus* 29, transl. Casson (1989: 67), Ἐπίνοσοι δὲ δεινῶς οἱ τόποι καὶ τοῖς μ ἐν παραπλέουσι λοιμικοὶ τοῖς δ ἐ ἐργαζομένοις πάντοτε θανατώδεις.

[261] The most famous among them being perhaps the report of Pliny (12.54), that the right to harvest frankincense was hereditary and reserved for 3000 families, that these families were considered sacred, and that they had to adhere to certain rules of purity when engaged in harvesting frankincense. Pliny's story is hardly consistent with the report in *Periplus* 29, that frankincense was handled by royal slaves and convicts.
[262] *Periplus* 30, 32, according to Schoff (1995: 133) probably the headland of Ras Fartak and of that follows that Omana was the Bay of Qamar. This identification has remained unchallenged. The bay of Omana mentioned in *Periplus* 32 should not be confused with the market town under Parthian influence of the same name mentioned in *Periplus* 27 and 36.
[263] Dioscorides interestingly mentions Συάγριος as a variety of frankincense in his first century *De Materia Medica* (I.68).
[264] *Periplus* 32, transl. Casson (1989: 69), ὅρμος ἀποδεδειγμένος τοῦ Σαχαλίτου λιβάνου πρὸς ἐμβολήν.
[265] The identification was first proposed by Theodore Bent (1895: 125). Schoff (1995: 140ff.) and Casson (1989: 170ff.) provide bibliographies and summaries of later evidence. The identification of Moscha with Khor Rori has since been strengthened by excavations at the site, see Albright 1982 and Avanzini 2002, but is far from agreed upon, see Wissmann 1977; Groom 1995: 184ff.; Costa 2002: 24f. Wissmann disagrees with the identification for textual reasons in the *Periplus* and Ptolemy's Geography. Costa follows much of the same line of argument and proposes a different candidate for the site of Moscha. The topographical parts of Ptolemy's geography must, however, be considered to be of a later, or at least of uncertain date, see Bagrow 1945: 385ff. and Mathew 1975: 155f. Groom's most important argument is a re-dating of the Khor Rori inscriptions proposed by Beeston (1976), who places them in the first or second century AD, thus providing a later possible date for the founding of Khor Rori than for the text of the *Periplus*. Recent excavations, however, suggest a much earlier date of foundation for the original settlement, Avanzini 2002: 21ff.
[266] *Periplus* 29.

already made clear about Kanê that "all the frankincense grown in the land is brought into it, as to a warehouse" in his description of *that* harbour.²⁶⁷ If his assumptions about which regions produced frankincense were correct, it would not make sense that the commodity was loaded at Moscha Limên in the bay of Omana before being brought to Kanê. Kanê would have been much closer in the first place.

Both Syagros and Moscha Limên had warehouses for the collection of frankincense.²⁶⁸ They were strategically located at the two ends of what is known as the main frankincense producing area today, and this is in itself a strong indication that it was the most important area also in the first century. Why does the *Periplus* place the frankincense producing area west of this? Are we misinterpreting the source? Was the bay of Omana in fact understood as a part of the region called Sachalitês by the author of the *Periplus*?

It does not seem so, for the text is pretty clear on the point that Sachalitês is a bay, and that after it comes another bay called Omana.²⁶⁹ In this case, however, archaeology can help us out. During the excavations at Khor Rori, inscriptions were found that identified the region as "Sakalan".²⁷⁰ The identification with Sachalitês is near at hand. It seems that the author of *Periplus* was mistaken, probably due to his lack of firsthand knowledge, and that the most important frankincense producing area was the same as it is today, though as Nigel Groom showed, the total area supplying the aromatic was somewhat larger than often assumed, and in this sense our unknown writer of the first century reported the truth.²⁷¹

Moscha Limên / Khor Rori / Sumhuram

Turning to the site of Khor Rori, probably the Moscha Limên of *Periplus*, history and archaeology meets in the core frankincense producing areas, near Salalah on the coast of modern Oman.

Khor Rori had a remarkable natural harbour in a lagoon sheltered from the ocean surf by a narrow inlet. The site itself is as much that of a fortress as of a city, surrounded by thick walls and with defence towers along the wall guarding the single entrance. In order to get in through the narrow gates, one had to change directions several times, and to pass through several doors. Thus, the inhabitants of Khor Rori and their possessions were well guarded. Several inscriptions on the walls of the monumental gate complex narrate the story of the foundation and later restoration of the town. We learn that the settlement was founded on royal initiative, and we get to know its name, Sumhuram and the name of the area, Sakalan. ²⁷² Beeston has pointed out that linguistically, Sumhuram is not a normal toponym but resembles personal names in form,²⁷³ in this case a personal name associated with Hadrami royalty.²⁷⁴ One of the inscriptions provides the additional information that that the new settlement was populated with emigrants from the Hadrami homeland.²⁷⁵ For palaeographic reasons, Pirenne dated the Khor Rori inscriptions to the first century BC.²⁷⁶ As a reasonable *terminus ante quem*, this date was supported by the discovery of Roman pottery datable to the first few decades after the turn of our era during the American excavations at the site in the 1950s.²⁷⁷ Radiocarbon dates, pottery and coins finds from the more recent excavations of the Italian Mission to Oman compares well with the dating of the inscriptions and the pottery, and indicate a date for this phase of settlement from the early first through the third century AD.²⁷⁸

The Italian excavations, however, also indicate that there had been an earlier Hadrami settlement on the site, probably dating from the third to the first century BC, with a brief period of abandonment between the two phases.²⁷⁹ In that case the inscriptions refer to later reconstruction and expansion of the settlement, or perhaps the re-establishing of a settlement that had been abandoned at some point. The gate, the walls and the large building described as the "palace-temple" all belong to this same period of the town's existence.²⁸⁰ The heavy reconstruction undertaken under the leadership of high ranking Hadrami officials and the use of a name connected with royalty for the settlement can only be read as a sign of royal or other outside initiative and interest in the site. It seems likely that the control of frankincense production was among the motives behind this initiative, and grains of frankincense were found all over the site by the American team.²⁸¹

---

²⁶⁷ *Periplus* 27:9.8-9, πᾶς δ' ὁ γεννώμενος ἐν τῇ χώρᾳ λίβανος εἰς αὐτὴν ὥσπερ ἐκδοχεῖον εἰσάγεται.
²⁶⁸ This is stated explicitly only with regard to Syagros (*Periplus* 30). The excavations at Khor Rori have, however, uncovered several large storehouses probably used for frankincense (Albright 1982: 33; Avanzini 2002: 36f.).
²⁶⁹ *Periplus* 29:9.29-31, Μετὰ δὲ Κανὴ, τῆς <γῆς> ἐπὶ πλεῖον ὑποχωρούσης, ἄλλος ἐκδέχεται βαθύτατος κόλπος, ἐπὶ πολὺ παρεκτείνων, ὁ λεγόμενος Σαχαλίτης, καὶ χώρα Λιβανωτοφόρος, "After Kanê, with the shoreline receding further, there next come another bay, very deep, called Sachalitês, which extends for a considerable distance, and the frankincense-bearing land", transl. Casson (1989: 67) and *Periplus* 32:10.26-27, Μετὰ δὲ τὸν Σύαγρον κόλπος ἐστὶν συναφής, ἐπὶ βάθος ἐνδύνων εἰς τὴν ἤπειρον, Ὄμανα, σταδίους ἔχων ἑξακοσίους τὸ διαπέραμα, "Immediately after Syagros is a bay indenting deeply into the coast, Omana, 600 stades across the mouth", transl. Casson (1989: 69).
²⁷⁰ Khor Rori 1 and Khor Rori 4 in Pirenne 1975: 82, 86ff.) = KR 2 and KR 5 in Avanzini 2002: 128ff, 132ff. Note that Avanzini has assigned new numbers to the Khor Rori inscriptions. references here are given with the relevant edition and number.
²⁷¹ Groom 1981: 109ff.

²⁷² KR2.
²⁷³ Beeston 1976: 39.
²⁷⁴ Avanzini 2002: 21f.
²⁷⁵ KR4.
²⁷⁶ Pirenne 1975: 91.
²⁷⁷ Comfort 1960.
²⁷⁸ Avanzini *et al.* 2001: 35f.Avanzini and Sedov 2005: 15f.
²⁷⁹ Avanzini and Sedov 2005: 15f.
²⁸⁰ Avanzini *et al.* 2001: 21ff.
²⁸¹ Albright 1980: 18f.

Zooarchaeological analysis has shown that the inhabitants of Khor Rori fed on range of marine, wild and domestic animals.[282] Among the finds at the site are several grinding stones and a hand mill,[283] showing that the diet of the inhabitants also included cereals. In the *Periplus* we learn that some grain was acquired by government officials from Indian ships happening to winter there.[284] Irrigated agriculture was possible near Khor Rori, and the technology was certainly familiar to the Hadramis. The Italian Mission to Oman identified irrigation walls and possible farmsteads near the walled city,[285] and we must expect that the inhabitants of a site occupied through centuries would take advantage of this opportunity, even though the growing seasons coincided with the harvesting of frankincense, which in the early 20th century, took place in two turns between March and August.[286] The important point is, however, that first century Sumhuram was not primarily an agricultural settlement, and neither a commercial one, except indirectly as suppliers of frankincense to the port of Kanê. The fortunes of a settlement maintained perhaps as long as seven centuries can of course not be explained by increased trade on the Indian Ocean alone,[287] and the economic foundation of the settlement will have varied over time. Situated far from the Hadrami core areas, with warehouses and fortifications as the most prominent features, and at one time populated by forced settlers, Khor Rori, however, emerges as a colony partly maintained for the purpose of controlling the frankincense production. This impression is strengthened by the report of Moscha Limên in the *Periplus*:

> "a designated harbour for loading the Sachalite frankincense, called Moscha Limên. Some vessels are customarily sent to it from Kanê; in addition, those sailing by from Limyrikê or Barygaza that passed the winter because of the season being late, by arrangement with the royal agents take on, in exchange for cotton cloth and grain and oil, a return cargo of frankincense, the Sachalite variety throughout, at a mole that stands there unguarded, thanks to some power of the gods who watch over this place. For, neither covertly, nor overtly can frankincense be loaded aboard a ship without royal permission; if even a grain is lifted aboard, the ship cannot sail, since it is against the god's will."[288]

Perhaps the most interesting aspect of the description of Moscha in the *Periplus* is the relative absence of trade at this port. While we do learn that ships from India wintered there because they missed the end of the summer monsoon that was to bring them home, Moscha was not their original destination,[289] and their trade has little resemblance with the exchange of high value goods for aromatics at Muza and Kanê. They exchanged necessities of life with the local garrison, and were paid in the only plentiful commodity at Moscha, frankincense. The main purpose of Moscha Limên was collection and transport, not trade. Most of the frankincense went by ship to Kanê.[290] Khor Rori / Sumhuram / Moscha thus emerges as a key economic centre in the first-century monsoon trade, but as a centre of production rather than commerce.

The Khor Rori inscriptions reveal that Sumhuram was built by levies of Hadrami colonists selected for emigration. Presumably this means that the settlers did not volunteer to go, and at the very least, it signifies a strong government effort to control the frankincense producing area. It seems to indicate the use of forced labour at least in the colony's first phase, and perhaps it even lends some meaning to a passage in the *Periplus* about frankincense production of Hadramawt stating:

> "The frankincense is handled by royal slaves and convicts. For the districts are terribly unhealthy, harmful to those sailing by and absolutely fatal to those working there – who, moreover die off easily because of the lack of nourishment."[291]

The author of the *Periplus* had almost certainly never set foot in these areas himself, and later travellers have voiced quite different opinions on the Dhofar region. It is not unlikely that the passage on the unhealthiness of the area is the result of disinformation designed to keep outsiders away. If other parts of the passage are interpreted literally, however, two details, are of particular interest: That workers died from lack of nourishment tells us that they were dependent on external (inadequate) supplies, and this lends credibility to the other important piece of information, namely that the frankincense was gathered by forced labour. The

---

[282] Wilkens 2002.
[283] Avanzini 2000: 209; Avanzini et al. 2001: 35.
[284] Periplus 32.
[285] Avanzini and Sedov 2005: 15.
[286] Naval intelligence Division 1946: 205f.
[287] Avanzini et al. 2002: 18ff.
[288] Periplus 32, transl. Casson (1989: 69ff.), ...ὅρμος ἀποδεδειγμένος τοῦ Σαχαλίτου λιβάνου πρὸς ἐμβολήν, Μόσχα λιμὴν λεγόμενος, εἰς ἣν ἀπὸ Κανὴ συνήθως πλοῖα πέμπεταί τινα καὶ παραπλέοντα ἀπὸ Λιμυρικῆς ἢ Βαρυγάζων, ὀψινοῖς καιροῖς παραχειμάσαντα, παρὰ τῶν βασιλικῶν πρὸς ὀθόνιον καὶ σῖτον καὶ ἔλαιον λίβανον ἀντιφορτίζουσιν παρ' ὅλον δὲ τὸν Σαχαλίτην χώματι κειμένῳ καὶ ἀφυλάκτῳ δυνάμει θεῶν τινὶ τοῦτον τὸν τόπον ἐπιτηρούντων· οὔτε γὰρ λάθρα οὔτε φανερῶς χωρὶς βασιλικῆς δόσεως εἰς πλοῖον ἐμβληθῆναι δύναται· κἂν χόνδρον τις ἄρῃ, οὐ δύναται πλεῦσαι τὸ πλοῖον ἀπὸ δαίμονος δίχα.

[289] Ships wintering at Moscha because they missed the end of the summer / SW monsoon must have put in at the port on their way eastwards at the end of a longer journey, if Moscha was their original destination they would have had to arrive with the northeast monsoon, in January-February and would have had several months before the SW monsoon turned unstable in late august, cf. Carsten Niebuhr who reported that when he left Mokha for Bombay on August 23. 1763, all Indian and British ships except the one he had bought passage on had already left, because they feared the changing winds (Niebuhr 2003: 461f.) See Seland 2008 and Gupta 2007 for opposing views of the role of Moscha in the trade between India, Southern Arabia and the Roman Empire.
[290] Periplus 27.
[291] Periplus 29, transl. Casson (1989: 67), Μεταχειρίζεται δὲ ὁ λίβανος ὑπὸ δούλων βασιλικῶν καὶ τῶν ὑπὸ τιμωρίαν πεμπομένων. Ἐπίνοσοι δὲ δεινῶς οἱ τόποι καὶ τοῖς μὲν παραπλέουσι λοιμικοὶ τοῖς δὲ ἐργαζομένοις πάντοτε θανατώδεις, ἔτι δὲ καὶ διὰ τὴν ἔνδειαν τῆς τροφῆς εὐχερῶς ἀπολλύμενοι.

Periplus, of course, refers to a period circa 50–100 years after the reconstruction and re-population of the town, according to the chronology of Khor Rori proposed by the Italian Mission to Oman.[292] The inhabitants of Sumhuram might have been forced colonists rather than actual prisoners, but with no real choice except to harvest frankincense. This all fits well with the picture of a quite small, fortified town far away from the Hadrami homeland where all trade had to pass through government hand, serving as a node in a frankincense trade tightly controlled by the Hadrami authorities.

Hadramawt – the picture of government control

To sum up, Hadramawt, like Saba-Himyar, was an inland-based kingdom despite its three ports. The areas producing an agricultural surplus capable of supporting a king, priesthood, an army and large population centres was in and near Wadi Hadramawt, behind the mountains rising from the coastal plain.

Again, like Saba-Himyar, Hadramawt maintained coastal settlements: the commercial centre of Kanê, a fortress and collection point for frankincense at Syagros and a colony with the same purpose at Moscha Limên.

Like myrrh was to Saba-Himyar, frankincense was vital to Hadramawt in securing a share in the trade on the Red Sea and Indian Ocean. Income from the frankincense trade must in turn have been instrumental in securing imported prestige goods for the king and the court in order to establish and maintain political superiority.
As in Saba-Himyar, maritime trade in Hadramawt was centred at one single port, the port closest to the capital, where the distance to the consumers of the imported goods was at its shortest, and the potential for control at its best.

In contrast to Saba-Himyar, the main area for the production of the most important export commodity was along the coast and far away from main population centres. While this seems to have resulted in a stronger coastal presence on behalf of the king in Hadramawt than in Saba-Himyar, it might also have made it easier for the king to control not only the sale, but also the production of the key commodity. There were no local elites in the frankincense producing regions, which could compete with the king for control with the resources, thus perhaps creating a situation closer to an export monopoly than was the case with myrrh in Saba-Himyar.

The picture given in the *Periplus* is that of strong government involvement in maritime trade: the king had farmed out Socotra to one group of merchants to the exclusion of all others.[293] He had invested in military and maritime installations at several coastal centres, but actual trade outside the main port of Kanê was very limited and only through government officials.[294] At the time of the *Periplus,* frankincense was gathered by slaves and convicts,[295] or perhaps rather by forced colonists as the inscriptions from Khor Rori could indicate.

This concludes the chapter on Southern Arabia. Through the account of the *Periplus,* a picture has emerged of South Arabian rulers eager to profit from maritime trade. This is particularly evident in their efforts to centralise trade to certain ports and in their wish to obtain certain key imports for themselves. The archaeological remains of port sites like Qana and Khor Rori supplement the impression from the *Periplus*: these ports reflect government investment in infrastructure in order to control trade and to profit from it. Rulers were also active in the supply side of the maritime trade. Tax levied in kind would make them major suppliers of aromatics and in the case of Hadramawt, the harvesting of frankincense seems to have been under state control.

---

[292] Avanzini 2002: 21ff.; Avanzini and Sedov 2005: 15f.
[293] *Periplus* 31.
[294] *Periplus* 32.
[295] *Periplus* 29.

Chapter 5: The African coast

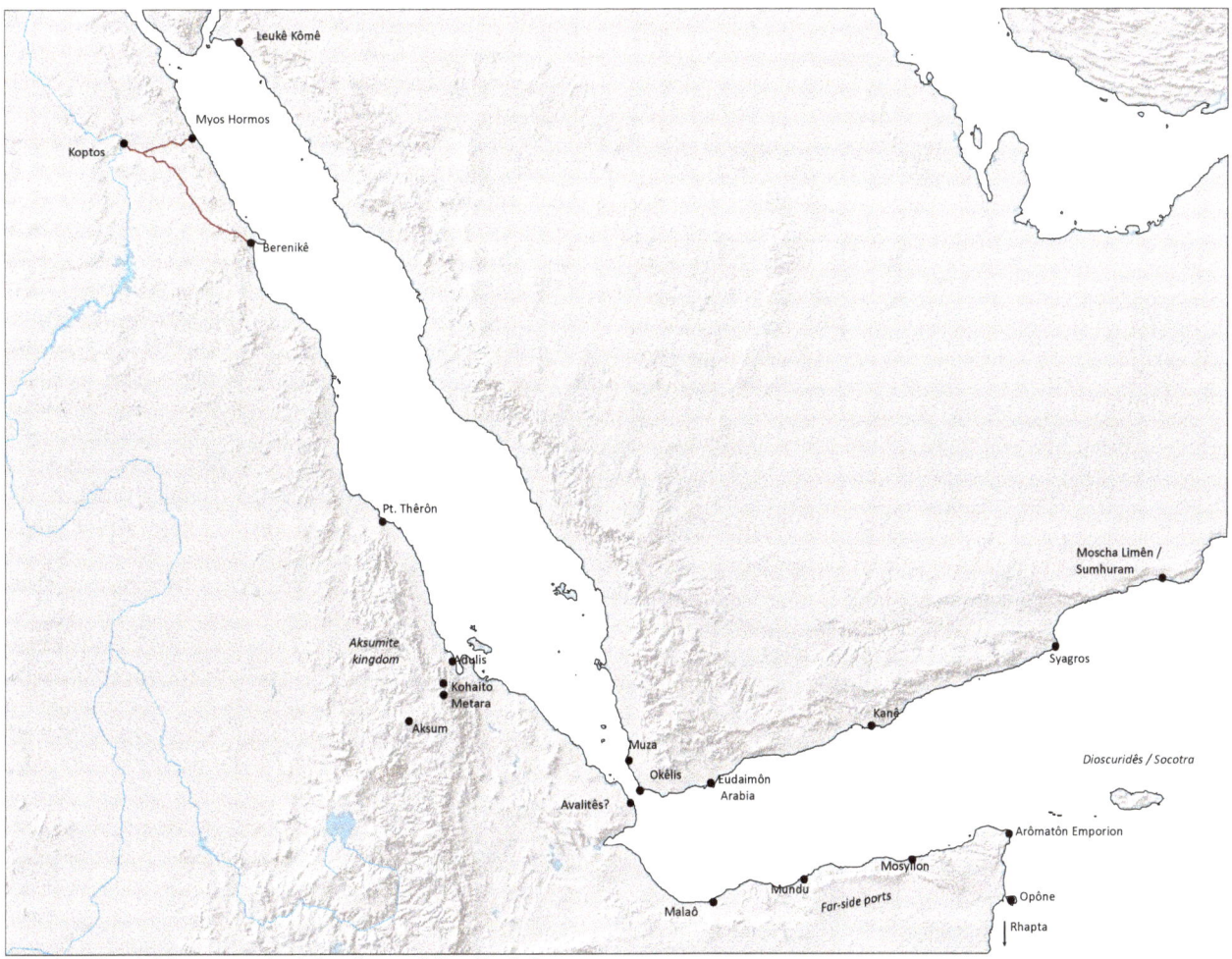

Fig. 3: The African coast at the time of the *Periplus*

Whereas most of the Arabian and Indian coasts were divided between inland kingdoms in the first century AD, the *Periplus* mentions only one centralised polity along the East African coast south of Egypt. This was the kingdom ruled by a certain Zôskalês, Aksum as it was later named after its capital in the highlands of northern Ethiopia. The kingdom of Meroë in modern Sudan is not known to have maintained any presence on the Red Sea coast. The African coast south of the Red Sea remains archaeologically under-explored. No indigenous literary sources from the period exist, neither are there contemporary South Arabian or Indian reports. The region is only sketchily described in Graeco-Roman geographic literature, leaving the *Periplus* the main source of information. According to the *Periplus* the rest of the African coast in the first century AD was inhabited by more or less nomadic tribes, dominated by Arabian states or organised in smaller chiefdoms. The absence of centralised power in most regions by no means hindered trade altogether, but could in some places make commercial activities uncertain or difficult, or foster alternative arrangements to facilitate trade. As we follow the description of the *Periplus* southwards from the Egyptian Red Sea ports, we shall study trading activities on the African east coast and the island of Socotra, with an eye toward how they related to political authority.

The Egyptian ports of Myos Hormos and Berenikê were the points of departure for Mediterranean traders engaged in trade with Africa, Arabia and India. Both were reached by overland travel from the Nile port of Koptos, on caravan roads where stations at regular intervals provided water and shelter for travellers. From Koptos, river transport northwards to Alexandria was possible. The road to Berenikê was constructed by Ptolemy II Philadelphus[296] (285-246 BC), after whose mother the port was named. Myos Hormos was situated further north and at a shorter distance from Koptos, but the longer sea voyage was a drawback. When ships returned from India in January-February, they had favourable southerly winds at their backs in the southern part of the Red Sea, but the upper part of the Red Sea is dominated by northerlies at

---

[296] Strabo 17.1.45.

that time of the year (or indeed at any time of the year.)²⁹⁷ Contrary wind and difficult waters could make it more attractive to put in at Berenikê, even if the overland haul to Koptos was longer. The prevailing northerly winds in the Red Sea north of 20° latitude were probably the reason why trade was centred at these southern ports, rather than at Arsinoê at the northernmost point of the Red Sea, where a canal connected the sea to the Nile,²⁹⁸ making cheaper water transport possible. Strabo referred to this problem in his *Geography*, reporting that the road to Berenikê was built through waterless desert, because "the Red Sea was hard to navigate, particularly for those who set out from its innermost recess".²⁹⁹

That the ports and the desert roads were of Ptolemaic origin show the importance of the Red Sea and Indian Ocean trade for the Ptolemaic and later Roman authorities of Egypt. Safe trade and travel, and the provision of water on the desert route to the harbours must have meant a considerable effort by the authorities, but it was obviously deemed necessary if trade and hence the customs and tax income were not to pass to other ports. These ports constituted the limits of Roman authority on the Red Sea coast. The coastline south of Berenikê is described as populated by different groups of *Barbaroi*, organised in chiefdoms, *tyrannida*.³⁰⁰ We hear of no trade in these parts before the description reaches the port of Ptolemais Thêrôn, situated near the modern border between Sudan and Eritrea.³⁰¹

Thêrôn means "of the hunts". According to Strabo, the settlement had been founded by a certain Eumedes, who was on a mission to the elephant hunting-grounds from the same Ptolemy II who built the desert roads.³⁰² The author of the *Periplus* explains that the port used to be the base of hunting expeditions when Egypt was under Ptolemaic rule, and "the king's hunters made their way inland" from this port.³⁰³ An important aim of these hunts was to provide elephants for the Egyptian army, as a Ptolemaic stele copied at Adulis in modern Eritrea by the sixth century traveller Cosmas Indicopleustes reported.³⁰⁴ The demand for African elephants decreased after the beasts performed less than convincing at the battle of Raphia in 217 BC.³⁰⁵ At the time of the *Periplus* the port, which offered tortoise shell and sometimes a little ivory to visiting traders,³⁰⁶ must have been long deserted by its Hellenistic settlers. No imports are mentioned, attesting perhaps to its limited importance in the monsoon and Red Sea trade in the first century. A later passage indirectly informs us that this part of the coast belonged to the kingdom of Zôskalês,³⁰⁷ the king who ruled the African coast from there to the straits of Bab al-Mandeb. There is, however, no trace of official authority at Ptolemais, nor any institutional or physical infrastructure for trade; and it is doubtful whether Zôskalês made his authority felt at the port.

Aksum – the kingdom of Zôskalês

The kingdom of Zôskalês was later to be known by the name of its capital, Aksum, in the Ethiopian highlands. The Aksumite kingdom controlled areas on both sides of the modern border between Ethiopia and Eritrea, where fertile highlands at 2000-2500 metres altitude and sufficient precipitation for dry farming in normal years provided the necessary agricultural basis for a number of urban centres.³⁰⁸ At least from the time of the *Periplus* and until the Arab sack of the Aksumite harbour of Adulis around 700 AD,³⁰⁹ the highland state also maintained a presence on the dry, hot coastal plain along the Red Sea. Adulis is more important than Ptolemais Thêrôn in this context. At the time of the *Periplus*, this was no more than a "village of moderate size",³¹⁰ but with a future ahead of it as one of the most important ports of the Red Sea trade until the Sasanian and later Muslim conquest of Southern Arabia cut Aksum off from the flow of Red Sea and Indian Ocean trade in the late sixth and seventh centuries.³¹¹ Extensive ruins and thick cultural deposits mark the location of ancient Adulis, about 56 km east and south of Massawa in modern Eritrea, where systematic surveys and excavations have revealed elite housing, churches, public buildings and sherds of glass and amphorae.³¹²

The Aksumite kingdom was not the first complex society in the region. As far back as perhaps 700 BC, a kingdom with strong cultural influence from Southern Arabia

---

²⁹⁷ Facey 2004: 9ff.
²⁹⁸ Redmount 1995.
²⁹⁹ Strabo 17.1.45, transl. Jones (2001: vol VIII, p. 119), διὰ τὸ τὴν Ἐρυθρὰν δύσπλουν εἶναι, καὶ μάλιστα τοῖς ἐκ τοῦ μυχοῦ πλοϊζομένοις.
³⁰⁰ *Periplus* 2:1.9-10.
³⁰¹ *Periplus* 3. Commentators disagree on the location of Ptolemais, see Casson 1989: 100f. Crowfoot (1911), however, made a strong case for Aqiq in modern Sudan, where he found what he was certain to be classical remains.
³⁰² Strabo 16.4.7.
³⁰³ *Periplus* 3:1.14-15, τῷ βασιλεῖ θηρεύοντες ἀνέβησαν.
³⁰⁴ Cosmas 2.58.
³⁰⁵ Polybius 5.84-6 (battle of Raphia); Burstein 1989: 10 (influence on Ptolemaic policy).
³⁰⁶ *Periplus* 3.

³⁰⁷ *Periplus* 5.
³⁰⁸ See Butzer 1981 on the agricultural basis of Aksum and its probable deterioration in later periods due to soil erosion and possibly a decrease in rainfall.
³⁰⁹ Kobischanow 1979: 116f.
³¹⁰ *Periplus* 4:2.6, κώμη σύμμετρος
³¹¹ Several good histories of Aksum are available. Selaisse (1972) and Kobischanow and Michels (1979) are now somewhat dated. Munro-Hay (1991); Phillipson (1998) and Finneran (2007) were able to include the results of the extensive archaeological excavations conducted after that, but especially Phillipson continues to rely mainly on archaeological material also for later periods, for which literary sources also exist.
³¹² See Munro-Hay (ed.) 1982 for a summary of available archaeological evidence up to that time, Paribeni (1907) for the Italian excavations in the early 20ᵗʰ century and Anfray (1974) for the a summary of the French excavations in the 1960s. An Eritreo-British team explored the site in 2004 and 2005, resulting in an extensive survey and the location of the probable ancient port (Peacock *et al.* 2004; Peacock and Blue 2007). The identification of this site with Adulis has been challenged by Lionel Casson, who proposed the site of modern Massawa instead (1989: 107f.). His evidence, however, is literary and geographical only, and has failed to win support due to the massive archaeological remains on the site traditionally thought to be Adulis, which Casson seeks to explain with a subsequent move of the city.

established itself in the highlands on both sides of the modern border between Ethiopia and Eritrea.[313] No political or cultural continuity can, however, be established between this "Kingdom of Damaat" and the later Aksumite state.[314]

The peak of Aksumite civilisation, of which its monumental stelae, royal tombs, huge elite residences, church ruins and gold coinage bear witness, dates mainly from the late third through the seventh centuries. A more active role of the Aksumites as middlemen in the Indian Ocean trade from the third century onwards seems to explain some of this prosperity. Kushan gold coins from the early third century found in a monastery northeast of Aksum[315] attest trade with India in a period when evidence of direct Roman trade with the subcontinent is scarce,[316] even if the context of these coins – a Christian monastery – is later.

The monumental phases of Aksum's history fall beyond the limits of this study, but the *Periplus* confirms that the kingdom was already an important regional power by the first century.[317] The author of the *Periplus* probably never visited the city of Aksum itself, but he knows its name, and he refers to it as a *mêtropolis*,[318] a term he reserves for places of royal residence only, and which puts it on equal standing with contemporary political centres in Southern Arabia and India. Excavations at Aksum have revealed that the site was settled as early as the first century AD.[319] The oldest structures in the large burial fields were constructed in that period,[320] and first-century glass of Roman origin was also found.[321] Reports of first century South Arabian coins found at Aksum[322] also contribute to the impression that exchange between coast and highland areas was already well established.

The *mêtropolis* of Aksum was situated a few days journey from the coast,[323] in the westernmost part of the highland kingdom. Stuart Munro-Hay has pointed out that the city was founded at the juncture of three regional trade routes,[324] and in an area where fertile soil and relatively plentiful and reliable rain made it possible to harvest twice a year.[325] The most important trade route was from Adulis to Metara or Qoohaito via Aksum and along the Takaze River to the Blue Nile, while other routes led southwards to modern Somalia, to the interior of modern Ethiopia and beyond and northwards to Aswan.[326]

The polity of Aksum was still in its infancy in the first century. The *Periplus* reveals that the kings Aksum held suzerainty over a large portion of the Red Sea coast,[327] but there is reason to suspect that its control over these areas was not very firm. In his description of Adulis, the author of the *Periplus* reports that attacks from the mainland had forced ships to anchor further away from the port than they used to.[328] The population of Adulis itself would hardly have wanted to attack ships coming to trade at their harbour and with their ruler, and we are left with an impression of the village itself as a safe haven, whereas the surroundings were not sufficiently subdued to leave traders in peace.

At the time of the *Periplus*, Adulis seems to have been a settlement maintained for commercial purposes, but that does not mean that the port was necessarily founded by the emerging power of Aksum. Italian excavations at Adulis in 1907 uncovered layers of cultural deposits more than 10 metres thick,[329] something which Munro-Hay has seen as an indication that the history of the site goes much further back than the first century, being perhaps a centre in its own right before the highland rulers from Aksum came to dominate it.[330] While rainfall is scarce on the coastal plain, the soil in the vicinity of Adulis is fertile, and a certain agricultural basis for the settlement would be possible through irrigation.[331] The stela copied at Adulis by Cosmas Indicopleustes, visiting Adulis in the early sixth century, had an inscription of Ptolemy III of Egypt (246-221 BC), commemorating his elephant hunts and those of his father.[332] This could be an indication that Adulis, like Ptolemais Thêrôn, was an old Ptolemaic hunting station or port, but the inscription has never been found by modern excavators, nor have other remains from the Ptolemaic period. This has led K.L. Kirwan to suggest that it had been moved from another spot, e.g. Ptolemais Thêrôn, before the time of Cosmas.[333]

---

[313] Fattovich 2004.
[314] Fattovich 2004.
[315] Kobishchanow and Michels 1979: 58.
[316] One of the few sources mentioning Roman travellers on the Indian Ocean in this period is the fourth century report of the adventures of a Theban lawyer in India, the *Epistola de Indicis Gentibus et de Bragmanibus* (sic). The letter is traditionally, but probably wrongly ascribed to a certain Palladius, see Coleman-Norton 1926; Derret 1962; Weerakkody 1997: 119ff. The lawyer reaches India on an Indian ship from the Aksumite kingdom (Palladius 7).
[317] But see Michels (2005: 113f.), who prefers to label Aksum in this period a chiefdom, reserving the state term for the period after 150 AD. In the end this of course comes down to which definition you chose to apply. In favour of calling Aksum a state speaks the evidence of the *Periplus*, characterising Aksum as a μετρόπολις (4:2.8) and reporting Zôskalês to βασιλεύει (5:2.19), "rule as a king", cf. Lidell, Scott and Jones (1996: 309b), putting Aksum on par with Indian and Arabian kingdoms.
[318] *Periplus* 4:2.8.
[319] Fattovich 1997: 68f, 70f.
[320] Munro-Hay and Phillipson 1989: 330f.
[321] Morrison 1989: 208.
[322] Breton and Munro-Hay 2002.
[323] The *Periplus*, 4, says eight days, but several routes were possible, see Munro-Hay 1991: 30ff. and Raunig 2004.
[324] Munro-Hay 1991: 33ff.
[325] Phillipson 1998: 11ff. describes the geographical and climatic setting of Aksum.
[326] Munro-Hay 1991: 33ff.
[327] *Periplus* 5.
[328] *Periplus* 4.
[329] Paribeni 1907: 448.
[330] Munro-Hay 1991: 47.
[331] Fattovich 2003: 17. Peacock and Blue (2007: 1) reports an annual precipitation of ca 200 mm., very close to the needs for dry farming. Nearby settlements today cultivate large fields, and it is reasonable to suspect that intensive irrigation and cultivation was possible in antiquity as well.
[332] Cosmas 2.58.
[333] Kirwan 1972: 171f.

While this is certainly possible, it is known that the Ptolemies established bases as far south and east as modern Somalia,[334] and there is no reason why their representatives should not have visited Adulis, considering the good possibilities for elephant hunting a few days inland from the port. The oldest known reference to Adulis, a passage in Pliny, probably also dates back to the Ptolemaic period:

> "The town of Adulis, founded by Egyptian slaves who had run away from their masters. Here is a very large market of the Trogodytes (sic) and of the Aethiopians, two days sail from Ptolemais.[335] They bring to it much ivory, rhinoceros horns, hippopotamus hides, tortoise shells, apes and slaves".[336]

Pliny's report on the foundation of Adulis is likely to be a spurious etymological conclusion and should not be taken too seriously.[337] Although his *Natural History* was published some 25 years after the *Periplus*, it is based on a number of older sources. Pliny gives no explicit reference for the description of Adulis, but it occurs among passages referring to a lost work of Juba,[338] a Roman client king of Mauretania from 25 BC onwards. The omission of the kingdom and city of Aksum in Pliny's work also point toward a first century BC or earlier date for this passage. This date could be taken to support Munro-Hay's notion that the history of Adulis goes as far back as Ptolemaic times.

Trade at Adulis

Be that as it may, by the time of the *Periplus*, Adulis had assumed the role that it would continue to exercise in the coming centuries as the main outlet of Aksumite maritime trade.[339] Like Muza on the Arabian side, it is described as an *emporion nomimon*, a "legally limited port of trade" in the *Periplus*,[340] implying some sort of official status. The extensive list of imports and exports provided in the *Periplus* is cited below in Lionel Casson's translation:

> "In this area there is a market for: articles of clothing for the Barbaroi, unused, the kind produced in Egypt; wraps from Arsinoe; colored *abbolai* [cloaks] of printed fabric; linens; double-fringed items; numerous types of glass stones and also of millefiori glass of the kind produced in Diospolis; brass, which they use for ornaments as well as cutting up for coins; copper honey pans[341] for cooking and for cutting up into armlets and anklets for certain of the women; iron which is expended on spears for elephants and the other wild animals as well as for war. Likewise there is also a market for: axes, adzes, knives; large round copper drinking vessels; a little Roman money for the resident foreigners; wine of Laodicea and Italy, limited quantity; olive oil, limited quantity. For the king, silverware and goldware fashioned in the local manner; in clothing, *abbolai* and *kaunakai* [heavy cloaks], with no adornment and modest in price".[342]

The inventory then continues with imports from the interior of the kingdom of Ariakê in Northwestern India, namely *iron, steel, lac dye* and a range of *textiles*, then the three exports from Adulis: *ivory, tortoiseshell and rhinoceros horns*.[343]

This is one of the most extensive lists provided in the *Periplus*. It attests a lively trade in quite everyday articles: tools, clothing, glass beads and inexpensive jewellery. Some of the trade was with the local population, some with resident foreign merchants and some with the king.

Metal in different forms seems to have been a significant import to Adulis, and three aspects of this trade are of special interest. Firstly, brass was imported and cut up in smaller pieces to be used as coins. Aksum did not issue its own coinage before ca 270 AD.[344] The existence of brass as a coin substitute at time of the *Periplus* gives us a glimpse into the local economy in Adulis at the time.

---

[334] Casson 1993: 255f.
[335] Some manuscripts read "five days", cf. Mayhoff 1906: 501, which would agree better with the distance between the ports given in the *Periplus* 4:1.19-20, 3000 stades or ca 540 kilometres.
[336] Pliny 6.172-173, *oppidum Aduliton - Aegyptiorum hoc servi profugi a dominis condidere. maximum hic emporium Trogodytarum, etiam Aethiopum - abest a Ptolemaide II dierum navigatione; deferunt plurimum ebur, rhinocerotum cornua, hippopotamiorum coria, chelium testudinum, sphingia, mancipia.* ΣΦΙΝΓΙΑ are attested as African monkeys, perhaps baboons, on the Nile Mosaic from Palestrina, see Meyboom 1995: 22.
[337] Based on the Greek verb ἀδούλέω, to have no slaves (Rackham 1997-2001: vol II, p. 466 note c.) The verb is known only from Strabo's account of Megasthenes' description of the Indian Brahmins (15.1.59), cf. Lidell, Scott and Jones (1996: 24b).
[338] Pliny 6.170, 175.
[339] Munro-Hay (1982) treats the foreign trade at Adulis in a diachronic perspective.
[340] *Periplus* 4:1.20.

[341] Casson (1989: 53 and 55, commentary p. 247) translates the Greek μελίεφθα χαλκᾶ (6:2.27) and μελίεφθα (8:3.28) as "honey pans". Huntingford (1980: 21 and 24, commentary p. 138) retains the Greek word but comments that it literally means, "copper cooked in honey" and possibly means "sheets of ductile or soft copper", as Schoff also translated it (1995: 24, 25, commentary p. 70). That it could be cut up into coins, νομίσματος, and armlets, at least gives us an idea of its use and nature.
[342] *Periplus* 6, transl. Casson (1989: 53), Προχωρεῖ δὲ εἰς τοὺς τόπους τούτους ἱμάτια Βαρβαρικὰ ἄγναφα τὰ ἐν Αἰγύπτῳ γινόμενα, Ἀρσινοϊτικαὶ στολαὶ καὶ ἀβόλλαι νόθοι χρωμάτινοι καὶ λέντια καὶ δικρόσσια καὶ λιθίας ὑ<α>λῆς πλείονα γένη καὶ ἄλλης μορρίνης τῆς γινομένης ἐν Διοσπόλει, καὶ ὠρόχαλκος, ᾧ χρῶνται πρὸς κόσμον καὶ εἰς συγκοπὴν ἀντὶ νομίσματος, καὶ μελίεφθα χαλκᾶ εἴς τε ἕψησιν καὶ εἰς συγκοπὴν ψελίων καὶ περισκελίδων τισὶν τῶν γυναικῶν καὶ σίδηρος ὁ δαπανώμενος εἴς τε λόγχας πρὸς τοὺς ἐλέφαντας καὶ τὰ ἄλλα θηρία καὶ τοὺς πολέμους. Ὁμοίως δὲ καὶ πελύκια προχωρεῖ καὶ σκέπαρνα καὶ μάχαιραι καὶ ποτήρια χαλκᾶ στρογγύλα μεγάλα καὶ δηνάριον ὀλίγον πρὸς τοὺς ἐπιδημοῦντας καὶ οἶνος Λαδικηνὸς καὶ Ἰταλικὸς οὐ πολὺς καὶ ἔλαιον οὐ πολύ· τῷ δὲ βασιλεῖ ἀργυρώματα καὶ χρυσώματα τοπικῷ ῥυθμῷ κατεσκευασμένα καὶ ἱματίων ἀβόλλαι καὶ γαυνάκαι ἁπλοῖ, οὐ πολλοῦ δὲ ταῦτα.
[343] *Periplus* 6.
[344] Munro-Hay 1991: 180ff.

The use of pieces of such a relatively low value metal for coins hints at a local economy where barter was not sufficient to facilitate the exchange of goods, and where low value transactions were conducted. This in turn implies that there was no such thing as a monopoly of import, export or trade at the *emporion nomimon* of Adulis. With only one or a few large participants, barter, helped by bullion of higher value if necessary, would have been sufficient to buy and sell goods.

Roman money, *dênarion*,[345] was imported for the resident foreigners at Adulis. Very few Roman coins have been found in Eritrea and Ethiopia, however, and the money mentioned in the *Periplus* was probably not intended for trade with the local population at Adulis if they preferred brass as the text seems to indicate, or with the inland authorities from Aksum. A separate monetised economy within what was probably a quite small foreign colony in Adulis also seems unnecessary and unlikely. It would appear that visiting merchants used the money in their dealings with the resident foreign merchant community, which secured local products throughout the year. The resident traders must have imported some of the goods in local demand for their trade with the Aksumites, but the balance, constituting their profit, would have been better paid in a currency they could use if they returned to the Mediterranean world, or that they could easily transfer to agents, patrons or business associates at home.

The third interesting metal import to Adulis was iron in the form of unworked metal and tools. David Phillipson has proposed that this must have been due to lack of technology in first century Aksum rather than to lack of raw materials, as finds from the third century onwards give ample proof of excellent local ironworking.[346] Now the *Periplus* seems to report that the iron was imported as raw material and then worked into spears after reaching African shores.[347] If that is correct, the demand for iron must have been founded on inadequate local supply of raw materials rather than on the lack of expertise in ironworking. In either case, the import of iron for weapons contributes to the picture of Aksum as a power in its infancy. If knowledge about ironworking or the availability of iron was poor in Eritrea and Ethiopia at the time, the import of weapons or iron could have given the Aksumites a strategic advantage in their struggles with their rivals. The *Periplus* confirms that such struggles took place, for the text says that the weapons were used not only for hunting but also for warfare.[348] The use of iron weapons for elephant hunting could, on the other hand, help the Aksumites to get the ivory they needed for their trade.

A little wine and olive oil was also imported at Adulis. It is not unlikely that local or highland elites consumed some of it. King Zôskalês is described as "acquainted with Greek learning",[349] and it would not be surprising if he had adopted Greek drinking habits as well. Still, some of the wine and oil could have been intended for the resident foreign merchants in Adulis; and up to the present, no remains of first-century amphorae have been found at Aksum although the archaeological evidence for wine trade in the third through seventh centuries is ample.[350]

Like other ports reported to be the maritime outlet of a royal court in the *Periplus*, Adulis too boasts a list of special imports for the king. He required silverware and goldware, probably intended for communal drinking or dining at the court or redistribution to followers and allies. Other royal imports were of less conspicuous nature, such as 'heavy cloaks without adornments and of modest price'. It is tempting to see this as clothing for the king's soldiers or other retainers, as night-time and winter temperatures in the highlands can be freezing.

The list of exports is relatively short, and thus the volume of the different commodities must have been quite substantial to pay for the imports. Tortoise shell, used by the Romans for inlays in expensive furniture,[351] for boxes, plaques and the like,[352] was readily available on the islands just outside the Bay of Zula, where Adulis was situated, and was brought there by the coastal population – the *Ichthyophagoi*[353] ("fish-eaters"). Obsidian was also found along this coast,[354] and can be seen scattered in the deposits from excavations at Adulis.

Ivory and rhinoceros horns were primarily inland commodities. Although the *Periplus* states that these animals inhabited the interior, they were sometimes seen and surely also hunted along the coast.[355] Ivory appears to have been the key export from Aksum, as myrrh was from Saba-Himyar and frankincense from Hadramawt. This is the very brief description the inland regions in the *Periplus* (*italics* added):

> "From Adulis it is a journey of three days to Koloê, an inland city that is the first trading post for ivory, and from there another five days to the metropolis itself, which is called Axômitês; *into it is brought all the ivory from beyond the Nile through what is called Kyêneion, and from there down to Adulis.*"[356]

---

[345] *Periplus* 6:2.32.
[346] Phillipson 1998: 77f.
[347] *Periplus* 6:2.29-30 σίδηρος ὁ δαπανώμενος εἴς τε λόγχας πρὸς τοὺς ἐλέφαντας καὶ τὰ ἄλλα θηρία καὶ τοὺς πολέμους, "iron spent for spears for elephants and other wild animals and wars".
[348] Ibid.

[349] *Periplus* 5:2.21-22, γραμμάτων Ἑλληνικῶν ἔμπειρος.
[350] Wilding 1989: 314f.
[351] Pliny 16.232.
[352] *Periplus* 30.
[353] *Periplus* 4.
[354] *Periplus* 5.
[355] *Periplus* 4.
[356] *Periplus* 4, transl. Casson (1989: 53), ἀφ' ἧς εἰς μὲν Κολόην μεσόγειον πόλιν καὶ πρῶτον ἐμπόριον τοῦ ἐλέφαντος ὁδός ἐστιν ἡμερῶν τριῶν· ἀπὸ δὲ ταύτης εἰς αὐτὴν τὴν μητρόπολιν τὸν Ἀξωμίτην λεγόμενον

Hence the *Periplus* underlines the importance of Aksum's position at the junction of trade routes. Ivory was highly sought after in the ancient world, and Aksum was able to control the bulk of its flow from the most important sources. Koloê has not been securely identified, but it might be identical with Metara, about halfway between Aksum and Adulis, where impressive Aksumite remains have been found.[357] Another candidate is constituted by extensive ruins on the site of Qohayto, on the edge of the highland plateau.[358] The old routes from the Red Sea coast to the highland plateau are still in use.[359] Local people at Senafe, near Metara, claim that the journey from Foro near ancient Adulis can be made in two days.[360] While this seems a rather demanding walk (ca 70 km), it contributes to the reliability of the report in the *Periplus* that the first leg of the journey to Aksum took three days.

Zôskalês

After the description of the whole coastline of Aksum, we are told that the region was ruled by a certain Zôskalês. Zôskalês is the earliest known king of Aksum, not surprisingly so as the *Periplus* is the first reference to the kingdom. The earliest Aksumite coins and inscriptions yet identified date from the third century, and what we can gather from *Periplus* description is all we know about him.

It is his rule of the coastal region that is stressed in the *Periplus*, not of the highlands. As the *Periplus* is primarily focused on coastal matters, this is not surprising, and does not rule out inland rule *per se*. Nevertheless, some commentators have suspected that Zôskalês was not actually *the* king of Aksum, but a vassal ruler of the coastal regions.[361] Lionel Casson ruled this out on linguistic grounds, noting that such sub rulers are called *tyrannoi* in other parts of the text, while Zôskalês is said to *basileuei* "rule as a king."[362] The fact that the royal imports included heavy cloaks (*kaunakai*)[363] has also been used to support that Zôskalês's kingdom extended to the highlands, as he would not need them in the hot coastal region.[364] The last argument is hardly conclusive, for Zôskalês, if he was a vassal king of the coastal regions, would still need suitable commodities for trade with or tribute to the highland region. Moreover, even if Zôskalês did not rule from Aksum, it is likely that he would have controlled parts of the highland plateau.

The coastal plain is only about 40-60 kilometers wide, and largely unsuitable for agriculture, while fertile and climatically more suitable areas were available at the edge of the plateau, relatively close to Adulis, while still relatively far from Aksum.

In the *Periplus* Zôskalês is described as "tight with his possessions and striving for more, but otherwise high-minded and acquainted with Greek learning."[365] This personal and ambivalent characteristic of the king, which balances Zôskalês' stinginess in economic matters with his liberal personality in other respects, is remarkable, and it does not fit well with a distant ruler in the remote and little known inland capital of Aksum. Maybe this indicates that Zôskalês was more directly interested in the trading activities of his kingdom than most rulers. He was obviously keen on getting as much out of it as possible, and perhaps the author of the *Periplus* had experienced him to be a hard bargainer. His residence in Adulis would explain both the personal knowledge of his character by the author of the *Periplus* and Zôskalês' abilities in the Greek language.

There is a third possible answer to the problem of Zôskalês' power base and residence. He could have been travelling between the coast and the highland, and be resident in different parts of his kingdom at different parts of the year. Similar arrangements are amply attested in other pre modern contexts, including not only later Ethiopian history, but also the Achamenid Empire, the empire of Charlemagne and Elizabethan England. Peripatetic courts ease control with large territories, strengthen ties between rulers and local elites, and facilitate collection of taxes and revenue in kind. For Zôskalês, a visit to the coast in the trading season would ensure control over trade and make a show of military power to his subjects. Nevertheless, as long as the *Periplus* remains our only source, the question of Zôskalês' position will remain a matter of conjecture. Structurally, the key aspect is that the export goods came from the inland centre of Aksum, and that this centre clearly ranked above Adulis politically, being labelled a *mêtropolis*. Although Adulis was a settlement of considerable size during its archaeologically best documented period from the fourth through seventh century, it is characterised as a village – *kôme*, at the time of the *Periplus*, which is hardly the ideal power base for a king no matter how important the trade was.

Aksum – the picture of government control

To sum up, the kingdom of Aksum in the first century was based on agricultural settlements in the highlands on both sides of the border between modern Ethiopia and Eritrea and with a commercial and political presence on the Red Sea coast. Foreign traders visiting the area

---

ἄλλων ἡμερῶν πέντε, εἰς ὃν ὁ πᾶς ἐλέφας ἀπὸ τοῦ πέρα<ν> τοῦ Νείλου φέρεται διὰ τοῦ λεγομένου Κυηνείου, ἐκεῖθεν δὲ εἰς Ἄδουλι.

[357] Anfray 1974: 753ff.
[358] Munro-Hay 1991: 47. Wenig (2003: 93ff.) rejects the identification of Qohaito with Koloê on grounds of the scattered pattern of habitation on the Qohaitoo plateau, not resembling the city structure expected for Koloê and the fact that Qohaito represents a detour on the two most attractive caravan routes from Adulis to Aksum.
[359] Raunig 2004.
[360] Personal communication.
[361] Huntingford 1980: 149ff. Casson (1989: 109f.) provides an extensive bibliography.
[362] Casson 1989: 109, cf. Lidell, Scott and Jones 1996: 309b.
[363] *Periplus* 6.
[364] Casson 1989: 110.

[365] *Periplus* 5:2.20-23, ἀκριβὴς μὲν τοῦ βίου καὶ τοῦ πλείονος ἐξεχόμενος, γενναῖος δὲ περὶ τὰ λοιπὰ καὶ γραμμάτων Ἑλληνικῶν ἔμπειρος.

needed royal protection to trade safely. This safety could be offered at Adulis, a "legally limited port of trade".

The most important export from Aksum was ivory. It was exchanged for products needed by the king and his household for both practical and prestige purposes. Metal for weapons was needed for elephant hunts and wars, expensive tableware for displays of power, redistribution or further trade. Trade thus seems to have been *one* instrumental way of maintaining the king's position.

Elephants were hunted in large areas of the Aksumite kingdom and beyond. Ivory was not only sold at Adulis, but also at Ptolemais Thêrôn further north and at inland markets. A royal monopoly on ivory trade seems unlikely. Still, the king must have been a major participant in this trade in order to acquire the goods he wanted from the foreign merchants. His highland power base at Aksum made the control of the flow of ivory from the inland and thus of the gross part possible. Whether he secured this ivory through trade, tax, tribute or royal hunts we cannot know, but a combination would certainly be a likely option.

As at Muza and Kanê, we have evidence of different flows of trade meeting at Adulis. Local and regional trade linked up with Red Sea and Indian Ocean networks. It might also be justifiable to speak of several spheres of trade: a prestige sphere where ivory was exchanged for objects of art with the king, and a lower sphere of trade with more everyday items, including commerce with the semi-sedentary population around Adulis in products like tortoise shell and obsidian.

The "Far-side Ports" – along the coast of the Somali Peninsula

Leaving the kingdom of Zôskalês, the author of the *Periplus* goes on to describe the ports along the coasts of modern Djibouti and Somalia (including Somaliland). These places were ruled by independent chieftains, *tyrannoi*,[366] but they are all grouped under the same heading, *ta peran emporia*[367] – "the markets across (the water)" / "the markets beyond",[368] or simply "the Far-side Ports" as Lionel Casson dubbed them, better describing their geographical situation.[369] "Far-side" refers to the other side of the Bab al-Mandeb straits when seen from the Red Sea perspective.

Northern Somalia is marked by a coastal plain, narrowing from about 100 kilometres near the border to modern Djibouti to only few kilometres east of modern Berbera, the ancient port of Malaô. South of the plain, mountains rise sharply, in their turn giving way an inland plateau of gradually decreasing altitude.[370] Due to limited precipitation, cultivation has always been secondary to pastoralism, but crops are raised in certain parts of the inland plateau.[371]

Avalitês

The first of the Far-side Ports was actually not very far-side at all. The *Periplus* places the port of Avalitês very near or at the straits themselves.[372] Modern commentators are not in agreement about the site of Avalitês, some placing it at or just before the straits, some quite a distance beyond them.[373]

Imports to Avalites, again according to the *Periplus*, included glass beads, clothing, unripe olives from Diospolis in Egypt, grain, wine and a little tin. Aromatics, a little ivory, tortoise shell and a small amount of an especially fine grade of myrrh were available for export.[374]

Trade at Avalites was different from the trade in what we could label *key imports and exports* at the ports of Muza, Kanê and Adulis. No product is identified as dominant, we learn that only small crafts and rafts put in there, and it seems that most trade was with the ports of Muza and Okêlis, just opposite on the Arabian side of the Red Sea.[375]

The author of *Periplus* perceived the population at Avalitês as somewhat "uncivilised" or "lawless" (*ataktoteros*),[376] but that some trade was conducted with Mediterranean traders is still evident from the fact that olives from Diospolis in Egypt were in demand.[377] All the other imports were also available from Egypt, if not exclusively; they could also have been acquired from Arabian ports like Kanê and Muza.

The exports from Avalites were certainly valuable, but the volume seems to have been limited and accordingly the imports not too impressive, wine being for instance the only commodity that seems particularly fit for elite consumption.

Malaô and Mundu

Malaô, identified with some certainty with modern Berbera on the Somali coast,[378] is briefly described in the next paragraph of the *Periplus*.[379] In contrast to Avalitês, the inhabitants of this port are characterised as "peaceful" (*eirênikôteroi*),[380] and imports as well as exports are of more value and potential interest than at Avalitês. To the list of imports to Avalitês is added more clothing,

---

[366] *Periplus* 14.
[367] *Periplus* 7:3.11.
[368] Cf. Lidell, Scott and Jones 1996: 1365a.
[369] Casson 1989: 55, 59, commentary p. 115.
[370] Foreign Office 1969: 2f.
[371] Colonial Office 1952: 127f.; Central Intelligence Agency 2002.
[372] *Periplus* 7.
[373] See extensive discussion in Casson 1989: 115ff.
[374] *Periplus* 7.
[375] *Periplus* 7.
[376] *Periplus* 7:3.21-22.
[377] Casson (1989: 249f.) commented that these were probably pressed, and the juice used as medicine.
[378] Fabricius 1883: 124; Schoff 1995: 79, the identification has never been challenged.
[379] *Periplus* 8.
[380] *Periplus* 8:3.24-25.

drinking vessels, soft copper sheets,[381] iron and some Roman silver and gold coins. Exports were myrrh, a little frankincense and cassia, a variety of cinnamon. Otherwise unknown products called *duka, kankamon* and *makeir* are also mentioned,[382] as are slaves. We learn that in addition to the trade with Roman merchants, Malaô also exported these goods to Arabia.[383] Mundu had the same imports and exports, and an additional unknown substance, *mokrotu*.[384]

The first two commodities, myrrh and frankincense, are well known from Arabia, and together with the island of Socotra, the hills behind the Somali coastal plain is the only place outside that region where larger concentrations of myrrh and frankincense trees grow naturally.[385] These aromatics were in heavy demand in the Mediterranean world, as well as in India, and must have been key products in the trade of the Far-side Ports, as they were in the Arabian trade.

The imports to Malaô are to a certain extent similar to those we find in the list for Adulis, but the range of products is smaller. Gold and silver tableware are two examples of commodities traded in most of the ports serving as the outlet of an established kingdom, but not at Malaô.

Again, the mention of Roman coinage, *dênarion*,[386] warrants comment. Unlike Adulis and Kanê, but as Muza and the Indian ports where coinage was imported, we do not get to know what this money was used for. At Adulis it was for the foreign traders resident there; at Kanê it was for the king. Lionel Casson argues that the money imported at Malaô was 'no doubt' for foreign traders resident there, as at Adulis.[387] There is nothing in the text to support his view. No colony of foreign merchants is mentioned at Malaô. That does not mean that there were no foreign merchants there, but the coins might just as well have been imported because the value of the exports was larger than the demand for the other relatively low value imports.

The next of the Far-side Ports was Mundu, identified with the modern site Heis,[388] where sherds of Roman pottery and glass have been found.[389] All we learn is that the imports and exports were the same as at Malaô, and that the author of the *Periplus* considered its inhabitants as "stubborn" (*sklêroteroi*),[390] presumably in their commercial dealings with visiting merchants.

Mosyllon, the Spice Market and Opônê

Mosyllon, two to three days under sail east of Mundu was probably the most important of the Far-side Ports, in terms of quantity of trade. This is indicated in the *Periplus*, where we learn that larger ships were sent there (than to the other Far-side Ports), on account of the large quantities of cassia available.[391] The imports were accordingly more expensive, including silver vessels and precious stones not imported by the other ports on this coast.

After Mosyllon and after turning Cape Guardafui, the easternmost point of Africa, came two more ports: *Arômatôn Emporion*, "the Market of Spices", and Opônê. They exported the same products as the other ports, but as in some of the other Far-side Ports, there were also some other products available, which modern commentators have found impossible to identify securely: *gizeir, asyphê, arôma, magla* and *môto*.[392]

A detour into the cassia yielding regions

The export of large quantities of cassia, a variety of cinnamon, from the ports on the Somali coast is one of the unsolved, and perhaps insolvable, problems of the ancient monsoon trade, but even so the issue cannot be completely ignored here.

To the ancients, cassia described different grades and qualities of products from the *Cinnamomum cassia* tree, found in parts of India, southern China and mainland Southeast Asia.[393] As far as we know, what we call cinnamon today, the bark from the *Cinnamomum zeylanicum*, now grown on Sri Lanka and in southern India, was not cultivated or harvested commercially in the ancient period.[394] Indeed, according to the *Periplus*, cassia was only to be found in the Far-side Ports. It is mentioned nowhere in the parts describing India and Southeast Asia.

Ancient authors from Herodotus onwards disagreed considerably as to where cassia and cinnamon originated. Most of them placed the source in areas corresponding to modern Yemen, Ethiopia / Eritrea or Somalia. A few, prominently Strabo, add India as a second possibility.[395]

In modern research this is reflected in two related lines of thought. The first is that cassia and cinnamon grew in Africa in the ancient period, either as now extinct

---

[381] See note 341 on Adulis, above.
[382] *Periplus* 8. Commentary in Casson 1989: 124ff. See Drake-Brockman 1912: 301ff. on the range of aromatics and resins harvested in British Somaliland in the early 20th century. These should be among the likely candidates for the unidentified commodities mentioned in the *Periplus*.
[383] *Periplus* 8.
[384] *Periplus* 9.
[385] See Groom 1981: 96ff, 138ff and Van Beek 1958 or Drake-Brockman 1912: 256ff. and 301ff. on Somalia in particular. Frankincence is also harvested in modern Ethiopia, see Phillipson (1998: 68f.), but is not attested as an Aksumite export.
[386] *Periplus* 8:3.28.. See also pp. 37, 53f., 64ff. and notes 242, 637 and 683 on the import of money to other ports.
[387] Casson 1989: 122.
[388] Casson 1989: 126; Schoff 1995: 81.
[389] Chittick 1979.

[390] *Periplus* 9:4.8-9.
[391] *Periplus* 10.
[392] *Periplus* 12. Casson (1989: 130) identified *gizeir, asyphê*, and *môto* as different grades of cassia.
[393] Casson 1984a: 225.
[394] Miller 1998: 75 though the leaves may have been harvested and sold as malabathrum in South Indian ports (Miller 1998: 74).
[395] Cf. Casson 1984a: 233. Strabo 15.1.22, 16.4.25.

varieties of the species, or that the ancients knew entirely different products native to Africa and Arabia under the names of cassia and cinnamon. Huntingford supported the former view in his commentary to the *Periplus*,[396] and Manfred Raschke was firm in his defence of the latter in his work on Roman trade with the east from 1978.[397] A second main view is that cassia *was* a variety of what we call cinnamon, and never has been a native product of Africa and Arabia. This idea goes back to W. Schoff;[398] and in more recent times, Lionel Casson has forcefully argued that cinnamon and cassia were the same products in antiquity as they are today, and that these species could never have grown in an African or Arabian climate.[399] As Graeco-Roman sources report the presence of cassia in African and Arabian ports, this implies that products of the *Cinnamomum cassia* tree native to Southeast Asia, were shipped to Somalia (and Arabia) by non-Roman traders.

The main argument against this view is that the products are not mentioned in the description of India in the *Periplus*. Casson believed that the products simply went unnoticed by our unknown author.[400] This explanation is not satisfying. Of course, the author of the *Periplus* might have failed to notice it, but he was only one of hundreds of Mediterranean merchants who visited the markets of India. To our knowledge, none of the others wrote down their experiences, as he did, but their knowledge should eventually have reached the ears of the ancient scholars interested in botany and geography. Amongst the ancient experts, areas corresponding to modern Ethiopia, Somalia and Arabia remained the favoured candidates throughout centuries of Mediterranean trade with India.

J. Innes Miller proposed an entirely different solution in *The Spice Trade of the Roman Empire* (1969). Based mainly on linguistic connections between Madagascar and South- and Southeast Asia, he postulated a southern cinnamon route across the Indian Ocean from Indonesia to East Africa.[401] Manfred Raschke dismissed this suggestion rather harshly and claimed that there is no proof of linguistic similarities between the areas before the sixth century, and that Southeast Asian emigration to Madagascar does not necessarily imply regular and large-scale commercial ties.[402]

Miller's southern trade route should have made cassia available at the port of Rhapta in East Africa described in the *Periplus*,[403] but it is not mentioned there. The problem thus remains unsolved. A third possible solution would be that Somalis traded with Southeast Asia, but this cannot be proven; for only scant and legendary evidence exists of Somali sea voyages in the ancient period.[404]

The problem of the Somali cassia will not be solved here. No matter what the actual provenance of the cassia sold at the Far-side Ports was, the *Periplus* does in fact describe trade between Somalia and India. Ships came to the Far-side Ports with a range of products "from the inner regions of Ariakê and (from) Barygaza".[405] Trade with the opposite coast of Arabia is also attested.[406]

Far-side Ports: trade and the state with no state

In conclusion, the impression of trade in the ports on the Somali coast differs somewhat from that presented by Kanê, Muza and Adulis. These three ports represented the main outlets of trade for the states of Hadramawt, Saba-Himyar and Aksum respectively. In different ways the three states exercised strict control over foreign trade. The *main flow* of foreign trade was limited to one port in each state, but all states had alternative ports: Moscha Limên, Okêlis and Ptolemais Thêrôn,[407] where trade was also conducted albeit on a smaller scale or subject to special regulations. The mainstay of the trade of these states was one particularly demanded commodity, frankincense, myrrh and ivory respectively. An important motivating force to participate in foreign trade seems to have been to acquire certain imported goods for royal consumption or military needs.

On the Far-side coast, we hear of no such attempts to limit the number of ports or to direct trade to one port in preference to others, although as we shall see in the following chapters, this seems to have been the pattern not only in Arabia and Eritrea / Ethiopia but also in India. Therefore, it is tempting to see the situation on the Somali coast as due to the lack of centralised power in these areas.

The Far-side Ports are also different in that they do not to the same extent offer one dominant main export. This had some impact on the pattern of trade. It seems that many traders travelling in this region tramped along the coast. The description is divided into *dromoi* ("runs")[408] indicating that the ships kept near the shore and put in at night, and the *Periplus* says outright that "some sail principally to these ports of trade, some sail along the coast and take on whatever return cargo come their way".[409] Here the source seems to reveal two separate trading networks: (1) a coastal network, presumably with smaller ships and with captains and merchants doing small scale trade in whatever goods are available on the spot and taking advantage of opportunities as they arise,

---

[396] Huntingford 1980: 134.
[397] Raschke 1978: 652ff.
[398] Schoff 1920.
[399] Casson 1984a: 233ff.
[400] Casson 1984a: 237.
[401] Miller 1998: 153ff.
[402] Raschke 1978: 652f.
[403] *Periplus* 16.

[404] Kobishchanow 1965.
[405] *Periplus* 14:5.9, ἀπὸ τῶν ἔσω τόπων τῆς Ἀριακῆς καὶ Βαρυγάζων.
[406] *Periplus* 8.
[407] If the latter port did indeed belong to the kingdom of Zôskalês in more than name.
[408] *Periplus* 9:4.1, 10:4.11, 11:4.14.
[409] *Periplus* 14:5.13-14, Καὶ οἱ μὲν προηγουμένως εἰς ταῦτα τὰ ἐμπόρια πλέουσιν, οἱ δὲ <κατὰ> τὸν παράπλουν ἀντιφορτίζονται τὰ ἐμπεσόντα.

and (2) a high seas trade with ships going directly to one port with the intention of securing a certain cargo.

The Far-side Ports, of course, also differed from each other. Ships were sent to Mosyllon on account of the large cargoes of cassia available there.[410] Although the text gives no clear answer, it seems likely that the largest quantities of far-side frankincense could be found at the market with the fragrant name of Arômatôn Emporion, which was situated closest to what the *Periplus* says is the most important frankincense producing area, Akannai near Cape Elephas.[411]

A significant point of difference between the Far-side Ports and the ports of Arabia and Eritrea is that the Far-side Ports can be described as primary centres in their respective regions. There were no inland political or agricultural centres dominating them, and with the important exception of cassia, which was probably imported, the products they offered for sale were to the best of our knowledge of local origin. The ports of trade of Saba-Himyar, Aksum, Hadramawt and as we shall see also the Indian kingdoms, on the other hand mobilised goods from extensive hinterland networks.

The absence of a centralised power does not mean that local rulers took no interest in the trade, but it may indicate that the conditions under which trade was to take place were more dependent on the arbitrary will of the local ruler than in some other ports. The attitudes of the "unruly" *Barbaroi* of Avalitês, the "quarrelsome" traders at Mundu and the "peaceful" inhabitants at Malaô, referred to in the *Periplus*, can probably be more satisfactorily explained by prevailing local conditions, than by difference in culture, nature, economy or political organisation between neighbouring communities. No such descriptions can be found for the ports serving as commercial outlets of established kingdoms, where, perhaps, more stable conditions could be expected.

Rhapta and the East African coast

Several days journey south of Opônê was Rhapta, which according to the author of the *Periplus,* was the last port of trade on the African coast.[412] Rhapta is not securly identified, but was probably situated in modern Tanzania, possibly near the delta of the Rufiji River,[413] and remains one of the most enigmatic ports described in the *Periplus*:

"Two runs beyond this island comes the very last port of trade on the coast of Azania, called Rhapta ["sewn"], a name derived from the aforementioned sewn boats, where there are great quantities of ivory and tortoise shell. Very big-bodied men, tillers of the soil [?], inhabit the region; these behave, each in his own place, just like chiefs. The region is under the rule of the governor [*tyrannos*] of Mapharitis, since by some ancient right it is subject to the kingdom of Arabia as first constituted. The merchants of Muza hold it through a grant from the king and collect taxes from it. They send out to it merchant craft that they staff mostly with Arab skippers and agents who, through continual intercourse and intermarriage, are familiar with the area and its language".[414]

Two points remain problematic in this passage, and are in fact still not completely understood. Although the issues will hardly be resolved here, they do call for a brief mention.

The first is a textual problem: whether the hapax *horatoi* of the manuscript[415] should be read as a "tillers of the soil" as Casson does in line three of the translation above, based on Giangrandes suggestion that it is a corruption of *arotai*, "ploughers" / "husbandmen" derived from *aroô*, to plough or to till,[416] or as a corruption of *peiratai*, "piratical", as earlier editors and translators preferred.[417] The question of whether piracy was a problem in these parts or not, is of course not unimportant for our discussion about the relationship between trade and the state, but Lionel Casson seemed to be on firm ground when he wrote that the reading *peiratai* seems to have "neither palaeographic nor other grounds to recommend it". Giangrande went as far as to label it "palaeographically violent."[418] Huntingford was well aware of the problem, but preferred "piratical" because he held that *arotai* implied the use of the plough, otherwise unknown in sub-Saharan Africa before the Europeans introduced it.[419] The Arabs dominating the coast around Rhapta could, of course, have introduced the plough to a limited area of East Africa, even if its use was

---

[410] *Periplus* 10.
[411] *Periplus* 11.
[412] *Periplus* 16.
[413] Chami 1999, but the location of Rhapta remains uncertain, see Horton 1990 and Casson 1989: 141f.
[414] *Periplus* 16, transl. Casson (1989: 61), Ἀφ' ἧς μετὰ δύο δρόμους τῆς ἠπείρου τὸ τελευταιότατον τῆς Ἀζανίας ἐμπόριον κεῖται, τὰ Ῥάπτα [τὰ] λεγόμενα, ταύτην ἔχον τὴν προσωνυμίαν ἀπὸ τῶν προειρημένων ῥαπτῶν πλοιαρίων, ἐν ᾧ καὶ πλεῖστός ἐστιν ἐλέφας καὶ χελώνη. Μέγιστοι δὲ ἐν σώμασιν περὶ ταύτην τὴν χώραν ἄνθρωποι ὁρατοὶ κατοικοῦσιν καὶ κατὰ τὸν τόπον ἕκαστος ὁμοίως τιθέμενοι τυράννοις. Νέμεται δὲ αὐτὴν, κατά τι δίκαιον ἀρχαῖον ὑποπίπτουσαν τῇ βασιλείᾳ τῆς πρώτης γενομένης Ἀραβίας, ὁ Μοφαρίτης τύραννος. Παρὰ δὲ τοῦ βασιλέως ὑπόφορον αὐτὴν ἔχουσιν οἱ ἀπὸ Μούζα καὶ πέμπουσιν εἰς αὐτὴν ἐφόλκια, τὰ πλείονα κυβερνήταις καὶ χρειακοῖς [καὶ] Ἄραψιν χρώμενοι τοῖς κατὰ συνήθειαν καὶ ἐπιγαμβρείαν ἔχουσιν ἐμπείροις τε οὖσιν τῶν τόπων καὶ τῆς φωνῆς αὐτῶν.
[415] *Periplus* 16:6.7. There is no doubt about the manuscript reading, CPG 398: 43v, 20.
[416] Giangrande 1975: 293f.; Lidell, Scott and Jones 1996: 245a and b.
[417] Fabricius 1883: 55; Huntingford (1980: 30, commentary pp. 63f.); Schoff (1995: 28) and Frisk (1927: 16:7.7) held on to πειραταὶ, derived from a suggested *possibility* in the commentary to Müller's edition of the Greek text and Latin translation from 1855 (1855: 271), and translated it as "piratical", (Fabricius: "räuberisch").
[418] Giangrande 1975: 293; Casson 1989: 253f.
[419] Huntingford 1980: 63f.

later forgotten. It seems more likely, however, that Huntingford overrated the discretion of the author of the *Periplus* in his use of agricultural terminology: it is quite possible that the Greek writer neither knew nor cared about whether local agriculturalists made use of the plough or not. Thus, even if we are still left in the dark concerning the plough, it seems safe to trust Casson and Giangrande in ruling out the pirates. Such choices do have consequences though. Jan Vansina has shown how postcolonial historians writing on East Africa in their reluctance to ascribe piratical behaviour to native Africans, have preferred the *arotai* option and thus postulated sedentary cultivators populating the coast of ancient East Africa on very slim evidence.[420] The best option remains to follow Vansina in leaving the question of what *horatoi* means open.

The second problem is the passage cited above, which states that the inhabitants of the area near Rhapta behaved "each in his own place, just like chiefs".[421] This time it is not the text itself, but its interpretation that is in question. Casson's translation cited above is the closest to the text and was also preferred by 19th century and earlier translators,[422] but both Schoff and Huntingford suggested a different solution, namely that "each place likewise has its own chief".[423]

The latter reading certainly lends more meaning to the passage, although Casson claimed that what the text implies is that there were in fact no native chiefs in the area because the Arab merchants of Rhapta ruled it and that they did not care much about the countryside. The native Africans were thus, in his opinion, left to do whatever they liked – to be their own rulers.[424] This interpretation is not satisfying. Arab rulers in a port city concerned only with trade would rather have the opposite effect; it would leave plenty of room for stratification and local rulers in agricultural communities nearby, if such did in fact exist, e.g. if the *arotai* reading discussed above is accepted. In another passage the *Periplus* reports the import of wine and grain to these areas "not for trade, but as an expense to win the good will of the Barbaroi".[425] This does point toward a certain degree of social organisation and stratification, which is incompatible with the "anarchy" of completely independent smallholders implied by Casson.[426] Such farmers would not constitute a force that needed to be pacified through gifts of wine and grain, unless they had leaders – most likely, their chiefs. These considerations left aside, the meaning of this passage continues to elude us; and it is quite possible that this is a result of our unknown author having had only vague notions about the social organisation prevalent in the area around Rhapta, as much as the obscurity of the text itself.

Trade at Rhapta

The key function of trade in the eyes of the ruler was to provide income in terms of goods for consumption by way of tax, tribute or trade. There was no state apparatus to deal with the traders at Rhapta or along the coast of East Africa, and this seems to have influenced the range of goods imported. These differ from the lists presented at ports such as Adulis, Muza and Kanê:

> "The principal imports to these ports of trade are: spears from Muza of local workmanship; axes; knives; small awls; numerous types of glass stones. Also, to certain places, wine and grain in considerable quantity, not for trade but as an expenditure for the good will of the Barbaroi. The area exports: a great amount of ivory but inferior to that from Adulis; rhinoceros horn; best-quality tortoise shell after the Indian; a little nautilus shell".[427]

We learn that even though Rhapta must have been the most important centre, Arabs lived in or visited several markets on this coast. The goods offered for sale or barter by the Arabs were relatively inexpensive, and not particularly suitable for ruler consumption or displays of power. Although redistribution of commodities like weapons, glass or tools would certainly be an option, the wine and grain mentioned were probably better instruments for demonstrating generosity. These goods were, as the passage states, needed in some places but not everywhere.

On the other side of the trade, and of the Indian Ocean, we find another state with a keen interest in the trade in the East African ports, represented by Charibaêl, the king of Saba-Himyar and Cholaibos, his vassal. There is no sign in the *Periplus* that they or their representatives took active part in the trade in the East African ports, as they probably did in their "home" port of Muza, but they certainly collected tribute from the traders in exchange for the right to trade with and tax their African possessions. This must have been a convenient arrangement for the King of Saba-Himyar. In this way he did not have to administer the area himself, and by farming it out to the merchants of his own port city, Muza, he could easily collect the tribute whenever they

---

[420] Vansina 1997.
[421] *Periplus* 16:6, 7-8, κατὰ τὸν τόπον ἕκαστος ὁμοίως τιθέμενοι τυράννοις.
[422] Fabricius 1883: 55 and his note 6 for translations older than his.
[423] Huntingford 1980: 30, commentary p. 63f. Schoff (1995: 28), using the words "separate chiefs for each place".
[424] Casson 1989: 142
[425] *Periplus* 17:6.17, οὐ πρὸς ἐργασίαν ἀλλὰ δαπάνης χάριν εἰς φιλανθρωπίαν τῶν Βαρβάρων.
[426] Huntingford (1980: 63f.) claimed that such an organisation of property is unknown in East Africa in later times, though he emphasises that we know nothing of the situation at the time of the *Periplus*.

[427] *Periplus* 17, transl. Casson (1989: 61), Εἰσφέρεται δὲ εἰς τὰ ἐμπόρια ταῦτα προηγουμένως ἡ τοπικῶς ἐν Μούζα κατασκευαζομένη λόγχη καὶ πελύκια καὶ μαχαίρια καὶ ὀπήτια καὶ λιθίας ὑαλῆς πλείονα γένη, εἰς δέ τινας τόπους οἶνός τε καὶ σῖτος οὐκ ὀλίγος, οὐ πρὸς ἐργασίαν ἀλλὰ δαπάνης χάριν εἰς φιλανθρωπίαν τῶν Βαρβάρων. Ἐκφέρεται δὲ ἀπὸ τῶν τόπων ἐλέφας πλεῖστος, ἥσσων δὲ τοῦ Ἀδουλι<ν>τικοῦ, καὶ ῥινόκερως καὶ χελώνη διάφορος μετὰ τὴν Ἰνδικὴν καὶ ναύπλιος ὀλίγος.

returned to Arabia, and could even ensure that a large part of the valuable exports from East Africa reached Muza, where he could get what he needed for the royal household through trade or taxation.

Rhapta: trade and the state with no state II

The most interesting aspect of the description of the East African coast in the *Periplus* is the reported Arabian rule over the port of Rhapta and the coast north of it. The foreign settlement at Rhapta constitute a clear example of what economic historians have called a trading diaspora.[428] Because the merchants from Muza intermarried with the local population and spoke their language, they were presumably settled abroad for longer periods of time, and they were, to borrow a term of P. Curtin's, the perfect "cross-cultural brokers".[429] What separated the Arabs at Rhapta from the typical trading-diaspora was, however, that they were not merely guests as such, for they obviously dominated the host region not only economically, but also politically.

The situation at Rhapta reflects a possible way out of the dilemma of trade and the state when there simply was no state to deal with. The key function of the state in the eyes of the traders was to provide security. At Rhapta they had to take care of that themselves. They relied mainly on social ties such as marriage, but also on friendship facilitated by gifts of wine and grain.

Dioscuridês / Socotra

125 nautical miles east of Cape Guardafui, the easternmost point of the African continent, is the large island of Socotra, the Dioscuridês of the *Periplus*.[430] Its description is not contained in the part of the *Periplus* dealing with Africa, but in the section describing the kingdom of Hadramawt, where we learn that "the island is subject to the aforementioned king of the frankincense-bearing land, just as Azania is to Charibaêl and the governor of Mapharitis".[431] It has been included in the discussion of Africa in this study because it constitutes a third example of areas outside state control that participated in the monsoon trade, and therefore better compared to Rhapta and the Far-side Ports than to mainland Arabia.

Dioscuridês,[432] is depicted in the *Periplus* as a desolate, unfriendly and dangerous place. It is described as infested with dangerous animals and void of agricultural products.[433] The inhabitants are said to be settlers from Arabia, India and the Greek world, who had come there in order to trade.[434] Socotra was surveyed and several sites excavated by a Russian-Yemeni team in 1985. The site of Hajrya on the northern side of the Island yielded pottery identified by Naumkin and Sedov as an amphora handle and red slipped pottery of probable Mediterranean origin, South Arabian pottery with a close resemblance to types found at the port of Qana / Kanê and black and grey ware of possible Indian or Persian Gulf origin.[435] The finds from Hajrya corroborate the *Periplus'* picture of varied and wide-ranging maritime contacts.

The chief export, again according to the *Periplus*, was tortoise shell in different varieties and large quantities, but cinnabar, also known as "Dragon's blood" and used as a drug and a strong red pigment,[436] was also locally available.[437] The island used to be frequented by ships from Muza, Limyrikê, i.e. the west coast of South India, and from Barygaza. They sold rice, grain, cotton cloth and female slaves,[438] goods that would be in demand in a trading settlement without a local agricultural and populational basis.

At the time when the *Periplus* was written, this situation had ceased, as the king of Hadramawt had farmed out the island, and he or the tenants had put it under guard. We do not know who they were, but it seems plausible that, just as Rhapta was leased to merchants from Muza, they came from Kanê or somewhere else in the Hadrami kingdom.[439] This would be an easy way to make sure that the king was not cheated of his rent or the possibility to tax the trade. Keeping a mountainous island of 1400 square kilometres under guard might seem ambitious, but in historical times natural conditions have restricted outside communication with the island to one anchorage, which was closed off during the SW monsoon.[440]

As at Rhapta, the *Periplus* reports the existence of foreign trading diasporas at Socotra, and as at Rhapta, they seem to have been in control of the situation at least until the king took over, though unlike most coastal stretches described in the *Periplus*, there is no mention of a local population of *Barbaroi, Ichthyophagoi* or the like. Still, we cannot rule out the possibility that there were other inhabitants on Dioscuridês even if the author of the *Periplus* did not know about them. How could he? He had probably never been there if the island was under guard and not open to Greek traders like himself. The

---

[428] See Curtin 1996: 1ff.
[429] Curtin 1996: 2.
[430] *Periplus* 30-31.
[431] *Periplus* 31:10.19-20, transl. Casson (1989: 69), Ὑποπίπτει μὲν οὖν, ὥσπερ ἡ Ἀζανία Χαριβαὴλ καὶ τῷ Μαφαρίτῃ τυράννῳ, καὶ ἡ νῆσος αὐτῷ τῷ βασιλεῖ τῆς Λιβανωτοφόρου.
[432] The name earlier thought to have been derived from Sanskrit, *Dvipa Sukhârdâ,* meaning "island abode of bliss" (Schoff 1995: 133ff). Beyhl (1998: 47ff.) has, however, shown that this has no valid etymological basis and that most of the island's several ancient and modern names could be derived from a word meaning "drip" or "exist in forms of drops" (60ff.) and might refer to the island's three resinous products: dragon's blood, frankincense and aloe. Beyhl maintains the Indian origin of the Greek form "Dioscuridês" and argues that the name has nothing to do with the *Dioskouroi* of Greek mythology. This does not mean, of course, that Greek travellers and Geographers did not make such a connection (61f.).
[433] *Periplus* 30.
[434] *Periplus* 30.
[435] Naumkin and Sedov 1995: 229.
[436] Schoff 1995: 137ff.
[437] *Periplus* 30.
[438] *Periplus* 31.
[439] Casson 1989: 169f.
[440] Naval Intelligence Office 1946: 613.

settlers were few, and if we take his word that they did not raise crops, it is safe to assume that they came there to trade, but who were the settlers to trade with, and what commodities did they come to trade in?

An earlier Greek source gives a different glimpse of what is probably Socotra. In his *On the Erythraean Sea*, Agatharchides of Cnidus, writing in the second century BC, describes what he calls *nêsoi eudaimones* – "The fortunate islands"[441] off the coast of Arabia where merchant vessels came from neighbouring countries, including Iran and the mouth of the Indus River. The work of Agatharchides has only survived in fragments, and is full of marvellous stories and hearsay, but his reports about the merchant ships still make it entirely plausible that it was Socotra he had in mind and that the island was populated.

Socotra is a sizable island, and large parts of it are difficult to access.[442] In the 20th century, the island supported a population of 6000-8000 individuals, equally distributed between pastoralists in the central mountain range and fishermen and traders of mixed Arab, Indian and African descent on the north coast.[443] The coastal population spoke Arabic, while the population of the interior maintained a language related to South Arabian languages.[444] When Cosmas Indicopleustes sailed by the island in the early sixth century, he knew it to have a Christian population, subject to the bishop of Babylon,[445] and when the Portuguese arrived almost a millennium later, certain Christian rites were still observed.[446] This of course shows only that Socotra was capable of sustaining a population of its own, independently of the mainland settlers and rulers who continued to come over from Southern Arabia also in later centuries,[447] and that this population was capable of holding onto aspects of Christian religion long after the rise of Islam. A native population at Socotra in the first century, which could collect tortoise shell and other products for exchange with the resident foreign merchants, would however, also make sense.

It seems that Dioscuridês used to be a meeting point for traders from different areas around the Indian Ocean before the time of the *Periplus*. The island had a name of Indian origin, which had entered into the Greek language,[448] and this should indicate that Indian traders had already been around for a while before the Greeks arrived at the island. Tortoise shell was a valuable commodity, but it was available around most of the Indian Ocean, it does not provide a satisfying explanation for why Indian, Arabian and Greek merchants came there to trade.

The description of the island in the *Periplus* seems almost designed to keep people away. Firstly, the island is described as barren and unfriendly. Secondly, it was placed under guard to prevent people from coming there; and, thirdly, the main export is said to be tortoise shell, which was also readily available in a number of ports in Africa and India. As the author of the *Periplus* never visited Dioscuridês, he must have learned this from someone who, it seems, did not want him to visit. Why?

The account of Dioscuridês has a similar air to it as the passages about the frankincense-bearing regions just opposite on the coast of Southern Arabia, and the port of Moscha Limên.[449] It is noteworthy that all these areas belonged to the same kingdom, Hadramawt, and that this was a kingdom that seems to have been extremely vigilant in controlling its trade and centring it in the port of Kanê, as near to the capital of Shabwa as possible.

Tortoise shell and cinnabar were probably not the only products available on Dioscuridês. The key is to be found elsewhere. Two products that the *Periplus* lists as exports from Kanê[450] are derived from plants native to the island, aloe and frankincense. The Oxford University expedition to Socotra in 1956 also reported valleys full of myrrh trees in bloom.[451] If these products were harvested at Socotra and then brought to Kanê, the secrecy and royal interest, as well as the island's earlier role as a meeting point for Indian, Arabian and Greek merchants all make more sense.

Dioscuridês: trade and the state with no state III

At Dioscuridês, as at Rhapta, we have an example of the possible organisation of trade in an area with no local polity capable of setting the terms of trade. In both places commercial activities were run by foreign diasporas, and in both places merchants farmed the right to exploit the area from a ruler, who over time could probably not have enforced his claims in any other way. At Dioscuridês, however, the arrangement seems to have been quite recent, and somewhat more strictly enforced than at Rhapta, for other traders were excluded altogether. This was perhaps easier because the area in question was not only closer to the homeports of the king, but also much smaller, and rendered unapproachable from sea by the monsoon throughout large parts of the year.

---

[441] Agatharchides 103 in Müller 1855.
[442] See Shinnie 1960: 100ff. who made personal experience as the archaeological expert of the 1956 Oxford University expedition.
[443] Naval Intelligence Office 1946: 612ff.
[444] Foreign Office 1969: 16f.
[445] Cosmas 3.65. He never landed on the island, and his claim that it had originally been colonised by settlers sent out by the Ptolemies can safely be dismissed on grounds of the reports of a mixed population with only a small Greek representation in *Periplus*. He is also in danger of overestimating the number of Christians on the island, when he states that there was a "multitude" (πλῆθος) of them, but there is less reason to doubt that he knew that the priests were sent there from Persia, as he was well informed and interested in churchly matters.
[446] Alvares 1961: 43.
[447] See Doe 1996: 136ff. on Arab records of Socotra, of which many repeat the report of Cosmas (3.65) that the island was originally populated by Greek settlers.

[448] Note [448], above.
[449] *Periplus* 29-32, cf. ch. 4, pp. 29ff., above
[450] *Periplus* 28.
[451] Botting 1958: 160ff. See also Foreign Office 1969: 38f.; Groom 1981: 104f. and Singer 2007 (only frankincense) on the presence of frankincense and myrrh on the island.

Once again, this conveys a picture of South Arabian states eager to secure income from inter-regional trade, and capable of taking measures to meet these ends.

The African coast - conclusions

The African coast is less homogenous than the Arabian side. Two significant areas discussed here, Rhapta and Socotra, could arguably also have been included in the section on the Arabian kingdoms, as Socotra is in the *Periplus*. When they are included in this chapter it is because they contribute to the picture of diversity drawn by the author of the *Periplus* in his reports about the African coast, which is not mirrored in other regions described in the work.

The ports and political units along the African coast can be divided into three groups. They show different degrees of political organisation and government involvement in trading activities:

1: The kingdom of Zôskalês, later to be known by the name of the highland capital of Aksum, with its ports of Adulis and possibly Ptolemais Thêrôn, had reached a state level of political organisation by the mid first century. The Aksumite state was, however, still in its infancy. We learn that Ptolemais Thêrôn belonged to the kingdom of Zôskalês,[452] but there is no trace of government presence or involvement at the port. At Adulis, ships at anchor had experienced attacks from the mainland,[453] confirming that the king's control of the region was not effective. Adulis was the only port on the African coast dubbed *emporion nomimon*, "legally limited port of trade", in the *Periplus*,[454] signifying that trade enjoyed some sort of state or law protection there.

The economic foundation of Aksum, here in terms of trade, but the same is true for agriculture, were the inland areas providing ivory, the single most important export of the African coast. Most commentators agree that Zôskalês must have been the ruler of the whole kingdom, not a vassal ruler of the coastal region, but he does seem to have taken a personal interest in the trade, and his presence at Adulis from time to time seems probable. The interest of the king seems to have been both in products suited for court life and displays of generosity or splendour and in practical products such as heavy cloaks and iron used for weapons.[455] Although iron was not imported exclusively for the king, such products could be useful for both political, economic and military purposes.

There are no signs of a state monopoly of trade at Adulis, neither on exports nor on imports. The use of low value metal pieces as coin substitutes[456] indicates that a large number of participants in a trade with low value goods were at least a part of the picture at Adulis. Ivory would be a difficult product to monopolise, because elephants were numerous in large parts of East Africa in the ancient period.[457] Nevertheless, the king appears to have been *a* major or *the* major supplier of the commodity, probably due to his control of Aksum, where trade routes from the interior intersected.

2: The Far-side Ports. Each of these ports along the coast of modern Somalia were separate political units. As far as we know, their economy, subsistence as well as commercial, was based on the sea, the coastal plain and its immediate hinterland. The ports were governed by independent chieftains,[458] and their importance as centres of commerce depended on the goods they offered, rather than political or administrative efforts to centre trade in one place.

Trade was dependent on the goodwill of the local ruler or the local population. No imported goods are described as reserved for the ruler although some imports must have been for the powerful or wealthy. There is no trace of monopolies, though rulers might well have been important participants in the trade.

The volume or value of different exports seems to have been quite balanced in most ports, at least in the sense that it is difficult to speak of one dominant commodity.

3: Rhapta and Dioscuridês. This third group has several important traits in common. There were no local rulers or political organisations capable of dictating the terms of trade. The regions were dominated, not only economically but also politically, by foreign trading diasporas. These diasporas consisted of Arabian merchants acting with permission from their kings. At Dioscuridês merchants outside the diaspora were excluded from trade. At Rhapta we witness the importance of social ties between traders and host society through intermarriage and gifts of wine and grain. Together, these regions offer a glimpse both of possible ways to organise trade in areas without complex societies and of the efforts of the Arabian kings to secure income from the monsoon commerce

---

[452] *Periplus* 5.
[453] *Periplus* 4.
[454] *Periplus* 4:1.20.
[455] *Periplus* 6.
[456] *Periplus* 6.

[457] Scullard 1974: 24ff.
[458] *Periplus* 14.

Chapter 6: From the Indus to the Konkan

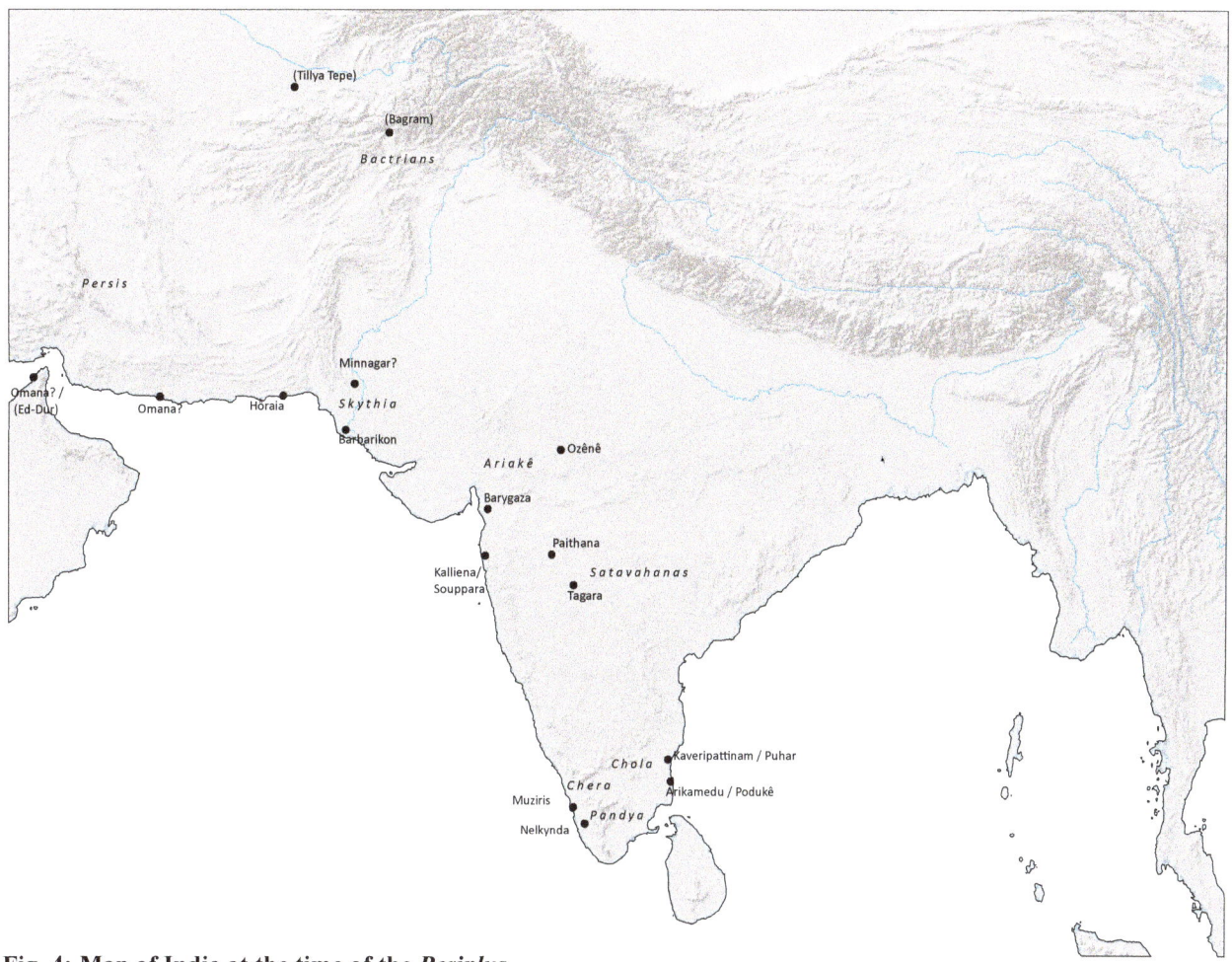

Fig. 4: Map of India at the time of the *Periplus*

Moscha Limên was the last market on the coast of Southern Arabia known to the author of the *Periplus*. Somewhere east of that port the territory of "the kingdom of the Persis" – the Parthian Empire – started. *Periplus* mentions two Parthian ports: The "legally limited port of trade", *emporion nomimon,* of Apologos near the mouth of the Euphrates[459] and the *emporion,* of Omana,[460] still not securely identified.[461]

After Omana and closer to the mouth of the Indus came the small port of trade, *mikron emporion,* of Hôraia in the country of the Parsidai. A seven-day journey inland from Hôraia was a *polis,* "city", with a royal residence.[462] The name of the city is missing from the manuscript.[463] The *Periplus* reports no long-distance trade from this market.

The description of the Persian Gulf and the coast of modern Iran is difficult to follow on the map, and chances are that our unknown merchant never visited these parts himself. It seems that he is describing a different trading network from the one he is taking part in himself, for he reports that large ships from Barygaza in India went to both these ports,[464] but says nothing about Egyptian shipping. The omission makes sense. Sailing from Egypt to the Persian Gulf would be both time-consuming and unnecessary. Roman trade with the Parthian Empire was more easily conducted over caravan routes terminating at the Syrian and Anatolian borders of the Roman Empire, for instance by way of the city of Palmyra which carried on a substantial trade with the

---

[459] *Periplus* 35.
[460] *Periplus* 36.
[461] Casson 1989: 180f. See also Salles 1995: 123f., who identifies Omana with Ed-Dur in modern U.A.E.
[462] *Periplus* 37.

[463] *Periplus* 37:12.18. The lacuna is marked in the margin of the manuscript (CPG 398:48r, 13) and must have been left out during copying.
[464] *Periplus* 36.

Persian Gulf and on the Indian Ocean at least from the second century onwards.[465] Thus we rejoin the author of the *Periplus* when his narrative reaches the ports of northwestern India. The Persian Gulf trade and other non-Roman networks as they appear in the *Periplus* will be discussed in Chapter 8.

Ports and kingdoms

As in Southern Arabia, good natural harbours were scarce along the west coast of India. Much of the coastline consists of rather shallow and sandy beaches, making anchorage difficult and unsafe. The terrain, with the mountains of the Western Ghats running parallel to the coast of the peninsula proper and with marshes and wastelands along parts of modern Gujarat, made pre-modern communication between coast and inland challenging.

In Southern Arabia and along the Red Sea, rocky promontories and coastal inlets offered a solution to the harbour problem. In northwestern India, river mouths offered sheltered anchorage, and river valleys and mountain passes in the Ghats served as means of overland communication. Riverine navigation was difficult except for the lower Indus, because the rivers originating in the Ghats fall steeply and bend sharply.[466] At the mouths of the rivers Indus and Narmada were ports with a strong royal presence, maintained at least partly in the interest of maritime trade, serving as commercial outlets of kingdoms with rich agricultural hinterlands.

Complex societies had long traditions in this region and it makes little sense to study the importance of the first century monsoon trade for the emergence of the state as an institution in this region. That does not mean, however, that trade was insignificant for the development or existence of the historical polities we encounter on this coastline.

At the time when the *Periplus* was written, the region seems to have been in a state of political turmoil. Rulers, their nationality and cities of residence had all been subject to recent change. Nevertheless, government interest in trade seems to have stayed firm, perhaps even firmer than in other ports described in the *Periplus*. These areas in modern Pakistan and India thus seem a good place to study the importance of trade for rulers under pressure.

On the coast of modern Punjab and Gujarat we encounter two kingdoms, called Skythia and Ariakê by the author of the *Periplus*. The Skythians, or Sakas as they were called in India were a group of Central Asian invaders, who gradually drove Alexander's Indo-Greek successors away from their possessions in modern Afghanistan and on the Indus plain, in the late second and first century BC.[467] The Greek name Skythia identifies this westernmost kingdom with the Saka, but the Skythia encountered in the *Periplus* was ruled by kings of Indo-Parthian origin.[468] Their dynasty was founded by the most well known of their kings, Gondophares, mentioned in the apocryphal *Acts of Judas Thomas*,[469] and believed to have ruled approximately 20 – 45 AD.[470] These Indo-Parthian rulers of Punjab and the Indus valley would in their turn eventually be ousted from Skythia by the Kushans, a new group of invaders from Central Asia, and probably already a power in the Kabul valley at the time of *Periplus*,[471] but by then still without direct influence on the shores of the Indian Ocean.

The second kingdom reported in the *Periplus* in this region was Ariakê in modern Gujarat.[472] This was probably the realm of the Saka rulers who called themselves the *Kshatrapas*, after the Arasacid and Achamenid governor title *satrap*. The Deccan, the highlands to the south and east of Ariakê, was ruled by a third dynasty, the Satavahanas (Andhras), a major power based in the inland city of Paithana, but as the Satavahanas were unable to maintain a coastal presence on the west coast at the time of the *Periplus,* they appear only indirectly in that source.

So Skythia was the northern and westernmost of the Indian kingdoms described by *Periplus* author. Maritime trade was conducted through the port of trade, *emporion*, of Barbarikon at the mouth of the Indus, and the capital, *mêtropolis,* of Minnagar was situated some distance upriver, but neither settlement has been securely identified by modern commentators.[473] The report is from a time of political instability, for we get to know that "the throne is in the hands of Parthians, who are constantly chasing each other off it."[474] The unrest mentioned could refer to the period immediately after the death of king Gondophares, which would coincide well with the mid first century date of the *Periplus.*

Like the other Indian Ocean states, Ariakê was inland based, its capital being upriver and inland from its principal port, the *emporion* of Barygaza. Up until what seems like a relatively short time before the *Periplus* was written, Barygaza had been ruled from "a city (*polis*)

---

[465] Gawlikowski (1994); Young 2001: 136ff.
[466] Ray 1986: 13ff.
[467] Tarn 1985: 320ff.
[468] Bopearachchi and Pieper 1998: 219ff.; *Periplus* 38.
[469] *Acts of Judas Thomas the Apostle* 2.17-29.
[470] Mitchiner 1976: 813; Tarn 1985: 353; Bopearachchi and Pieper 1998: 222. The Syriac *Acts of Thomas* is, however, first known in the fourth century. Indigenous traditions of the origin of the Indian Orthodox Church as it now exists in Southern India are all post-Portugese (Brown 1982: 48ff.).
[471] It has been proposed that they were identical with 'the most warlike people of the Bactrians', μαχιμώτατον ἔθνος Βακτριανῶν, mentioned in the *Periplus* 47:16.6 (Schoff 1995: 184ff.).
[472] *Periplus* 41.
[473] See, however, Kervan 1999 on the different possible sites of Barbarikon.
[474] *Periplus* 38, transl. Casson (1989: 75), βασιλεύεται δὲ ὑπὸ Πάρθων, συνεχῶς ἀλλήλους ἐκδιωκόντων.

called Ozênê, in which the royal residence used to be".⁴⁷⁵ Ozênê is identified with modern Ujjain, about 200 miles northeast of the port at Barygaza, the latter being situated near modern Broach / Bharuch.⁴⁷⁶ This had, however, changed, and by the time of the *Periplus*, the capital, *mêtropolis,* of Ariakê was at a place called Minnagara.⁴⁷⁷ This poses a possible problem, for the name is almost identical to the *mêtropolis* above Barbarikon – Minnagar.⁴⁷⁸

Commentators have approached this in different ways. Fabricius saw them as two different cities.⁴⁷⁹ Schoff followed him in this and commented that the etymology of the name is "city of the Min", "Min" being an Indian name for the Sakas.⁴⁸⁰ This suggests that Minnagar / Minnagara was a generic name, connected with the inhabitants or perhaps rather the rulers, rather than the city itself. Huntingford interpreted the references to be to the same single city,⁴⁸¹ whereas Casson believed them to be separate.⁴⁸² The distance between a city on the Indus and a city inland from Barygaza would be so large that confusion seems unlikely. Nevertheless, as long as the places are not securely identified, no certain conclusion can be reached, and we have three capitals, one of them abandoned, for two kingdoms.

Trade at Barbarikon / Minnagar

Returning now to account of the *Periplus*, the description of India starts with the mouth of the Indus:

> "Vessels moor at Barbarikon, but all the cargoes are taken up the river to the king at the metropolis. In this port of trade there is a market for: clothing, with no adornment in good quantity, of printed fabric in limited quantity; multicolored textiles; peridot; coral; storax; frankincense; glassware; silverware; money; wine, limited quantity. As return cargo it offers: costus; bdellium; *lykion*; nard; turquoise; lapis lazuli; Chinese pelts, cloth, and yarn; indigo. Those who sail with the Indian [sc. winds] leave around July, that is, Epeiph. The crossing with these is hard going but absolutely favorable and shorter".⁴⁸³

---

⁴⁷⁵ *Periplus* 48:16.12-13, πόλις λεγομένη Ὀζήνη, ἐν ᾗ καὶ τὰ βασίλεια πρότερον ἦν.
⁴⁷⁶ *Periplus* 48; Huntingford 1980: 113, 110; Casson 1989: 199f., 206.
⁴⁷⁷ *Periplus* 41.
⁴⁷⁸ *Periplus* 38.
⁴⁷⁹ Fabricius 1883: 150 and 153, and also for the 19th century debate.
⁴⁸⁰ Schoff 1995: 180 and 165f. relevant in this respect is also Isidore of Charax' mention of a *Min polis* as the metropolis of the Saka in the eastern section of his *Parthian Stations* (Isidore 18).
⁴⁸¹ Huntingford 1980: 110.
⁴⁸² Casson 1989: 189 and 199.
⁴⁸³ *Periplus* 39, transl. Casson (1989: 75), Τὰ μὲν οὖν πλοῖα κατὰ τὴν Βαρβαρικὴν διορμίζονται, τὰ δὲ φορτία πάντα εἰς τὴν μητρόπολιν ἀναφέρεται διὰ τοῦ ποταμοῦ τῷ βασιλεῖ. Προχωρεῖ δὲ εἰς τὸ ἐμπόριον ἱματισμὸς ἁπλοῦς ἱκανὸς καὶ νόθος οὐ πολύς, πολύμιτα καὶ χρυσόλιθον καὶ κοράλλιον καὶ στύραξ καὶ λίβανος καὶ ὑαλᾶ σκεύη καὶ ἀργυρώματα καὶ χρῆμα, οἶνος δὲ οὐ πολύς. Ἀντιφορτίζεται δὲ κόστος,

The port of Barbarikon was situated at the mouth of the Indus. The estuary of this river, one of the world's largest, has changed over the course of two millennia.⁴⁸⁴ The author of the *Periplus* reports that the river had seven mouths, but that only the middle one was navigable. This was where Barbarikon was placed.⁴⁸⁵ The northern Minnagar was seemingly situated not very far inland and on the river.⁴⁸⁶

On the list of goods for which a visiting merchant could find a market at Barbarikon / Minnagar, several products of high value are attested: coral, used for jewellery, *chrysolithon,* "golden stone", a gem that Casson tentatively translates as peridot,⁴⁸⁷ storax, a resin used as incense and as a drug,⁴⁸⁸ frankincense, presumably from Kanê in Hadramawt or from the Far-side Ports, glassware, silverware and wine. Textiles of apparently rather unexceptional value were also imported, as were money, which will be discussed below together with the import of money to Barygaza.

Among the exports, several commodities are of special interest, mainly because of their origin. Barbarikon offered costus, bdellium, lykion, nard, turquoise, lapis lazuli, indigo and Chinese pelts, silk cloth and yarn. Costus was probably a drug based on a herb from Kashmir.⁴⁸⁹ Lykion was also a drug,⁴⁹⁰ maybe based on plants found in the western Himalayas.⁴⁹¹ Nard, or spikenard, although unimportant today, was among the most expensive eastern plant-products in the Roman Empire at this time,⁴⁹² used both in oil and leaf form, the plant grows on the slopes of the Himalayas.⁴⁹³ Bdellium was available locally,⁴⁹⁴ and, as Pliny reports, a resin so sought after that the Indian variety was sometimes adulterated with almonds.⁴⁹⁵ The source of turquoise was probably mines in modern eastern Iran, and lapis lazuli came from the northeastern part of modern Afghanistan.⁴⁹⁶ Indigo, a natural dye, was extracted from a number of plants native to western India.⁴⁹⁷

βδέλλα, λύκ<ι>ον, νάρδος καὶ καλλεανὸς λίθος καὶ σάπφειρος καὶ Σιρικὰ δέρματα καὶ ὀθόνιον καὶ νῆμα Σιρικὸν καὶ Ἰνδικὸν μέλαν. <Ἀν>άγονται δὲ καὶ αὐτοὶ οἱ πλέοντες μετὰ τῶν Ἰνδικῶν περὶ τὸν Ἰούλιον μῆνα, ὅς ἐστιν Ἐπίφι· δυσεπίβολος μὲν ἐπιφορώτατος δὲ ἐκείνων καὶ συντομώτερος ὁ πλοῦς.
⁴⁸⁴ Kervan 1999.
⁴⁸⁵ *Periplus* 38.
⁴⁸⁶ Casson 1989: 189; Kervan 1999.
⁴⁸⁷ See his discussion of the word, Casson 1989: 190. The translation has found later support, see Wendrich *et al.* 2003: 56.
⁴⁸⁸ Casson 1989: 163f.
⁴⁸⁹ Casson 1989: 191f.
⁴⁹⁰ Pliny 12.31.
⁴⁹¹ Casson 1989: 192f.
⁴⁹² Cf. the biblical story of Mark (14.3-5), where a jar of genuine spikenard is said to be worth 300 *denarii*.
⁴⁹³ Warmington 1995: 194ff.
⁴⁹⁴ Casson 1989: 185f.
⁴⁹⁵ Pliny 12.35.
⁴⁹⁶ Casson 1989: 194; Schoff 1995: 170f.
⁴⁹⁷ Thus identified by Schoff (1995: 172f.) The Greek Ἰνδικὸν μέλαν (39:13.11-12) means simply "Indian black", which Huntingford (1980: 67) translated as "Indian ink".

Skythia was not only active in overland trade and in the maritime trade with Arabia, Africa and Roman Egypt. The Persian Gulf, and the coasts of modern Iran, Pakistan and India constituted a second axis in the monsoon system. This trade is not directly attested in the *Periplus* with regard to Skythia, though it is mentioned that Barygaza in Ariakê carried on trade both with the Persian Gulf[498] and with Southern India.[499] Maritime trade with Skythia by way of the Persian Gulf is, however, mentioned in inscriptions from the Syrian city of Palmyra. The inscriptional record from the city reveals that its merchants frequently went to the Parthian city of Vologesias on the Euphrates and to the port of Charax on the Persian Gulf,[500] where they apparently linked up with this axis of the monsoon network. Two inscriptions from the year 157 AD, also commemorates the successful return of Palmyrene ships from Skythia.[501]

Why enter into details about the origins of the commodities exported at the mouth of the Indus? Because their provenance attests the presence and importance of inland and transit trade northwards. Bdellium and indigo were locally available in this region, others were perhaps available in the northern parts of Skythia. Nevertheless, some of the gems and the Chinese pelts and silk were products of a long-distance trade along the Indus, northwards to modern Afghanistan and across the mountain passes to central Asia and beyond. The spectacular finds of Iranian, Chinese, Indian, Mediterranean and Central Asian artefacts from the Kushan palace storerooms of Bagram and the chieftain graves at Tillya Tepe[502] testify not only to the expanse of these networks, but also the potential of long-distance trade as a means of social stratification for the elites supplying and facilitating the maritime and overland networks.

The route down the Indus to Barbarikon, its eastwards extension by way of the Ganges represented an alternative to northern caravan routes through Central Asia and Parthia for the export of Chinese and Central Asian products to the Mediterranean world. Although it is not clear how the different land and sea routes interacted, it seems that the rulers of Skythia actively sought to centralise trade and mobilise resources from the different networks at their capital. In the *Periplus*, we learn that "vessels moor at Barbarikon, but all the cargoes are taken up the river to the king at the metropolis."[503] This way the kings at Skythia could conveniently control the overland trade, while getting their share of the monsoon trade on the Indian Ocean at the same time.

Supportive evidence for such practices can perhaps be found in the ancient Indian handbook in statesmanship, *Arthasastra*. The *Arthasastra* offers rulers advice on how they should rule their kingdoms, including just laws and organisation of civil service. Economic activity and trade is not a prime concern in the work, but the sections on revenue also present rulers with a range of options as to how trade and production can be organised in order to benefit their kingdoms. Uncertainties regarding the date and origin of the *Arthasastra* preclude direct comparison,[504] but the work still alludes to the pool of traditional knowledge and practice rulers in this part of the world were able to draw upon.

In the *Arthasastra*, a government official, called the *panyādhyaksa* fills the functions both of a regulator and of a facilitator of commerce, and as an agent of royal trade. Prominent among his duties are the establishment and control of markets,[505] in order to ensure taxation, income from sale of foreign imports and and collection of domestic products. It is also suggested that caravans arriving at the borders of the kingdom should be registered and the custom officials in the capital notified,[506] these take care of the actual taxation on arrival.[507] The report of the royal monopoly at Barbarikon / Minnagar and the centralisation of trade at the capital, might well resemble arrangements like these.

Trade and the state in Skythia

Barbarikon and Minnagar offer perhaps the clearest example of administered trade attested in the *Periplus*. The king here went one step further than for instance in the Arabian kingdoms. Not only was trade centred at one city and some goods reserved for the king, as was frequently the case, but in Skythia trade took place at the capital rather than at the port city, and the king is explicitly mentioned in connection with "all the cargoes" rather than for certain goods only.

---

[498] *Periplus* 36.
[499] *Periplus* 54.
[500] See Gawlikowski (1994: 32f.) who lists all 34 known inscriptions related to the Palmyrene caravan trade.
[501] Inv. X 96 and Gawlikowski 1994: no. 24, published in Cantineau 1933: 187.
[502] Hiebert and Cambon (eds. 2008) The finds from both sites are contemporary with the *Periplus* (Mehendale 2008: 131f. (Bagram); Schlitz 2008: 225f. (Tillya Tepe).
[503] *Periplus* 39:13.5-6, transl. Casson (1989: 75), Τὰ μὲν οὖν πλοῖα κατὰ τὴν Βαρβαρικὴν διορμίζονται, τὰ δὲ φορτία πάντα εἰς τὴν μητρόπολιν ἀναφέρεται διὰ τοῦ ποταμοῦ τῷ βασιλεῖ.

[504] The *Arthasastra* is traditionally ascribed to Kautilya, the mentor of the Mauryan emperor Chandragupta who ascended to the throne ca 320 BC. Even if the work is now believed to have been composed considerably later (Trautmann 1971: 183f.), the alleged authorship and historical context seems to connect the *Arthasastra* with the heartland of that empire, the Ganges plain and the smaller kingdoms that succeeded the Maurya empire there, rather than the Saka kingdoms, even if these also in time came to encompass large parts of the same area. The work cannot, however, be considered to be the free composition of one author in one place, regardless of whether he lived in the fourth century BC or in the second century AD. The *Arthasastra* represents a long tradition of ancient Indian political science (Kangle 1988: 1ff., 40ff.), as is also acknowledged in the first paragraph of the work itself (*Arthasastra* 1.1.1). It is likely that ideology and practice expressed in the *Arthasastra* was known in the region touching on the Indian Ocean.
[505] *Arthasastra* 2.16.4, also 2.22.9 on the regulation of sale.
[506] *Arthasastra* 2.21.24-26.
[507] *Arthasastra* 2.21.1, 2.21.24-27.

The extra effort put into controlling trade shows its importance to the rulers, and even if not all goods were for the king and his household, this arrangement would make him confident of having the first pick among the imported goods, and perhaps more importantly, it facilitated taxation of trade. An echo of such an arrangement can be found in the merchantile code of Qataban, which gives the king supervisory authority in all transactions and over all goods passing through his territory.[508] Some of the products imported at Barbarikon seem fit for the conspicuous consumption connected with court life: silverware, glassware and wine. In the case of the wine, the limited quantity imported[509] could imply that the king wanted to keep control of this resource. Other products, for instance textiles, might have had a broader distribution as an article of redistribution or continued trade.

Ariakê and Barygaza

"The bottom in some places has sheer drops, in others is rocky and sharp, so that the anchors lying parallel [i.e., dropped from the bows], thrust out to withstand [sc. the difficult waters], get cut loose and some even get smashed on the sea floor. An indication of these [sc. dangers] to vessels coming from the sea are the snakes, huge and black, that emerge to meet them. In the areas beyond, and around Barygaza, snakes that are smaller and yellow and golden in color are met with".[510]

The passage above is only a short excerpt from the detailed description in the *Periplus* of the navigational difficulties encountered in approaching Barygaza, the chief port of the next kingdom along the Indian coast after Skythia, Ariakê. The mention of snakes of different colours coming out to meet the ships adds to the credibility of our unknown author, as 17th and 18th century European travellers report that captains of their day used the same sign to determine their distance to the coast when approaching Surat and Bombay.[511] The author of the *Periplus* has devoted almost a sixth of his work, sections 41-52 out of 66, to this part of the Indian coast. In addition to his evident familiarity with the coastal waters and the coastline, he mentions what he believed to be remains of Alexander's expedition that could be seen in the area,[512] (Alexander never ventured this far east), and his knowledge of recent political events leaves us with little doubt that he writes from personal experience.

Barygaza was one of the most important ports involved in the monsoon trade as it is described in the *Periplus*.[513] It is mentioned 29 times in the short text, and we learn of its connections with trade with both Arabian kingdoms,[514] Socotra,[515] Aksum,[516] the Far-side Ports,[517] the Parthian Empire[518] and Southern India.[519] Given the importance of the port, most of the description of Barygaza is cited here in Lionel Casson's translation:

> "Alexander, setting out from these parts, penetrated as far as the Ganges but did not get to Limyrikê and the south of India. Because of this, there are to be found on the market in Barygaza even today old drachmas engraved with the inscriptions, in Greek letters, of Apollodotus and Menander, rulers who came after Alexander.
>
> There is in this region [sc. of Barygaza] towards the east a city called Ozênê, the former seat of a royal court, from which everything that contributes to the region's prosperity, including what contributes to trade with us, is brought down to Barygaza: onyx, agate; Indian garments of cotton; garments of *molochinon*; and a considerable amount of cloth of ordinary quality. Through this region there is also brought down from the upper areas the nard that comes by way of Proklais (the Kattyburinê, Patropapigê, and Kabalitê), the nard that comes through the adjacent part of Skythia, and costus and bdellium.
>
> In this port of trade there is a market for: wine, principally Italian but also Laodicean and Arabian; copper, tin, and lead; coral and peridot; all kinds of clothing with no adornment or of printed fabric; multicolored girdles, eighteen inches wide; storax; yellow sweet clover (?); raw glass; realgar; sulphide of antimony; Roman money, gold and silver, which commands an exchange at some profit against the local currency; unguent, inexpensive and in limited quantity. For the king there was imported in those times precious silverware, slave musicians, beautiful girls for concubinage, fine wine; expensive clothing with no adornment, and

---

[508] Res 4337c 11-14, transl. Avanzini 2004: 290. Cf. p. 25, above.
[509] Periplus 39.
[510] Periplus 40, transl. Casson (1989: 75), Ὁ δὲ βυθὸς ἔν τισι μὲν ἀπόκοπος ἐν τισιν δὲ πετρώδης καὶ ἀπόξυρος, ὥστε τέμνεσθαι τὰς παρακειμένας ἀγκύρας ἀντέχειν ἀποκοντουμένας, ἃς δὲ καὶ συντριβομένας ἐν τῷ βυθῷ. Σημεῖον δ' αὐτοῖν τοῖς ἀπὸ πελάγους ἐρχομένοις οἱ προαπαντῶντες ὄφεις ὑπερμεγέθεις καὶ μέλανες· ἐν γὰρ τοῖς μετὰ ταῦτα τόποις καὶ τοῖς περὶ Βαρύγαζαν μικρότεροι καὶ τῷ χρώματι χλωροὶ καὶ χρυσίζοντες ὑπαντῶσι.
[511] Valle 1665: 5; Niebuhr 1774: 452. Both authors refer to the *Periplus* in this connection. Further references on sea snakes and herpetological details in Casson 1989: 187f.
[512] Alexander off course never ventured this far east and south, but even so firsthand knowledge of the author of the *Periplus* seems plausible. The remains might be from Alexander's Indo-Greek successors, as W. Tarn held (1985: 148f.), or they might have been wrongly ascribed to Alexander on grounds of local traditions of his campaign. In either case, the author of the *Periplus* might have sseen something he believed to be remains of Alexander's Indian expedition.
[513] See also Gokhale 1987, who summarises Indian references to Barygaza.
[514] Periplus 21, 27, 32.
[515] Periplus 31.
[516] Periplus 6 (mentioning Ariakê, not Barygaza).
[517] Periplus 14.
[518] Periplus 36.
[519] Periplus 54 (mentioning Ariakê, not Barygaza).

choice unguent. This area exports: nard; costus; bdellium; ivory; onyx; agate; *lykion*; cotton cloth of all kinds; Chinese [sc. silk] cloth; *molochinon* cloth; [sc. silk] yarn; long pepper; and items brought here from the [sc. nearby] ports of trade. For those sailing to this port from Egypt, the right time to set out is around the month of July, that is Epeiph".[520]

Like most ports, Barygaza has a list of special imports for the king, but we are informed that this was "in those times", (*kat' ekeinous tous kairous*),[521] and this must refer to earlier days, when Ozênê was the seat of the royal court. The abandonment of Ozênê as a seat of royal residence seems to have had a dramatic influence on the trade at Barygaza. Whereas formerly a range of luxury goods for the king had been among the imports at the port, the imports at the time of *Periplus* were more modest than at most ports, not just in quantity or range, but also in quality and value, as a brief tabulation of goods that occur on both lists reveals:

Table 2: Quality of imports to Barygaza - past and present

Imports for the king:	General imports:
49:16.27: Fine wine (*diaphoros oinos*).	49:16.20: Wine (*oinos*), principally Italian but also Laodicean and Arabian.
49:16.27: Expensive, unadorned clothing (*himatismos haplous polutelês*).	49:16.22: unadorned clothing of all kinds (*himatismos haplous pantoios*).
49:16.28: Choice unguent (*muron exochon*).	49:16.25: Unguent, inexpensive and in limited quantity (*muron ou barutimon oude polu*).

Wine, clothing and unguents figure on both lists, but in the list of imports for the king, their exceptional quality is underlined, whereas in the list of general imports, it is rather their plainness that attracts attention. This seems to reflect that a change in the nature of the trade at Barygaza had indeed taken place.

The expensive goods that were once in demand were no longer attractive to the local market. If the finer grades of wine, unguents and clothing had still been in demand after the royal court moved from Ozênê, there would have been little reason to mention the inferior quality of the general imports. The author of the *Periplus* presumably had the experience of a long professional life to draw upon when he composed his work. If the change in demand at Barygaza was relatively recent, it is understandable that he included it in his guide to trade on the Indian Ocean. It had an important bearing on which goods merchants should bring to India. The slave musicians, female slaves for the harem and expensive silverware that traders used to bring to the port for the king[522] are examples of commodities that must have had a very limited market once the royal court disappeared.

As at Babarikon, it is possible to trace many of the products sold at Barygaza to their point of origin, thereby reconstructing the overland trading networks that connected with the Indian Ocean trade. Just as the Indus offered opportunities for riverine communication from Barbarikon, the Narmada valley made overland communication and trade between inland and coast possible from Barygaza.[523] *Periplus* 48 (cited above) tells us not only of products originating in Ariakê, e.g. gems such as onyx and agate,[524] and different varieties of textiles, but also of trade with areas further north, represented with varieties of spikenard, costus and bdellium. In *Periplus* 49 (also cited above) more exports are mentioned in addition to those in the previous paragraph: ivory, silk cloth and yarn, *lykion*, long pepper[525] and "items brought here from the ports of trade",[526] which might refer to the other coastal markets in Ariakê, namely Akabaru, Suppara and Kalliena.

As in other regions, the *Periplus* attests how the political centre took control over the flow of trade goods from inland sources to the port city on the coast; and this situation seem to have continued, even after the royal residence was moved to another city:

> "There is in this region towards the east a city called Ozênê, the former seat of a royal court,

---

[520] *Periplus* 47-49, transl. Casson (1989: 81), ... Καὶ Ἀλέξανδρος ὁρμηθεὶς ἀπὸ τῶν μερῶν τούτων ἄχρι τοῦ Γάγγου διῆλθε, καταλιπὼν τήν τε Λιμυρικὴν καὶ τὰ νότια τῆς Ἰνδικῆς, ἀφ' οὗ μέχρι νῦν ἐν Βαρυγάζοις παλαιαὶ προχωροῦσιν δραχμαί, γράμμασιν Ἑλληνικοῖς ἐγκεχαραγμέναι ἐπίσημα τῶν μετὰ Ἀλέξανδρον βεβασιλευκότων Ἀπολλοδότου καὶ Μενάνδρου. Ἔνι δὲ αὐτῆς καὶ ἐξ ἀνατολῆς πόλις λεγομένη Ὀζήνη, ἐν ᾗ καὶ τὰ βασίλεια πρότερον ἦν, ἀφ' ἧς πάντα τὰ πρὸς εὐθηνίαν τῆς χώρας εἰς Βαρύγαζαν καταφέρεται καὶ τὰ πρὸς ἐμπορίαν τὴν ἡμετέραν, ὀνυχίνη λιθία καὶ μουρρίνη καὶ σινδόνες Ἰνδικαὶ καὶ μολόχιναι καὶ ἱκανὸν χυδαῖον ὀθόνιον. Κατάγεται δὲ δι' αὐτῆς καὶ ἀπὸ τῶν ἄνω τόπων ἡ διὰ Προκλαΐδος καταφερομένη νάρδος ἡ Καττυβουρίνη καὶ ἡ Πατροπαπίγη καὶ ἡ Καβαλίτη καὶ ἡ διὰ τῆς παρακειμένης Σκυθίας, ὅ τε κόστος καὶ ἡ βδέλλα. Προχωρεῖ δὲ εἰς τὸ ἐμπόριον οἶνος προηγουμένως Ἰταλικὸς καὶ Λαοδικηνὸς καὶ Ἀραβικός, καὶ χαλκὸς καὶ κασσίτερος καὶ μόλυβος, κοράλλιον καὶ χρυσόλιθον, ἱματισμὸς ἁπλοῦς καὶ νόθος παντοῖος, πολύμιται ζῶναι πηχυαῖαι, στύραξ, μελίλωτον, ὕελος ἀργή, σανδαράκη, στίμι, δηνάριον χρυσοῦν καὶ ἀργυροῦν, ἔχον ἀλλαγὴν καὶ ἐπικέρδειάν τινα πρὸς τὸ ἐντόπιον νόμισμα, μύρον οὐ βαρύτιμον οὐδὲ πολύ. Τῷ δὲ βασιλεῖ κατ' ἐκείνους τοὺς καιροὺς εἰσφερόμενα βαρύτιμα ἀργυρώματα καὶ μουσικὰ καὶ παρθένοι εὐειδεῖς πρὸς παλλακείαν καὶ διάφορος οἶνος καὶ ἱματισμὸς ἁπλοῦς πολυτελὴς καὶ μύρον ἔξοχον. Φέρεται δὲ ἀπὸ τῶν τόπων νάρδος, κόστος, βδέλλα, ἐλέφας, ὀνυχίνη λιθία καὶ σμύρνα καὶ λύκιον καὶ ὀθόνιον παντοῖον καὶ Σηρικὸν καὶ μολόχινον καὶ νῆμα καὶ πέπερ<ι> μακρὸν καὶ τὰ ἀπὸ τῶν ἐμπορίων φερόμενα. Ἀποπλέουσιν δὲ κατὰ καιρὸν οἱ ἀπὸ τῆς Αἰγύπτου εἰς τὸ ἐμπόριον ἀναγόμενοι περὶ τὸν Ἰούλιον μῆνα, ὅς ἐστιν Ἐπῖφι.

[521] *Periplus* 49:16.25, Casson 1989: 81. Schoff's translation, "into those places" (1995: 42), is based on an unfounded emendation by Fabricius (1883: 90, line 13).

[522] *Periplus* 49.

[523] The Narmada today is not navigable beyond Barygaza, modern Bharuch (Ray 1986: 21f.).

[524] This identification is not certain, see Casson 1989: 207.

[525] Greek: πέπερ<ι> μακρὸν (49:16.30), the Latin *Piper longum*, native to many parts of India (Casson 1989: 210) and according to Pliny (12.28-29), more expensive in Rome than the black pepper bought in South India. See also Warmington's compilation of the prices of eastern plant products mentioned *en passant* by Pliny (1995: 226ff.).

[526] *Periplus* 49:16.30-31, τὰ ἀπὸ τῶν ἐμπορίων φερόμενα.

from which everything that contributes to the region's prosperity, including what contributes to trade with us, is brought down to Barygaza".[527]

It seems that exports were gathered in Ozênê before they were sent to Barygaza. This way the political centre could control and tax the flow of trade.

On the list of general imports to Barygaza[528] were wine, copper, tin, lead, coral, peridot, clothing, girdles, storax, yellow sweet clover,[529] raw glass, and realgar,[530] sulphide of antimony,[531] Roman money (*dênarion*) and unguent. The mix is much the same as at Barbarikon: plant products for drugs and cosmetics, textiles, corals and gems for jewellery, money and wine, in addition comes base metal – copper, tin and lead – and raw glass. We have to assume that these products were raw material for local manufacture. Raw glass could be used for beads and metal for personal adornments, coins, statues and figurines.

Apart from the wine, these products were not particularly suitable for the conspicuous consumption that the *Periplus* connects with rulers in other ports, and which in no other place is more clearly pointed out than in the list of *former* imports for the king and the court at Ozênê. It is noteworthy that expensive tableware is missing, a commodity that appears to have been imported to all other ports where local kings and chieftains were involved in the trade.

This does not mean that the goods imported at Barygaza were of low value or uninteresting for a ruler as objects of trade, consumption or taxation, only that with the possible exception of the wine, they did not belong to the group of prestige goods that it would be in a ruler's interest to monopolise.

Like at all other ports described in the *Periplus* as commercial outlets of kingdoms, coin was imported both at Barbarikon and Barygaza. A reasonable explanation seems to be that from the Mediterranean perspective, trade on the Indian Ocean was primarily an import trade. The demand for Mediterranean goods in Arabia, India and Africa was simply not large enough enough to balance the demand for Indian Ocean commodities in the Roman Empire. Pliny's complaint about the large amounts of money drained by the trade springs to mind: "in no year does India absorb less than fifty million sesterces of our empire's wealth, sending back merchandise to be sold with us at a hundred times its prime cost".[532] Regardless of the actual size of any such trade deficit – the figure would be even less possible for us to estimate than for Pliny – the need to pay in coin could be a further indication of the administrative nature of the trade in several of the ports taking part in the monsoon exchange. As many imports to Africa, Arabia and India seem to have been reserved for royal consumption, the demand is likely to have remained restricted.

The way around this obstacle was to pay in cash. At Kanê, money was mentioned among the imports for the king.[533] At Barbarikon all imports were for the king. At Barygaza there is no such mention of royal interest in imported money, but another highly interesting piece of information: among the imports are "Roman money, gold and silver, which commands an exchange at some profit against the local currency".[534]

This puzzle has not been satisfactorily solved. These parts of India had their own silver based currency,[535] and there should be no reason for paying more for the Roman coins than their weight in gold or silver, unless the prices of precious metals were higher in Barygaza than within the Roman Empire.

Manfred Raschke held that this was due to the high quality of Roman coins before the reforms of Nero.[536] Casson believed that the text reflects a temporary situation: "perhaps Western merchants came out somewhat ahead by using local currency to buy whatever Indian products they had to".[537]

Raschke also maintained that the trade in money at Barygaza was insignificant, as much larger numbers of coins have been found in South India.[538] The problem is that the archaeological record has little to do with what was imported, and more to do with what was buried, never recovered and thus found in modern times. Among other places, money is also mentioned as an import to Barbarikon,[539] the main ports of Southern Arabia,[540] and to Adulis,[541] in South Arabia with the addition that the quantity was considerable.[542] Still, finds of Roman money are even scarcer in South Arabia and within the ancient kingdom of Aksum, than in Northern India.[543]

---

[527] *Periplus* 48, transl. Casson (1989: 81), Ἔνι δὲ αὐτῆς καὶ ἐξ ἀνατολῆς πόλις λεγομένη Ὀζήνη, ἐν ᾗ καὶ τὰ βασίλεια πρότερον ἦν, ἀφ' ἧς πάντα τὰ πρὸς εὐθηνίαν τῆς χώρας εἰς Βαρύγαζαν καταφέρεται καὶ τὰ πρὸς ἐμπορίαν τὴν ἡμετέραν.
[528] *Periplus* 49.
[529] The identification is not certain, but probably a variety with medicinal properties (Casson 1989: 207f.).
[530] Red sulphide of arsenic, used as a dye and as medicine (Casson 1989: 208).
[531] Used both for eye-cosmetics and as medicine, (Casson 1989: 208f.).
[532] Pliny 6.101, transl. Rackham (1997-2001: vol 2, 417), *nullo anno minus HS|D̄| imperii nostri exhauriente India et merces remittente quae apud nos centiplicato veneant.*
[533] *Periplus* 28, cf. note 241.
[534] *Periplus* 49, transl. Casson (1989: 81), δηνάριον χρυσοῦν καὶ ἀργυροῦν, ἔχον ἀλλαγὴν καὶ ἐπικέρδειάν τινα πρὸς τὸ ἐντόπιον νόμισμα.
[535] Mitchiner 1976; Bopearachchi and Pieper 1998.
[536] Raschke 1978: 630.
[537] Casson 1989: 209.
[538] Raschke 1978: 630f.
[539] *Periplus* 39.
[540] *Periplus* 6.
[541] *Periplus* 24, 28 and 6.
[542] Kanê: πλείονα – "more" (*Periplus* 28:9.16). Muza: ἱκανός – "considerable" / "sufficient" (*Periplus* 24:8.5).
[543] Cf. Turner 1989 for the Indian situation.

In Southern Arabia[544] as well as in Northern India,[545] local coinage was issued in this period. That does not necessarily mean that foreign coins were not accepted, the metal value was after all the same. Rulers probably allowed foreign coins to circulate in their kingdoms, even if they issued their own coinage, at least the presence of old Indo-Greek drachmae at the market in Barygaza mentioned in the *Periplus*[546] seems to indicate this.

Nevertheless, coins were powerful means of propaganda, and over time, we would expect that Roman coins imported to north-western India would be melted down, as would older Hellenistic issues. Although the development of coinage was under way also in South India, it had not reached a comparable level in the first century, consisting of punch marked coins of small denominations.[547]

The rationale behind the arrangement at Barygaza might have been fiscal. The critical question is whether the prices of goods were the same in Roman money as in Indian. Fixed prices were not unknown in the ancient world. Setting fair prices, for instance, is high on the list of the duties of *panyādhyaksa* ("director of trade") in the ancient Indian handbook in statecraft, *Arthsastra*,[548] Diocletians well-known price edict of AD 301 aimed to establish uniform prices in the Roman Empire at the turn of the fourth century, probably without success.[549] If prices in local currency were lower than prices in foreign coinage, visiting merchants would make a profit by changing their money before buying Indian goods, rather than using Roman money directly. This way the king could control the influx of foreign money, at a relatively reasonable cost, as long as the profit on the exchange was not too high. If this was the case the exchange rate between Roman and Indian money contributes to explaining the low density of Roman coins in the archaeological record of the area.

Royal involvement in trade at Barygaza

At most other ports visited by the author of the *Periplus*, royal involvement seems to have taken the form of different kinds of monopoly or restrictions on trade, the control of inland routes gathering commodities of interest to the maritime trade, and the concentration of foreign trade to one port only, where the necessary physical and institutional infrastructure was in place. Direct royal participation in trade at Barygaza is only described in the *Periplus* as a thing of the past; but in controlling trade, the rulers of Barygaza went one step further and extended their operations offshore.

In the rather detailed description of the coast between Barbarikon and Barygaza and of the entrance to the Gulf of Khambhat, the bay leading to the latter port, we are told that these waters were dangerous due to strong tides and currents, reefs and shoals, but also because the coastline had few good landmarks for anyone who approached from the sea.[550] Like many Indian ports, Barygaza was placed some distance from the actual river mouth. The *Periplus* provides the figure 300 stadia,[551] about 54 kilometres or 29 nautical miles.

In order to get approaching ships safely to the port at Barygaza, the king provided a pilot service that met the arrivals at some distance outside the river mouth:

"For this reason local fishermen in the king's service[552] come out with crews and long ships (…) to meet vessels and guide them up to Barygaza. Through the crew's efforts, they maneuver them right from the mouth of the gulf through the shoals and tow them to predetermined stopping places".[553]

This not only shows royal interest in trade, but reveals that without royal effort, or other organisational structure, trade at Barygaza would hardly have been possible at all. Without it, visiting ships or Indian ships returning to Barygaza after trade with Parthia, Arabia or Africa, would not be able to get safely through the shallows and tides. In the *Arthasastra*, income from ports, roads, ferries and river guards are mentioned as possible sources of revenue,[554] and it is likely that the pilot services outside Barygaza also came at a price.

The next mention of royal control with maritime trade comes in the description of the ports on the coast south of Barygaza: Akabaru, Suppara and Kalliena. The author of the *Periplus* tells us that these ports were in the region called Dachinabadês, perhaps related to the modern name Deccan.[555] At least from the early first century BC onwards, the interior of the Deccan was controlled by the Satavahanas, who established their capital at Paithana on the Godvari River[556] and gradually enlarged their realm to an empire stretching from coast to coast.[557]

---

[544] Munro-Hay 2003.
[545] Mitchiner 1976; Bopearachchi and Pieper 1998.
[546] *Periplus* 47.
[547] Hall 1999: 433ff.
[548] *Arthasastra* 2.16.1-10.
[549] Potter 2004: 334ff.
[550] *Periplus* 40-46.
[551] *Periplus* 44.
[552] The term translated as "fishermen in the king's service", βασιλικοὶ ἁλιεῖς, could also be translated as "royal sailors / rowers", cf. Lidell, Scott and Jones (1996: 309b and 65a), which would convey an even stronger message of royal involvement. Cf. the royal slaves, δοῦλοι βασιλικοί, in *Periplus* 29:9.28.
[553] *Periplus* 44, transl.Casson (1989: 79), Τούτου χάριν περὶ αὐτὸν τὸν εἴσπλουν βασιλικοὶ ἁλιεῖς ἐντόπιοι πληρώμασιν μακρῶν πλοίων (…) ἀφ' ὧν ὁδηγεῖται τὰ πλοῖα μέχρι Βαρυγάζων. Κλίνουσιν γὰρ εὐθὺς ἀπὸ τοῦ στόματος τοῦ κόλπου διὰ τὰ τενάγη τοῖς πληρώμασιν καὶ ῥυμουλκοῦσιν αὐτὰ σταθμοῖς ἤδη τεταγμένοις.
[554] *Arthasastra* 2.6.3.
[555] Schoff 1995: 195.
[556] Ray (1986: 85) argues that Paithana was probably not the capital of the kingdom from the start of the Satavahana period, its status at the time of the *Periplus* is not clear, but it *is* mentioned as a royal residence, βασίλειον, by Ptolemy (7.1.82).
[557] Ray 1986: 50, 208f.

Control of the western coast, however, shifted between the Sakas to the Satavahanas several times. The state of affairs at the time of the *Periplus* has been subject to debate. The key to understanding the situation is given in paragraphs 50-52:

The city, *polis,* of Kalliena, had once been an *emporion enthesmon,* a "lawful port of trade".[558] The term reminds of the term *emporion nomimon,* "legally limited port of trade", which was used for Adulis, Muza and Apologos. But this was earlier, and now "after Sandanês occupied it, there has been much hindrance. For the Greek ships that by chance come into these places are brought under guard to Barygaza".[559]

These ports have been seen as Satavahana (Andhra)[560] possessions serving as outlets for trade coming through the passes in the Western Ghats, but blockaded by the Saka by the time of the *Periplus*.[561] In his *Sakas versus Andhras in the Periplus Maris Eythraei,*[562] Lionel Casson summed up the debate which has evolved around this passage and concluded that the text says just what it appears to be saying: that these three ports were Saka possessions at the time of the *Periplus,* but that they were relatively recent acquisitions.[563] The Saka control of these ports seems also to be attested in an inscription from Nasik in western India.[564]

Casson's interpretation seems reasonable, and rather than a blockade of hostile ports, we witness an example of government effort to concentrate trade at one port, the one closest to the political centre and further away from the hostile Satavahanas, who controlled the hinterland of these ports. Allowing trade to be conducted from these ports would be contrary to the interests of the Sakas. Not only would they lose traffic to their chief port, but, more importantly, it would supply their rivals with prestigious imported goods, for there were few other potential buyers in the neighbourhood of these ports.

Casson, however, also commented upon an earlier passage in the *Periplus,* describing overland trade from the cities of the Deccan to Barygaza: "From these there is brought to Barygaza, by conveyance in wagons over very great roadless stretches, from Paithana large quantities of onyx and from Tagara large quantities of cloth of ordinary quality".[565] Now the logical outlet for these Satavahana cities would have been the ports occupied by the Saka, especially Kalliena that had earlier served as a "lawful market". The passage is coherent with the trade blockade of the west coast ports indicated in *Periplus* 52, but why were the goods sent north to Barygaza?

Casson proposed that this was on account of smuggling, that the Satavahanas, who still controlled the mountain passes leading down to the coastal cities they had recently lost to the Saka, would prevent trade from their area from reaching these cities.[566] This interpretation has no direct support in the text. While the Sakas would probably have had no scruples about trading in goods from the Andhra realm as long as they could make a profit, it is less clear that the goods were smuggled. The Satavahanas would have had only theoretical interest in diminishing the value of Saka trade by withholding goods from areas under their control. Much more could be gained by continuing trade even after they had lost their coastal possessions and had to trade through their rivals. The reason for this trade to pass through Barygaza rather than the coastal settlements of Kalliena, Suppara or Akabaru must have been the desire of the Sakas to centre trade at one single port, where they could control it and tax it, not an Andhra desire to keep trade away. There would be little or no advantage for the Satavahanas in sending goods to their lost coastal possessions if foreign ships were not allowed to call there. Such a practice would also be reminiscent of the policy of centralising trade to certain markets suggested in the *Arthasastra,*[567] although, as emphasised above, no direct comparison is possible.

Networks meeting at Barygaza

The primary interest of the author of the *Periplus* was the trade with Egypt; yet, passages throughout the work reveal the trade and trade routes of Arabian, Parthian and Indian merchants. A number of "local ports of trade" (*emporia topika*) are briefly mentioned along the Konkan coast south of Barygaza,[568] and apart from Egyptian shipping, the *Periplus* reveals trade on Indian as well as Arabian keels from Barygaza or Ariakê with Adulis,[569] the various Far-side ports,[570] Kanê, Moscha Limên, Muza,[571] the island of Dioscuridês / Socotra,[572] Parthian ports and Southern India.[573] There is no reason to assume that the list is exhaustive, as we cannot expect our anonymous author to be fully informed about the Indian trade.

This trade involved both staple goods such as grain,[574] oil[575] and rice,[576] and goods of medium or high value, like

---

[558] *Periplus* 52:17.19.
[559] *Periplus* 52, transl. Casson (1989: 83), μετὰ γὰρ τὸ κατασχεῖν αὐτὴν Σανδάνην ἐκωλύθη ἐπὶ πολύ· καὶ γὰρ τὰ ἐκ τύχης εἰς τούτους τοὺς τόπους ἐσβάλλοντα πλοῖα Ἑλληνικὰ μετὰ φυλακῆς εἰς Βαρύγαζαν εἰσάγεται.
[560] Older literature often use the term *Andhra*, rather than *Satavahana*. See Ray 1986: 173f. on the relationship between the two: Andhra being the name of a *jati* (caste group) and Satavahana a clan within this *jati*.
[561] As for instance Palmer 1947: 138.
[562] Casson 1984b.
[563] Casson 1984b: 220.
[564] Gokhale 1987: 70.
[565] *Periplus* 51, transl. Casson (1989: 83), Κατάγεται δὲ ἐξ αὐτῶν πορείαις ἀμαξῶν καὶ ἀνοδίαις μεγίσταις εἰς τὴν Βαρύγαζαν ἀπὸ μὲν Πιθήνων ὀνυχίνη λιθία πλείστη, ἀπὸ δὲ Ταγάρων ὀθόνιον πολὺ[ν] χυδαῖον.
[566] Casson 1984b: 218f.
[567] *Arthasastra* 2.16.4, 2.22.9.
[568] *Periplus* 52-53.
[569] *Periplus* 6.
[570] *Periplus* 14.
[571] *Periplus* 27, 32 and 21.
[572] *Periplus* 31.
[573] *Periplus* 36 and 54.
[574] *Periplus* 14, 31, 32.
[575] *Periplus* 14, 23.

textiles,[577] metals,[578] hardwood and slaves.[579] Typical prestige goods like tableware, jewellery, wine and gold are absent among the goods exported from Barygaza, although expensive textiles might have belonged to a similar elite sphere.

These maritime links were linked up with overland routes. Caravans made their way inland from the ports on the western coast, over the passes in the Western Ghats and to the Satavahana centres further inland.[580] These are the very routes that appear to have been blocked at the time when *Periplus* was written, so that the flow of trade with the West to and from the Deccan had to go through Barygaza.

Skythia and Ariakê – the picture of government control

In conclusion, Skythia and Ariakê as depicted in the *Periplus* were both states where the government put much effort into controlling trade. In both kingdoms long-distance maritime trade was restricted to one port. This echoes the arrangements described in Aksum, Saba-Himyar and Hadramawt. Both states also controlled the flow of inland commodities towards the coast. In Skythia trade was centred in the capital,[581] in Ariakê most goods came by way of the capital of Minnagara or the earlier royal residence city of Ozênê before they were transported to the coast.[582]

Whereas the Skythian king maintained some kind of monopoly on foreign trade and imported prestige goods that could be invested in the political process, traces of direct royal participation in trade at Ariakê belonged to the past, probably the period before the Sakas took over. Government interest in trade at Barygaza at the time of the *Periplus* was thus probably limited to different kinds of taxation. The removal of the royal court from Ozênê[583] seems to have had an effect on the volume and range of the commodities imported at Barygaza, and this supports the notion that rulers were important consumers of imported goods.

In Ariakê the rulers were faced with a potential problem through competition with the Satavahanas in the Deccan. The potential competition was not about prices, but about which port traders would visit and thus who would gain access to imported goods and who would be able to tax the trade. The problem was solved by active intervention, such as a pilot service at Barygaza[584] and a blockade of alternative markets.[585] Such policies show that trade was considered an important source of income by the rulers of Ariakê.

The active measures taken to guide ships to the port at Barygaza[586] and to direct inland commodities towards the coast,[587] show not only that trade was important to the state, but also that a working state apparatus was important to the existence of long-distance maritime trade.

---

[576] *Periplus* 14, 31.
[577] *Periplus* 6, 14, 31, 32.
[578] *Periplus* 6, 36.
[579] *Periplus* 36, 31 (slaves).
[580] Ray 1986: 70; Deshpande 1994: 175f.
[581] *Periplus* 39.
[582] *Periplus* 41, 48.
[583] *Periplus* 48.
[584] *Periplus* 44.
[585] *Periplus* 52.
[586] *Periplus* 44, 52.
[587] *Periplus* 41, 48.

Chapter 7: The Malabar and Southern India

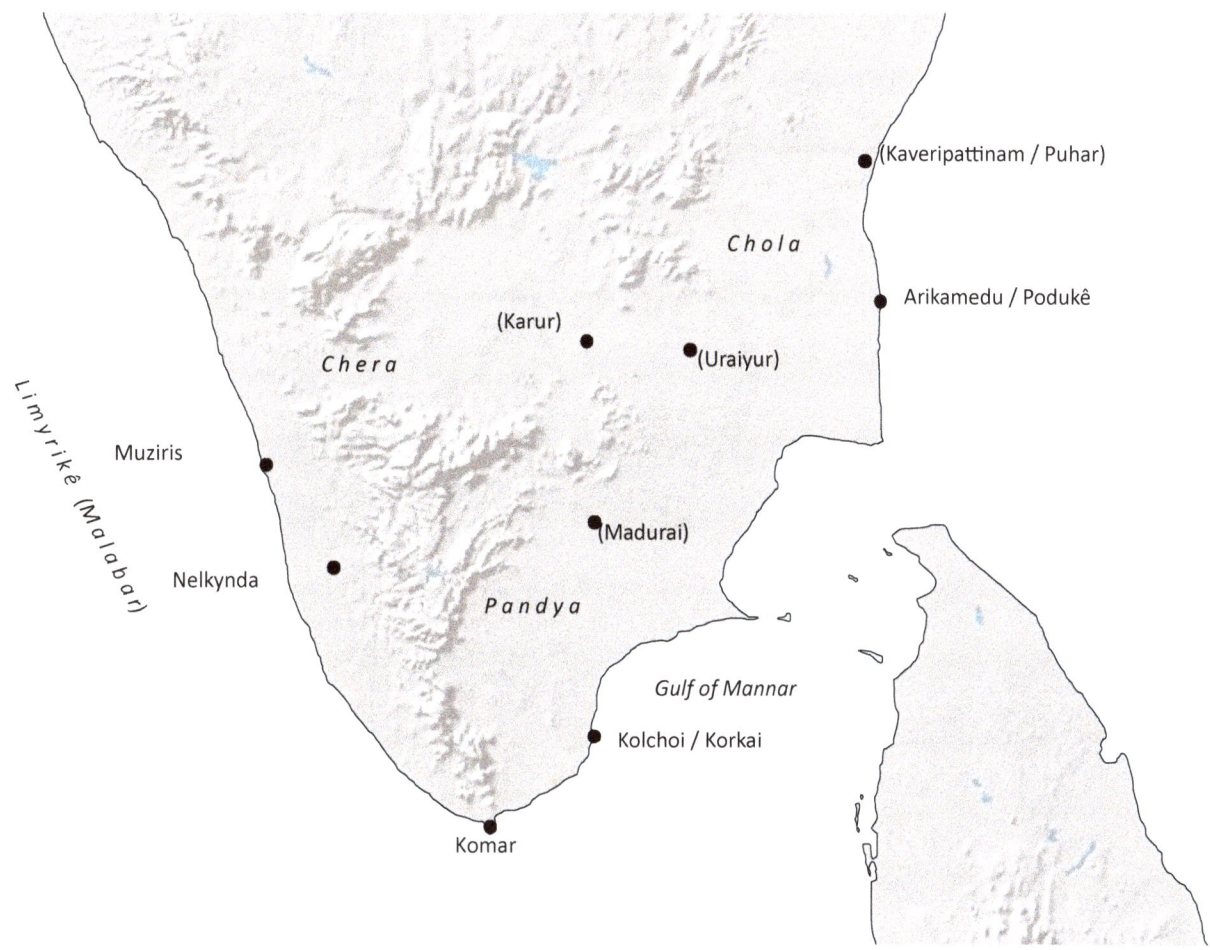

Fig. 5: Map of Southern India at the time of the *Periplus*

In southernmost India, three kingdoms emerged in the centuries before the turn of our era. They were known by their ruling dynasties as the *Chera*, situated on the west coast with its hinterland, the *Pandya* in the south, and finally the *Chola* on the east coast. The kingdoms met in central South India, where the capitals of the Chera and the Chola were situated in the fertile Kaveri Valley, while Madurai of the Pandyas was on the Vaigai River, some 130 kilometres further south. The Deccan and the Krishna and Godvari valleys were dominated by the Satavahana dynasty, which, however, seems not to have maintained any coastal presence on the western coast of India at the time of the *Periplus* (cf. p. 55, above).

Southern ports and kingdoms

The Chera kingdom on the Malabar Coast of Southern India was known to the author of the *Periplus* as *Kêprobotos*,[588] probably related to the modern name Kerala,[589] whereas the Malabar Coast as such was called *Limyrikê*. The kingdom had at least two ports, Tyndis and Muziris, of which only Muziris was active in the monsoon trade at the time of the *Periplus*. Muziris figures prominently among the ports described in that work[590] and is also known from Tamil poetry,[591] Pliny's *Natural History*,[592] a second century Egyptian papyrus[593] and from the fourth century Roman roadmap known as the *Tabula Peutingeriana*.[594] According to the *Periplus*, Muziris was situated 20 stades, ca 3.6 kilometres, from the river mouth.[595] Here the port would be sheltered from the ocean surf, and the Periyar river and the backwaters of Kerala facilitated communication further inland. The

---

[588] *Periplus* 54:17.29.
[589] Casson 1989: 217f.
[590] *Periplus* 54-56.
[591] *Purananuru* 343, *Ahananuru* 149.
[592] Pliny 6.104-105.
[593] P. Vindob. G40822.
[594] Tab. Peut. Seg. 12.
[595] *Periplus* 54:18.3, ἀπὸ δὲ τοῦ < στόματος ποταμοῦ τοῦ > κατ' αὐτὴν εἴκοσι. Or rather twenty stadia away from something, as the sound manuscript reading (CPG 398: 52r, 1) seems to be missing a few words. The interpolation cited here and first proposed by Müller (1855: 297b) seems plausible and is agreed upon by all modern translators: Huntingford 1980: 50; Casson 1989: 85; Schoff 1995: 44. See Fabricius (1883: 95 note 7) for older suggestions.

coastline of the Malabar has undergone considerable changes since the ancient period, but the site of Muziris has probably been identified at Pattanam, near Kodungallur, where excavations have uncovered remains of wharves and warehouses along with significant quantities of imported ceramics from the first century BC through the fifth century AD.[596]

The potential for inland communication must have been an important asset, for the *Periplus* reveals that "the kings themselves of both ports of trade[597] dwell in the interior".[598] Ptolemy mentions a royal residence of the *Kêrobothros* (sic) named Karoura in this region,[599] and in Tamil literature the seat of government of the Chera kingdom goes under the two names of Karuvur and Vanji. The identification of Karuvur / Vanji remains controversial, but could be identical with modern Karur on the Amaravati River,[600] a tributary to the Kaveri, about 70 kilometres from the modern city of Tiruchirapalli.[601] The convenient route from Muziris to the capital was thus an overland journey through the Palghat pass into the Coimbatore region. Interestingly, locations along this corridor have yielded the bulk of the finds of several thousand Roman coins in South India.[602]

The Pandya kingdom figures most prominently among the Tamil kingdoms in Graeco-Roman literature. Both Pliny and Alexander's second century biographer Arrian relate a mythological story of the kingdom being founded by Hercules, who installed his daughter Pandaea after whom the kingdom was named on the throne.[603] Less mythological was the kingdom's fame for its pearls, which Arrian in the same passage reveals was known to Megasthenes who wrote in the fourth century BC.

The capital of the Pandya realm was Madurai, still a thriving city today. Second century AD Madurai is described in great detail in the Tamil poem *Maduraikanchi*, and is mentioned as the capital of the Pandians by both Pliny[604] and Ptolemy.[605] Tamil literature names Korkai on the Gulf of Mannar as the main port of the Pandian Kingdom.[606] The port is also attested in the *Periplus*,[607] but at the time of that work, the main outlet of Pandian maritime trade was Nelkynda on the Malabar Coast.[608] Nelkynda has not beeen securely identified. Schoff placed it at modern Kottayam,[609] a centre for the Nestorian Indian Church, which, according to later legend, was founded by St. Thomas approximately at the time of the *Periplus*.[610] Schoff's identification has been supported by Gurukkal and Whittaker,[611] while Casson favoured a position slightly further south.[612] If either of these identifications is correct, communication between coastal and highland areas of the kingdom was possible either by riverine transport and the southern passes in the Ghats, or along the coast to Alagankulam and upriver along the Vaigai towards the capital from there. Like Muziris, Nelkynda is reported to have been situated at some distance from the river mouth.[613] We learn that ships actually loaded their cargoes at a roadstead called Bakarê at the mouth of the river. The river up to Nelkynda was shallow and contained sandbanks, which presumably made it dangerous for ships leaving fully loaded and on an ebbing tide.[614]

The *Periplus* reports several coastal sites along the Pandian coast after Nelkynda, which he calls *Paralia*, "the Seaboard".[615] First came a village (*kômê*) called Balita, of which we learn nothing more than the fact that it had a good harbour.[616] After Balita came Komar, a port primarily identified with worship and pilgrimage in the *Periplus*. The name suggests the undisputed identification with modern Cape Comorin / Kanyakumari, the southernmost point on the Indian subcontinent.

After Komari came Kolchoi, identified with the Korkai refered to as a Pandyan harbour in Tamil literature.[617] Kolchoi was a centre for pearl fishing. The Pandya Kingdom controlled the Indian side of the shallow Gulf of Mannar, separating India and Sri Lanka, and still important for its rich pearl fisheries.[618] According to the *Periplus*, these fisheries were worked by convicted criminals.[619]

Alagankulam is the modern name of a fourth coastal site in the ancient Pandian kingdom. The port was situated on

---

[596] Cherian, Selvakumar and Shajan 2007; Tomber 2008: 140ff.; Cherian et. al. 2009.
[597] That is Muziris in the Chera kingdom and Nelkynda in the Pandya kingdom, further south.
[598] *Periplus* 55:18.11-12, transl. Casson (1989: 85), Αὐτοὶ δὲ οἱ βασιλεῖς ἀμφοτέρων τῶν ἐμπορίων ἐν τῇ μεσογαίῳ κατοικοῦσιν.
[599] Ptolemy 7.1.86, Κάρουρα, βασίλειον Κηροβόθρου.
[600] Champakalakshmi 1999: 118ff. Karur has also been identified several sites closer to the coast. See, however, Champakalakshmi (1999: 118) on why these identifications have been abandoned and on the identification of Karuvur and Vanji as the same place. A different solution is suggested by Rajan (1996: 100ff.), who proposes that the location of the capital has changed over time.
[601] Which by the way is identified by most commentators as the ancient Uraiyur, capital of the Chola kingdom (Casson 1989: 226ff.).
[602] Cf. Turner 1989: 119.
[603] Pliny 6.76; Arrian, *Indika* 7-11.
[604] Pliny 6.105.
[605] Ptolemy 7.1.89.
[606] Iyengar (1982: 296f.) collects and cites references.

[607] *Periplus* 59, Kolchoi, cf. Casson 1989: 226.
[608] Pliny 6.106, *Periplus* 54, 56.
[609] Schoff 1995: 208.
[610] Brown 1982: 48ff.
[611] Gurukkal and Whittaker 2001: 348f.
[612] Casson 1989: 297ff.
[613] *Periplus* 54.
[614] *Periplus* 55.
[615] *Periplus* 58:19.14.
[616] *Periplus* 58.
[617] See Schoff 1995: 237 on the identification of Kolchoi (Schoff: Colchi) with Korkai and the mythological past of the port and Iyengar 1982: 296f. on Korkai in Tamil sources.
[618] See Schoff 1995: 239ff. on ancient, medieval and modern pearl fishing in the area and Sarma 1978: 423ff. on the ecological side of the issue.
[619] *Periplus* 59:19.23-24. Κατακρίσιμος, "condemned", used as a noun, is a form only known from this passage (Lidell, Scott and Jones 1996: 896a), but the meaning seems to be clear. See, however, Fabricius (1883: 103 note 4) who abstained from emendation but suggested that it might be the result of a scribal error.

the mouth of the Vaigai River, providing sheltered anchorage and possibilities for inland communication with Madurai on and along the river. The port is not mentioned in the *Periplus*, but it could be identical with a certain Saliyur mentioned in Tamil literature,[620] which again has been identified with the Salour Emporion of Ptolemy.[621] Excavations at Alagankulam have yielded pottery that attest to coastal exchange with the Bengal and Andhra coasts, and late Roman coins indicate direct or indirect commercial contact with the Mediterranean.[622]

The third kingdom of Tamil South India was ruled by the Chola dynasty. Their ancient capital was a city called Uraiyur in Tamil sources, probably identical with the Argaru mentioned in the *Periplus*.[623] The Greek source presents Argaru as a region, *chôra*, rather than as a city, and as a production centre for textiles and a collection point for the pearls harvested in the area.[624] The change from the Pandya kingdom to the Chola is perhaps reflected in the *Periplus* by a different name for the coast after Kolchoi, *Aigialos*, "the Strand"[625] after *Paralia*, "the Seaboard" for the Pandyan Coast;[626] but except for the mention of three ports on the Coromandel Coast,[627] this is all we get to know about the Chola kingdom in the *Periplus*. Unlike the Chera (*Periplus*: *Kêprobotos*) and the Pandya (*Pandiôn*), not even the name of the kingdom is traceable. This is probably because the author of the *Periplus* lacked firsthand knowledge, and may indicate that Roman merchants rarely travelled beyond Cape Comorin in this period, but stayed on the west coast.[628]

The *Periplus* does, however, reveal that the Coromandel Coast maintained direct contact with Southeast Asia,[629] and the Chola kingdom belonged to an integrated coastal and overland trading network in South India, where both the import of Mediterranean goods and the supply of export products for the monsoon trade played important roles.

In Tamil sources we are told that the main port of the Cholas was Kaveripattinam. In more than 300 lines the poem *Pattinapalai*, probably composed ca 190 AD,[630] describes the city during the reign of King Karikala Cholan. *Pattinam* means "city", and Kaveripattinam was situated on the Coromandel Coast, where the delta of South India's largest river, the Kaveri, meets the sea. *Pattinapalai* describes the town, its temples, its trade with inland and overseas regions, the warehouses where merchandise was stored, the various inhabitants of the city, including its merchants, and the great king of the Chola. An even more elaborate description of the city is given in the later epic of *Silappadikaram*, probably dateable to the fifth century.[631] The site of Kaveripattinam is today believed to be the village of Poompuhar, ca 350 kilometres south of Chennai, but archaeological excavations have so far not been able to support the identification.[632]

In contrast to the ports described in the *Periplus* and in Tamil poems, the site of Arikamedu near Pondicherry must now be said to have been thoroughly excavated.[633] The site has yielded evidence of a considerable bead making industry and commercial contact with the Mediterranean, Mesopotamia and other regions over a span of several centuries. Arikamedu is situated in an area usually ascribed to the Chola kings, but the site has also been identified with one of the many lesser chieftains mentioned in the Tamil poems.[634] This might also have been the case with many of the other coastal sites in Southern India, for the process of centralisation in the Tamil kingdoms had not yet come very far by the first centuries of our era.[635]

The *Periplus* on trade in the Tamil kingdoms

Along with passages in Tamil literature, the *Periplus* give a glimpse of three interrelated trading networks in the Tamil kingdoms of Southern India: one joining the Malabar Coast with Egypt, East Africa, Arabia, Mesopotamia, Iran and Western India, a regional network connecting the Tamil areas by coastal and overland trade, and a third network connecting Southern India with Sri Lanka, the Satavahana kingdom, the Ganges delta and Southeast Asia.

At the time of the *Periplus*, the western entrepôts of this system were the ports of Muziris and Nelkynda on the Malabar Coast, belonging to the Cheran and Pandyan kingdom respectively. The trade of the two ports is dealt with in the same passage by our unknown author:

> "Ships in these ports of trade carry full loads because of the volume and quantity of pepper and malabathron. They offer a market for: mainly a great amount of money; peridot; clothing with no adornment, in limited quantity; multicoloured textiles; sulphide of antimony; coral; raw glass; copper, tin, lead; wine, in limited quantity, as much as goes to Barygaza; realgar; orpiment; grain in sufficient amount for

---

[620] Champakalakshmi 1999: 133.
[621] Warmington 1995: 62; Ptolemy 7.1.11.
[622] Champakalakshmi 1999: 133f.
[623] *Periplus* 59:20.1 uses the form Ἀργαλου, see Casson 1989: 266 for the emendation, Schoff 1995: 241f. on the identification and Maloney 1975: 32 for a different view.
[624] *Periplus* 59.
[625] *Periplus* 59:19.25.
[626] *Periplus* 58:19.14.
[627] *Periplus* 60, Kamara, Podukê, Sôpatma.
[628] As I argue in detail in Seland 2007, based on the scanty knowledge of these parts reflected in the *Periplus* (60-66), Strabo's statement on the infrequency of Roman contacts with the east coast (15.1.4), and the apparent lack of reliable data on these regions in the theoretical chapters of Ptolemy's *Geography* (1.13-14). See, however, Tomber (2008: 149) for a different view.
[629] *Periplus* 60.
[630] Zvelebil 1973: 78f. 99ff.; Zvelebil 1975: 78f. 96.

[631] Zvelebil 1975: 110ff.
[632] Maloney 1975: 29; Champakalakshmi 1999: 127.
[633] Wheeler, Gosh, and Deva 1946; Casal 1949; Begley *et al.* 1996.
[634] Champakalakshmi 1999: 135.
[635] Champakalakshmi 1999: 24ff.

those involved in shipping, because the [sc. local] merchants do not use it.

They export pepper, grown for the most part in only one place connected with these ports of trade, that called Kottanarikê. They also export: good supplies of fine-quality pearls; ivory; Chinese [i.e., silk] cloth; Gangetic nard; malabathron, brought here from the interior; all kinds of transparent gems; diamonds; sapphires; tortoise shell, both the kind from Chrysê Island and the kind caught around the islands lying off Limyrikê itself. For those sailing here from Egypt, the right time to set out is around the month of July, that is, Epeiph".[636]

Unlike the main ports of other kingdoms, no separate lists of imports for the kings or their vassals can be found at Muziris and Nelkynda, although commodities like money[637] and wine might have been of interest to local rulers. This should not be taken to mean that the Tamil kings were uninterested in long-distance trade. To get an impression of how the Tamil states and their rulers related to the Indian Ocean trade, we have to look further; and when the list of imports fails us, the obvious place to start looking is the list of exports.

That the traders from Roman Egypt considered the Malabar markets among the most important ports of call in the Indian Ocean is clear from the statement about the large volume of the shiploads and from the fact that these were the only ports where the Romans could acquire black pepper, a spice of almost universal popularity in cooking and medicine in the Roman Empire.[638] We are told that pepper grew only in one area nearby, Kottonarikê. Pepper is still an important export from the Malabar Coast. The pepper plant is a climber, growing as a parasite on other trees. It requires a combination of high temperatures, moist climate and high altitude unique to the Southern Ghats of modern Kerala and Tamil Nadu.

Pearls and ivory were other prominent exports from Nelkynda and Muziris, both products native to the region. Different kinds of gems were also on offer. These could be found in South India and on Sri Lanka, and some of them must have been from the rich beryl mines in the modern Coimbatore region,[639] near the Chera capital of Karur.

Pearls represent a highly interesting commodity in the context of trade and political authority. They were harvested in all the Tamil kingdoms, but as far as we know, the best pearl fisheries were in the Gulf of Mannar and the Palk Strait.[640] These coasts were controlled by the Pandya and the Chola. The *Periplus* gives the following report on pearl fisheries near Kolchoi in the Pandian kingdom: "Beyond Komar the region extends as far as Kolchoi, where diving for pearls goes on; it is carried out by convicts."[641] In the description of the Chola kingdom, if it is indeed identical with the "Strand" of the *Periplus*, we learn that "After Kolchoi...comes the Strand, bordering a bay with, inland, a region named Argaru. In one place...along it...pearls are gathered".[642]

That pearls were collected by convicts, *katakrisimoi*, tells us that the harvesting of this resource was under government control in some way or the other.[643] It is also significant that pearls were not sold from Kolchoi where they were harvested, but from Nelkynda and / or Muziris on the west coast. This way the king could ensure that no trade happened outside his control so that he got his cut. When we read that all pearls harvested in the neighbouring Chola kingdom were gathered in one place, it could be a similar arrangement. What we witness is government effort to control the flow of a valuable key commodity in order to profit from both trade and production. It is tempting to draw parallels to Hadramawt, where the existence of a valuable trading commodity on the coast, frankincense, appears to have caused an inland based government to invest in infrastructure and military presence in otherwise

---

[636] *Periplus* 56, transl. Casson (1989: 85), Πλεῖ δὲ εἰς τὰ ἐμπόρια ταῦτα μεστὰ πλοῖα διὰ τὸν ὄγκον καὶ τὸ πλῆθος τοῦ πιπέρεως καὶ τοῦ μαλαβάθρου. Προχρεῖ δὲ εἰς αὐτὴν προηγουμένως [δὲ] χρήματα πλεῖστα, χρυσόλιθα, ἱματισμὸς ἁπλοῦς οὐ πολύς, πολύμιτα, στῖμι, κοράλλιον, ὕελος ἀργή, χαλκός, κασσίτερος, μόλιβος, οἶνος δὲ οὐ πολύς, σώσει δὲ τοσοῦτον, ὅσον ἐν Βαρυγάζοις, σανδαράκη, ἀρσενικόν, σῖτος δὲ ὅσος ἀρκέσει τοῖς περὶ τὸ ναυκλήριον διὰ τὸ μὴ τοὺς ἐμπόρους αὐτῷ χρῆσθαι. Φέρεται δὲ πέπερι, μονογενῶς ἐν ἑνὶ τόπῳ τούτων τῶν ἐμπορίων γεννώμενον πολύ, λεγομένη Κοττανάρική. Φέρεται δὲ καὶ μαργαρίτης ἱκανὸς καὶ διάφορος καὶ ἐλέφας καὶ ὀθόνια Σηρικὰ καὶ νάρδος ἡ Γαγγιτικὴ καὶ μαλάβαθρον ἐκ τῶν ἔσω τόπων εἰς αὐτὴν λιθία διαφανῆς παντοία καὶ ἀδάμας καὶ ὑάκινθος καὶ χελώνη ἥ τε Χρυσονητιωτικὴ καὶ ἡ περὶ τὰς νήσους θηρευομένη τὰς προκειμένας αὐτῆς τῆς Λιμυρικῆς. Πλέουσι δὲ εἰς αὐτὴν οἱ κατὰ καιρὸν ἀναγόμενοι ἀπ' Αἰγύπτου περὶ τὸν Ἰούλιον μῆνα, ὅ ἐστιν Ἐπῖφι.

[637] The *Periplus* here uses the term χρήματα, plural of χρῆμα, "money", but also with a wider sense, possibly meaning things like goods, property, or simply something one needs, cf. Lidell, Scott and Jones (1996: 2004f.) Casson's translation as "money" is, however, nowhere more justified than in South India, where large amounts of Roman coin have come to light.

[638] Cf. Warmington 1995: 182ff. Pliny (12.29) despairs at the popularity of Indian pepper. It appears in a number of recipes in Apicus' book of recipes, *De re coquinaria*. Three and a half centuries after Pliny 3000 Roman pounds, ca 1000 kg, of pepper figure prominently on the list of Rome's ransom to Alaric in 408 AD (Zosimus 5.41.4). Among the prices of spices given *en passant* in book 12 by Pliny and compiled by Warmington (1995: 228), pepper comes out among the more inexpensive, this perhaps in part explaining its popularity. More than 3000 peppercorns have been found at Berenikê in Egypt (Cappers 2006: 114) smaller quantities are reported from other sites in the Eastern Desert, Germany, France and Britain (2006: 117ff.).

[639] Warmington 1995: 250f.

[640] Sarma 1978: 423ff.

[641] *Periplus* 59 transl. Casson (1989: 87), Ἀπὸ δὲ τοῦ Κομαρεῖ ἐκτείνουσα χώρα μέχρι Κόλχων, ἐν ᾗ κολύμβησις τοῦ πινικοῦ ἐστίν, ἀπὸ δὲ κατακρισίμων κατεργάζεται.

[642] *Periplus* 59:19-20.24-2 transl. Casson (1989: 87f.): Μετὰ δὲ Κόλχους ἐκδέχεται † πρότερος † Αἰγιαλὸς ἐν κόλπῳ κείμενος, ἔχων χώραν μεσόγειον, λεγομένην Ἀργαλου· ἐν ἑνὶ τόπῳ † τερονειτε παρ' αὐτήν τῆς ἠπιοδώρου † συλλεγομένον πινικόν, The latter passage is partly corrupt in the manuscript, the important words, "in one place" (ἐν ἑνὶ τόπῳ) and "are gathered" (συλλεγομέν) are however legible, the question of where the pearls were gathered, we can leave open.

[643] Cf. note 619 on the term Κατακρίσιμος.

unattractive areas.⁶⁴⁴ While the coast of Southern India had a far greater potential for littoral agriculture than Southern Arabia, the special ruler interest in both cases seems to have been fostered by a desire to control a valuable export commodity.

The Chinese cloth (silk)⁶⁴⁵ probably reached the Tamil areas through Central Asia by way of the Ganges and down the Indian east coast. The last legs of the route is reported by the *Periplus*,⁶⁴⁶ while the connection to the trade routes across the mountains to Central Asia is confirmed by the presence of silk also at the northwestern ports of Barbarikon and Barygaza.⁶⁴⁷ The silk traded from these ports came by way of the Indus, but from there overland trade routes led on to the Ganges Plain, with its easy communication to the east coast. Alternatively the silk could have reached Southern India through the trade with Chrysê – the Malay Peninsula,⁶⁴⁸ attested elsewhere in the *Periplus*.⁶⁴⁹

Gangetic nard exported from Muziris and Nelkynda was a variety of the Spikenard available from Barbarikon and Barygaza.⁶⁵⁰ The author of the *Periplus* supplies the place of origin as it was known to him, i.e. the Ganges, revealing that like the silk, it came down the Ganges and from there down the east coast.⁶⁵¹

Malabathron was probably a product from the leaf of the cinnamon tree.⁶⁵² Casson argues on grounds of the *Periplus* that our unknown author believed it to come from areas that seem to have been near the border between modern India and Burma.⁶⁵³ Nothing indicates that the author of the *Periplus* had been there himself, and his report has a mythical ring to it. Still, this reveals that the malabathron had reached Southern India through coastal or trans-oceanic exchange on the Bay of Bengal. Thus it was not a product of the cinnamon tree native to Southern India, which is the commercially important species today.⁶⁵⁴ We are told that malabathron was brought to Muziris and Nelkynda from "places in the interior",⁶⁵⁵ indicating that it must have been transported overland from the Coromandel Coast. Finally the tortoise shell attests the maritime trade further eastwards as we learn that some of it came from Chrysê.

Why enter into detail about the origin of the different exports from the Malabar Coast? Of all the exports mentioned, only pepper, ivory and some of the gems were available in the immediate hinterland of Muziris and Nelkynda. All the other products had a shorter or longer journey behind them before they were traded with the foreign merchants who called at the two west coast ports of trade. Thus they show local administrative or commercial efforts, whether by rulers or merchants, to mobilise resources in order to participate in the monsoon trade. The list of exports in the *Periplus* provides an outline of a trading network along the east coast of India to the Ganges and beyond, and across the Bay of Bengal. This network connected with the trade on the western Indian Ocean in the harbours on the Malabar Coast, just as the Red Sea and Indian Ocean trade met the Mediterranean economic system at the Red Sea ports of Egypt

The picture of the *Periplus* can be contrasted with that of ancient Tamil literature. Although almost 150 years later than the *Periplus,* the description of Kaveripattinam in the *Pattinappalai* belongs to a time in which the monsoon trade seems to have operated along the same patterns.⁶⁵⁶ While describing the flows of goods meeting at the Chola port, the author recognises the trading links along the coast, north to the mouth of the Ganges and beyond, south to Sri Lanka and possibly eastwards across the Bay of Bengal, as well as regional exchange between coast and inland in the Chola kingdom.⁶⁵⁷ The *Pattinappalai* gives an impression of a respected, wealthy and active class of merchants,⁶⁵⁸ and also describes the work of customs agents monitoring and taxing the flow of imports and exports through royal warehouses.⁶⁵⁹

The *Pattinappalai* is unique among the Tamil poems in its detailed description of trade, but it is not the only piece of poetic evidence available. The heroic *Purananuru* 343 describes the port of Muciri, probably the Muziris of the Graeco-Roman sources. In his praise of the Cheran hero-king Kuttuvan, the poet mentions the exchange of rice for fish, the import of golden tableware by sea, and the trade in pepper. The king is extolled for his generosity in giving out gifts of goods from the mountains as well as goods from the sea. Royal generosity is a frequent motif in Tamil poetry,⁶⁶⁰ but in

---

⁶⁴⁴ Cf. ch. 4, pp. 31f.
⁶⁴⁵ *Periplus* 56:18.24, ὀθόνια Σηρικά, "Sêric cloth", could mean either "Chinese" or "silken" cloth (Lidell, Scott and Jones 1996:1594b, σηρικός = "Seric" or "silken"). The translations of Casson (1989: 85), and Huntingford (1980: 52) to "Chinese", rather than "silken" are supported by the adjective being used also for hides in *Periplus* 39:13:11, Σιρικὰ δέρματα.
⁶⁴⁶ *Periplus* 64.
⁶⁴⁷ *Periplus* 39, 49, 64.
⁶⁴⁸ Gerini 1974: 77ff., but see Casson 1989: 235f. for an updated bibliography.
⁶⁴⁹ *Periplus* 56, 60.
⁶⁵⁰ *Periplus* 39, 49.
⁶⁵¹ *Periplus* 63.
⁶⁵² Casson 1989: 220.
⁶⁵³ Casson 1989: 241f.; *Periplus* 65.
⁶⁵⁴ The problem of cinnamon and its three ancient varieties, cinnamon, cassia and malabathron remains unsolved, but see ch. 5, pp. 40f., on the cinnamon trade from the Far-side Ports on the Horn of Africa and Casson 1984a, where sources, botanical evidence and the scientific debate is discussed.
⁶⁵⁵ *Periplus* 56:18.25, ἐκ τῶν ἔσω τόπων.

⁶⁵⁶ Whereas the *Periplus* is older than the description of Kaveripattinam in the *Pattinappalai*, which is dated to ca 190 AD (Zvelebil 1975: 78f. and 107), the so called "Muziris Papyrus" (P. Vindob. G 40822), is more or less contemporary. The Papyrus attests that Muziris was still a major entrepôt for Roman trade to India in the mid second century, and that the goods traded in were at least in part the same as at the time of the *Periplus,* spikenard, ivory and textiles.
⁶⁵⁷ *Pattinappalai* 212-224.
⁶⁵⁸ *Pattinappalai* 225-252.
⁶⁵⁹ *Pattinappalai* 134-152.
⁶⁶⁰ Champakalakshmi (1999: 97f.) discusses the role of gift-exchange in the early Tamil kingdoms.

this case the generosity is explicitly linked to the flows of goods from the interior, and from abroad (the sea), and the king is positioned as a mediator between the two. The poem thus seems to stress the important position of the king in the long-distance trade, an impression absent from the *Periplus,* but echoed by the description of the royal warehouses of Kaveripattinam in the *Pattinappalai*. The passage, however, also shows the redistributive use of trade goods, and thus their potential function in the political system of the Chera kingdom. Some imported goods, such as gold and silver coins, could be directly redistributed to followers, hoarded or used for further trade or wages for soldiers. Others, especially wine, were fit for the conspicuous consumption connected to court life as other Tamil poems suggest.[661]

The ecology and economy of Southern India

A large number of local dynasties are mentioned in Tamil literature.[662] In time, three of them evolved into kingdoms.[663] States are not characterised only by their trading activities. The natural environment in which the polity evolves defines the basis for agricultural production and commercial exchange. The three kingdoms of Southern India were all riverine polities.[664] The Cheras were based on the Periyar Valley and on the upper Kaveri, the Pandyas on the Vaigai and Tambraparani Rivers and the Cholas on the Kaveri Plain and Delta. These are the main rice growing areas of Southern India, providing the kings with necessary control of an agricultural surplus.

The three kingdoms each had access to the coast and to at least one good harbour. As elsewhere in India, good natural harbours were scarce along the Malbar and Coromandel coasts, and river mouths offered the best possibility for safe mooring.[665] The coastal region not only supplied the possibility to participate in trade, but also offered resources itself, such as salt and fish.[666] Finally, all three states had access to mountain terrain and woodland that provided many of the goods demanded in the coastal and overseas trade – fragrant woods, spices and precious stones.

The possibility of dividing the South Indian kingdoms into identifiable ecological zones is a feature they share with most other regions, but South India is special insofar as these zones and their natural resources were recognised and reflected both in Tamil poetry and in the early medieval literary theory that evolved from it.[667] Ancient Tamil poetry divides the Tamil regions into different ecological zones with different qualities, to which the poets themselves and their somewhat later commentators attributed different romantic feelings. An excerpt of relevant features from this model of an "interior landscape", as Kamil V. Zvelebil has called it, is given below:

Table 3: Regions reflected in Tamil love-poetry (adapted after K. Zvelebil)[668]

Landscape	Mountains	Forest/ pasture	Cultivated countryside	Seashore	Wasteland
Occupation	Guarding millet fields, honey gathering	Pastoral occupation, fieldwork	Agriculture	Drying fish, selling salt	Wayfarers, robbery, fighting
Settlements	Small hamlet, village	Town, city, hamlet, village, pastoral village	Big village, big town	Harbour-town, small hamlet, seaside village	Stronghold
Food	Millet, mountain rice	Millet	Rice	Fish	

Directly, the table does not tell us very much about trade, or about the basis of statehood. It is based on an idealised and theoretical description of ancient South India as expressed in its poetry and interpreted in early medieval commentaries. However, it does systematise some aspects of the Tamil kingdoms that could help us understand their political and commercial layout. The table shows how the regions had access to different resources. Exchange between the ecological zones appears to have been an everyday occurrence. Fish, salt, pearls and imported goods from the coast, rice from the river valleys, spices, wood and gems from the mountain and forest tracts entered into a regional system of exchange.

The South Indian three-kingdom structure remained remarkably stable for centuries,[669] even through frequent periods of warfare.[670] The interregional difference between the Chera, Pandya and Chola kingdoms can perhaps contribute to understanding how they all managed to keep their position in the Indian Ocean exchange. The kingdoms each held control of key commodities in the monsoon exchange. The Chera controlled the flow of gems from mines in the Coimbatore district, near their capital of Karur. The

---

[661] *Ahananuru* 149; *Purananuru* 56.
[662] Smith (1914: 439f.) mentions the figure 120.
[663] But see Champakalakshmi (1999: 205), who holds that these polities are better described as chiefdoms. The question of course comes down to which state-definition to apply, cf. ch. 2, pp. 7ff.
[664] Champakalakshmi 1999: 94.
[665] Ray 1995: 98.
[666] Salt: *Narrinai* 4, 187, 183, 254, 331; *Ahananuru* 390; *Perumpanattrupadai* 75-79. Fish: *Narrinai* 331; *Purananuru* 343.
[667] Zvelebil 1973: 85ff.
[668] Zvelebil 1973. Adapted and edited excerpt from his chart 10, p. 100 with translations and commentaries from pp. 96-101. His chart is in turn based on three of the early Tamil commentaries and grammars with probable outer limits to their date between the fourth and the eight century AD (Zvelebil 1973: 85ff.).
[669] According to conservative chronologies such as that of Sastri (1976: 118ff.), names of monarchs are known back to the second century AD, but the three state structure itself is probably older and is reflected in the *Periplus*. The end of the three kingdoms came some time in the period 300 – 600 AD, of which little is known in South India (Sastri 1976: 9f.; Champakalakshmi 1999: 36f.).
[670] Sastri 1976: 134ff.; Champakalakshmi 1999: 98.

Pandya controlled the bulk of the pearl fisheries between Sri Lanka and India. The Chera and Pandya shared control of the areas, which today produce most of the worlds pepper, but what about the Cholas? Through their strategic situation on the east coast they were in a position to control the transit trade in northern and eastern goods that came down the east coast from the mouth of the Ganges, Krishna and Godvari rivers as well as across the Bay of Bengal from Southeast Asia.

The impact of trade

R. Champakalakshmi has studied the process of urbanisation in South India over the very long period from around 300 BC to 1300 AD.[671] Champakalakshmi emphasises the beginning of exchange of subsistence goods between the littoral, riverine and highland regions as an agent of social change, which led to the establishment of settlements as focal points of interregional contacts.[672] As imported prestige goods entered the system, it became interesting to the emerging rulers. Even if agricultural income was clearly important, the kings lacked and continued to lack systems of regular taxation and tribute for agricultural land. In this way income from maritime trade became a potentially important instrument in maintaining and expanding political power.[673] Thus, Champakalakshmi holds forth the emergence of maritime trade as the central agent of socio-political change in early historic South India. The need for prestige goods, which could be employed in redistributive processes made control with coastal regions an important priority to south Indian rulers.[674]

The *Periplus* does not show the same active ruler intervention in trade in the Tamil areas as it did in Arabian and northwest Indian areas, but it does hint in that direction. Other sources, however, arguably underline Champakalakshmi's last point – that the control of coastal areas became an objective for the Tamil kings.

Pliny, his sources being from approximately the same time as the description in the *Periplus*,[675] gives us a picture of changing local conditions on the Malabar Coast in the mid-first century AD. His description is compatible with the account of the *Periplus* in important details, but the two sources diverge in other respects.

> "To the first market of India, Muziris, not desirable because of nearby pirates who occupy a place called Nitrias and also not rich in merchandise. Moreover the anchorage for the ships is far from land, and cargo is fetched and brought by boats. As I published this,[676]
> Caelobothras ruled there. Another, more serviceable port, of the Neacyndon tribe, is called Becare. Pandion ruled there, in a city which is called Modura, far inland from the market. The region, however, from which pepper is brought to Becare by boats made of single logs, is called Cottonara".[677]

Outwardly, the situation is much the same as in the *Periplus*.[678] There are two markets belonging to two different kingdoms. Pliny refers to the tribe Neacyndon rather than to the market Nelkynda, and he names the Pandian market as Becare, whereas the Bakarê of the *Periplus* is a mere anchorage and loading place for ships leaving from or heading to Nelkynda.[679] Still they both refer to the same arrangement for loading and unloading ships by smaller boats, even if Pliny reports that this happened at Muziris and *Periplus* says Nelkynda / Bakarê. The similarities between the texts strengthen the credibility of both sources, while their differences give them independent authority.

The text of Pliny, however, also reflects a change in situation compared to the *Periplus*. The *Periplus* reports two ports of great and seemingly equal importance in the monsoon trade. In Pliny, Muziris is described as a less desirable port of call, pestered by pirates, and with insufficient amounts of goods available for export. The use of force in order to keep the ships of other rulers away is also mentioned in Tamil poetry,[680] and the pirates might have been subjects of local rulers operating to disrupt Chera trade.[681] Their presence shows that the Chera king at this time failed to provide the security needed to participate successfully in maritime trade, and to achieve the control of the coastal region that Champakalakshmi pointed out as a critical political asset for the Tamil kingdoms.[682] That Muziris was "not rich in merchandise" hints at a second problem, namely that the Chera king at the time was not able or willing to mobilise hinterland resources and transport them safely to the coast.

---

[671] Champakalakshmi 1999.
[672] Champakalakshmi 1999: 28.
[673] Champakalakshmi 1999: 29, 97f.
[674] Champakalakshmi 1999: 94.
[675] De Romanis 1997b: 163.
[676] We unfortunately have no clue as to whether the use of the first person imperfect, *proderem*, refers to Pliny himself or is of derivative nature.
[677] Pliny 6.104-105, ...ad primum emporium Indiae Muzirim, non expetendum propter vicinos piratas, qui optinent locum nomine Nitrias, neque est abundans mercibus; praeterea longe a terra abest navium statio, lintribusque adferuntur onera et egeruntur. regnabat ibi, cum proderem haec, Caelobothras. alius utilior portus gentis Neacyndon, qui vocatur Becare; ibi regnabat Pandion, longe ab emporio in mediterraneo distante oppido quod vocatur Modura; regio autem, ex qua piper monoxylis lintribus Becaren convehunt, vocatur Cottonara. An example of a dugout canoe, perhaps of the type here described by Pliny, has been fopund during the excavations of Pattanam (Cherian et. al. 2009).
[678] *Periplus* 54–55.
[679] *Periplus* 55.
[680] *Purananuru* 126.
[681] An example of Tamil rulers resorting to violence is preserved in *Patirruppattu* II, 4-10, commemorating the deeds of Cheran king Netunceral, transl. Zvelebil (1956: 404): "having captured the uncivilised Yavanas of harsh speech, poured oil on (their) heads, tied (their) hands to (their) backs and took (their) precious beautiful vessels and diamonds." Netunceral ruled in the second century AD (Sastri 1976: 118; Zvelebil 1995: 536.
[682] Champakalakshmi 1999: 94.

Roman Coins in Southern India

In the previous chapter, Pliny the elder was cited on the drain of currency from the Roman Empire to India. While the significance and size of this trade deficit remains uncertain, the *Periplus* reports that Roman coins[683] were imported at Adulis,[684] the Far-side Ports,[685] Muza,[686] Kanê,[687] Barbarikôn,[688] Barygaza[689] and Muziris and Nelkynda.[690] In short, coins were imported to all the ports serving as maritime outlets for an established or emerging state, and also to the smaller chiefdoms on the Horn of Africa. Finds of Roman coins in East Africa and Southern Arabia are, however, very scarce. In India the situation is different, but together with the Satavahana realm, the area once controlled by the Chola, Chera and Pandya kings in antiquity stands out, with more than 6000 Roman coins reported from the modern states of Kerala and Tamil Nadu.[691]

Very simply put, but sufficient for the purposes of this study: the number both of finds and of coins from the Tamil kingdoms show a chronological peak with issues of the emperors Augustus to Nero (the Julio-Claudian period),[692] and a geographical concentration to the Coimbatore district, once the heartland of the Chera kingdom, with extensions through the Palghat pass westwards to the Malabar Coast.[693] Numerous attempts have been made to use the fluctuations in the number of coins over time as an archaeological indicator for the structures of and changes in Roman trade with South India.[694] As J.C. Meyer has pointed out, that approach is methodologically dangerous: with the import of coins documented in written sources at a large number of ports around the Indian Ocean, their survival in South India must be due to local conditions rather than changes in the pattern of Roman trade.[695] The absence of Roman coins in other areas and the absence of Roman coins from certain periods in South India thus have no independent significance outside the South Indian context. The question remains, however, whether the coins can tell us much about the issues that interest us in South Indian history?

Table 4: Rule of emperors mentioned in Chapter 7

Augustus	31 BC – 14 AD
Tiberius	14 – 37
Gaius	37 – 41
Claudius	41 – 54
Nero	54 – 68
Vespasian	69 – 79
Domitian	81 – 96
Trajan	98 – 117
Hadrian	117 – 138
Antoninus Pius	138 – 161
Commodus	161 – 192
Caracalla	211 – 217

Most interesting in this context are the finds of first-century AD coins. They constitute the bulk of finds from the are controlled by the Tamil kingdoms, the vast majority of coins in terms of numbers, and were issued (although not necessarily deposited) in approximately the same period as our dateable sources belong to.

In 1989, Paula Turner published her analysis of the finds of *Roman Coins in India*, along with a complete catalogue.[696] Her maps and tables based on this catalogue[697] reveal that of the 43 finds in India containing mainly Julio-Claudian coins, 26 come from the ancient Tamil areas.[698] In addition, three finds of post Julio-Claudian coins have been reported from the Tamil region.[699] Of these 29 finds, 21 come from the area extending from Karur, the ancient Chera capital and through the Palghat Pass,[700] westwards to the Malabar Coast. In other words 21 of the 29 finds in Tamil South India come from within the approximate borders of the Chera Kingdom.

As some of these finds were made as far back as the 18th century, and were described simply as "many" or "hundreds" in the reports Turner based her work upon,[701] it is impossible to break these figures into absolute numbers, but we can divide the finds between hoards – finds consisting of two or more coins, and finds of single coins. The rationale behind such a division is that single coins might have been lost by accident, while hoards are more likely to have been deposited on purpose. This is of course not a categorial rule; single coins could have been

---

[683] For Adulis (6:2.32), Malao (6:3.28) and Barygaza (49:16.23) the term δηνάριον is used. For Muza (24:8.5), and Barbarikôn (39:13.9) , χρῆμα, for Kanê (28:9.17), Muziris and Nelkynda (56:18.18), the plural χρήματα. Only δηνάριον, identifying the Roman coin, can be translated with money with near absolute certainty. The other identifications, however, also seem sound; see notes on the respective ports, n. 242 (Kanê and Muza) and n. 637 (Muziris and Nelkynda).
[684] Periplus 6.
[685] Periplus 8.
[686] Periplus 24.
[687] Periplus 28.
[688] Periplus 39.
[689] Periplus 49.
[690] Periplus 56.
[691] Raschke 1978: 665. Turner (1989) catalogues known finds.
[692] Turner 1989: 123ff.
[693] Turner 1989: 118ff.
[694] Bolin 1958: 65ff.; Raschke 1978: 666f.; Turner 1989: 16ff.; Burnett 1998: 184ff.; Mac Dowall 2004: 9ff.; Mitchiner 2004: 20ff.
[695] Meyer 2007.

[696] Turner 1989.
[697] Turner 1989: 118ff.
[698] The exact borders of the Tamil kingdoms are not known and were probably not clearly defined. I have counted mainland finds south of the Kunda Hills which constitute a natural barrier in the western part of South India, thus excluding finds from modern Karnataka. Further east the distances between finds are greater. Turner's nos. 37 and 42 are the northernmost finds included here.
[699] Turner's 28 and 39. No. 25, Kadmat on the Lakshadweep Islands, has also been included, as these coins must have been on their way to Tamil ports.
[700] The finds excluded being Turner's nos. 25, 28, 34, 37, 39, 42, 61, 66.
[701] Cf. Turner 1989: 123.

deposited e.g. as votive gifts or in connection with burials, but as a description of a tendency it seems reasonable. As almost no finds in Tamil South India were results of archaeological excavations, their context is unknown. Elsewhere in India and Pakistan, Roman coins have been found in Buddhist Stupas,[702] signifying a possible votive function. No such structures are known from the Tamil kingdoms, and the division between coins probably lost by accident and coins probably deposited on purpose thus seems the soundest we can make. The result of such a division is that seven of the 29 finds from the Tamil area were single coins,[703] 22 were hoards, each consisting of anything from 2 to more than 500 coins.[704]

When we study the composition of these hoards, coins issued during the reigns of Augustus and Tiberius are the most numerous. Coins of all emperors up to and including Nero are common.[705] Nevertheless, three hoards included coins of the emperors Vespasian,[706] Domitian,[707] and Trajan respectively.[708] One hoard ends with Hadrian,[709] one with Commodus,[710] and one hoard is even reported to have contained a coin of Caracalla, and possibly several of Antoninus Pius.[711] Three of these hoards containing late coins also included issues of emperors from the whole period from Augustus to Nero, while one included no issues earlier than Claudius and Nero.[712]

All but four of the 22 hoards[713] included issues of more than one emperor. Hoards were of course not deposited before the date of issue of their most recent coin. Even if the issues of late emperors like Trajan, Domitian and Vespasian are insignificant in terms of number, their presence in hoards of the Julio-Claudian emperors show that these hoards were deposited relatively late.

Almost no silver *denarii* post-dating the debasements carried through by Nero have been found in India.[714] Julio-Claudian coins found in India are of a small range of distinct types and not representative of the coinage circulating within the Empire.[715] The older coins in Indian hoards are often much worn, but of high silver purity. This has led to the conclusion that coins were specially selected for export to India,[716] and exported a long time after they were issued, perhaps towards the end of the first century AD in the case of the Julio-Claudian *denarii*.[717]

Together with the hoards ending with coins of late emperors like Commodus and Caracalla, this indicates that the depositing of Roman Coins in Tamil South India took place from the late first century and throughout the second century AD. This means that the coins found in Southern India postdate the report of the *Periplus* that large amounts of money were imported to this area[718] by anything from several decades to more than one and a half century. The finds of Roman coins from Southern India are thus not directly comparable to the description of Southern India in the *Periplus*, and the coins.

How can we explain that the coins imported at the time of the *Periplus* do not show up in the archaeological report, and why is there a relative absence of Roman coins from other areas of Tamil South India than the Chera kingdom? Why have almost all Roman coins been found within the relatively limited area of one kingdom, when the Pandya and Chola kings were just as active in the monsoon trade with the west? The Pandya controlled Nelkynda on the Malabar Coast. The Chola participation might have been indirect, but that Roman coins reached the kingdom is attested by the *Periplus*, here about the ports along the Tamil part of the Indian east-coast:

"There is a market in these places for all the [sc. Western] trade goods imported by Limyrikê, and, generally speaking, there come to them all year round both the cash originating from Egypt and most kinds of all the goods originating from Limyrikê and supplied along this coast".[719]

Very few finds from Southern India have come as results of archaeological excavations. The distribution of finds is thus not due to more extensive archaeological activity in some areas compared to others. In a 1926 study of hoards from the Germanic areas, Sture Bolin pointed out that hoards are in all likelihood the results of war or unrest in the period when the coins were deposited.[720] Hoards indicate that the persons who deposited the coins were never able to retrieve them, or to tell anyone where they were hidden. Stray finds would be explicable from the owners' pure bad luck; a pattern like the one we find in South India, however, needs an explanation. The reason could be that the Chera kingdom experienced frequent violence starting in the late first century AD and

---

[702] Salihundam (Turner 1989: 77). Manikyala (Mac Dowall 1998: 89).
[703] Turner's nos. 6, 17, 39, 42, 45, 58, 60, cf. Turner 1989: 118, 123, 125.
[704] Turner 1989: 123, 125.
[705] 5 hoards end with coins of Nero, 1 with Claudius, 10 with Tiberius, 1 with Augustus, cf. Turner 1989: 123. These numbers include only hoards and only finds from the Tamil areas, cf. note 698, above.
[706] Pudukottai (Turner 1989: 74ff.).
[707] Madurai Hills (Turner 1989: 64f.).
[708] Iyyal, (Turner 1989: 55f.).
[709] Karivalamvandanallur (Turner 1989: 58).
[710] Kadmat (Turner 1989: 57).
[711] Kottayam (Turner 1989: 62f.) The late coins of this find are not securely attested, and to remain on the safe side, they are left out of the discussion, as they will not alter the conclusions drawn from the rest of the material.
[712] Madurai Hills (Turner 1989: 64f.)
[713] Vellalur 1931, Annamalai, Coimbatore 1912, Koneripatty, cf. Turner 1989: 123.
[714] Mac Dowall 1998: 83.
[715] Raschke 1978: 667; Mac Dowall 1998: 83.

[716] Raschke 1978: 669; Burnett 1998: 184; Mac Dowall 1998: 83, 91.
[717] Burnett 1998: 184; Mac Dowall 1998: 89.
[718] *Periplus* 56.
[719] *Periplus* 60, transl. Casson (1989: 89), Προχωρεῖ δὲ εἰς τοὺς τόπους τούτους πάντα τὰ εἰς τὴν Λιμυρικὴν ἐργαζόμενα, καὶ σχεδὸν εἰς αὐτοὺς καταντᾷ τό τε χρῆμα τὸ ἀπ' Αἰγύπτου φερόμενον τῷ παντὶ χρόνῳ κα<ὶ> τὰ πλεῖστα γένη πάντων τῶν ἀπὸ Λιμυρικῆς φερομένων <καὶ> διὰ ταύτης τῆς παραλίας ἐπιχορηγουμένων. The term translated with cash is χρῆμα, cf. note 683, above.
[720] Bolin 1926: 207ff.

continuing into the second century. The large finds of coins still indicate that these conflicts never disrupted trade for longer periods of time. The likely aggressors in such conflicts would be the neighbouring kingdoms of Chola and Pandya. War between the kingdoms is amply reflected in Tamil literature,[721] but the problems of dating connected to the poetic material make the identification of specific poems with the conflicts possibly reflected in the numismatic material difficult.

The Roman numismatic material in South India allows the following tentative conclusions:

The chronological and geographical distribution of coins suggests substantial political unrest in the Chera kingdom in the late first and throughout the second century AD. Trade was, however, not seriously disrupted. A struggle for control of areas important in regional and maritime exchange could have been an instigator of this unrest, but other causes are conceivable.

Roman coins cannot attest fluctuations in the volume of Roman trade with South India,[722] nor can they be used to determine the relative importance of the Chera kingdom in the monsoon trade compared to the other Tamil kingdoms or the relative importance of South India compared to other regions in the monsoon trade.

Roman coins *can*, however, show traces of the political structure of the area where they were found. Coins are found all over the ancient Chera kingdom. The concentration of finds in the Coimbatore region seems to mirror a connection between a political centre inland and the coastal region where the coins were imported.

Local punch-marked coins of copper and silver are attested from the Tamil Kingdoms in the period.[723] Nevertheless, it is possible that Roman coins circulated in the regional system of South India. Roman coins could accommodate the needs of a higher sphere of exchange or redistribution in absence of local gold and silver coinage of comparable high denominations and quality.[724]

The Malabar and Southern India – the picture of government control

In conclusion to this brief survey of the three Tamil kingdoms, each had access to good agricultural regions, coastal areas with suitable harbours and natural resources demanded in the maritime trade. Population centres and political centres were situated in the interior, while maritime exchange was restricted to one port in each kingdom. This reflects the situation found in other regions bordering the Indian Ocean. Access to maritime trade seems to have been a possible motive for struggles between the Tamil kingdoms, reflected both in Tamil poems[725] and by the discrepancies between the descriptions of the Malabar Coast in *Periplus*[726] and by Pliny.[727]

Rulers took steps to mobilise resources for maritime exchange, both through active involvement in production, as the government interest in pearl harvesting in the Pandya and Chola kingdom indicates,[728] and through regional and interregional exchange, as attested in the *Periplus* and in Tamil literature.[729] The three Tamil kingdoms each held control of key commodities in the Indian Ocean exchange. The Chera kingdom had perhaps the best access to gems and pepper. The Pandyans were famous for their pearls, whereas the Cholas could control the flow of commodities from east-coast and Bay of Bengal commerce. Tamil kings seem to have held a key position both in foreign and regional exchange. Rulers levied dues on the movement of trade goods, but also figure as mediators of trade themselves.[730] Imported commodities were employed by Tamil rulers in displays of wealth and power,[731] stressing the political significance of the Indian Ocean exchange to South Indian rulers.

---

[721] Large parts of the *Puram* anthologies, *Purananuru* and *Patirruppattu* and some of the *Pattupattu*, esp. *Porunararrupatai* and *Mullaipattu* are concerned with war and warfare.
[722] Meyer 2007.
[723] See Hall 1999: 433f. on the development of coinage in South India.
[724] Cf. Hall 1999: 434, see Meyer 2007 for a different view.
[725] *Purananuru* 126.
[726] *Periplus* 54-56.
[727] Pliny 6.104-105.
[728] *Periplus* 59.
[729] *Purananuru* 343; *Pattinappalai* 211-222.
[730] *Purananuru* 343; *Pattinappalai* 211-222.
[731] *Purananuru* 56.

Chapter 8: Indian, Parthian and Arabian networks in the *Periplus*

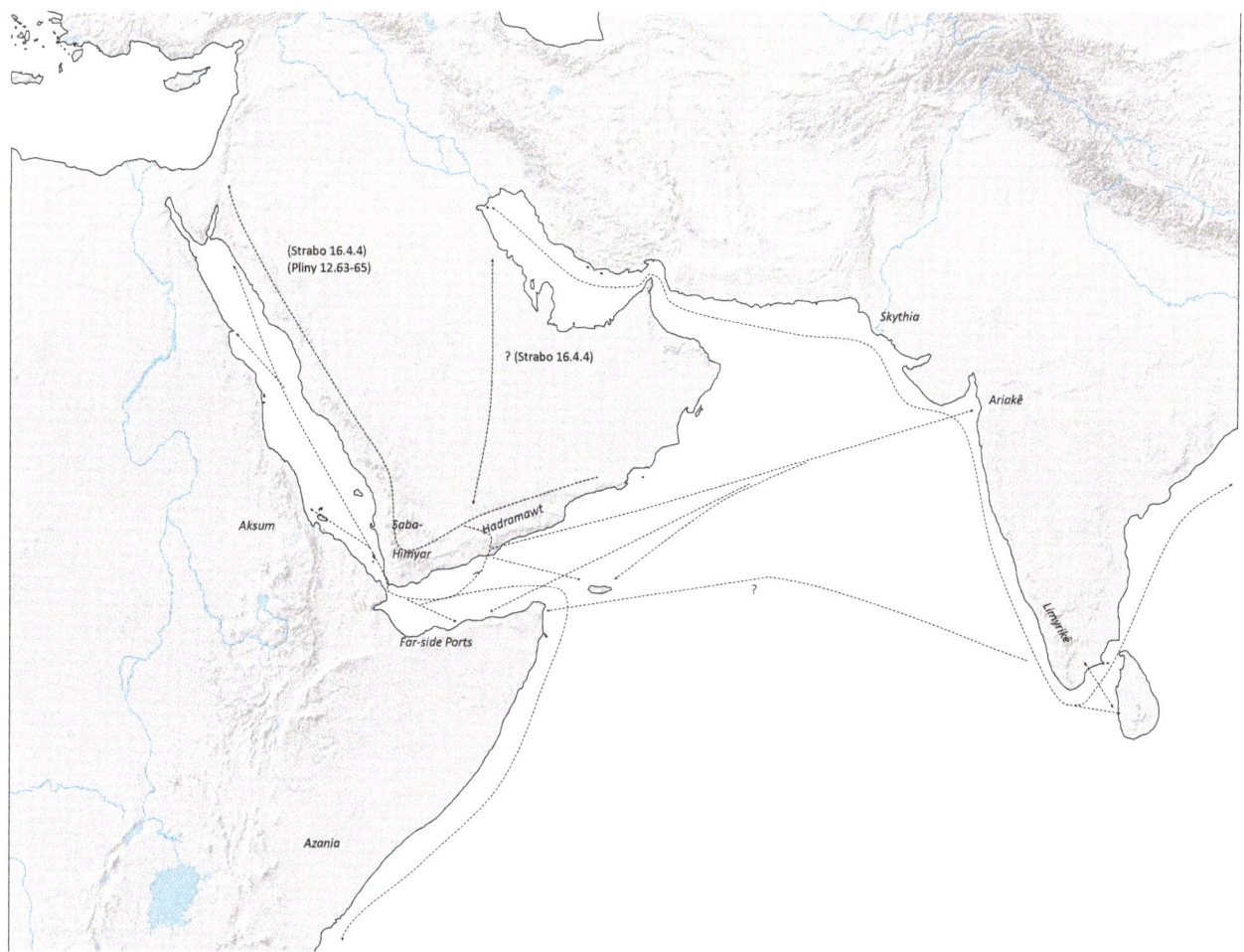

Fig. 6: Map of Indian, Parthian and Arabian trade routes in the Graeco-Roman sources

This study takes the *Periplus of the Erythraean Sea* as its point of departure, not primarily as a source for Roman trade in the Indian Ocean, but rather to approach the relationship between politics and economy in societies on the Indian Ocean rim. The *Periplus*, however, is one text only, written by an author with limited knowledge, personal prejudices and cultural bias. A risk therefore exists, that information derived from the *Periplus* reveals more about that work, its author and the context he wrote in, than about the ports and kingdoms described in the work. While this problem is inherent to any literary source, there are ways to address it. With regard to the *Periplus* and the Indian Ocean, the descriptions of maritime networks other than the one the author of the *Periplus* took part in represent a possible test-case. If these resemble the network of which the author of the *Periplus* had firsthand knowledge, the validity of the finds presented in the previous chapters is strengthened as characteristic of Indian Ocean societies and Indian Ocean trade in general.

"After sailing by the mouth of the gulf, six runs further on you come to another port of trade of Persis called Omana. Customarily the merchants of Barygaza deal with it, sending out big vessels to both of Persis's ports of trade [sc. Apologos and Omana], with supplies of copper, teakwood, and beams, saplings and logs of sissoo and ebony; Omana also takes in frankincense from Kanê and sends out to Arabia its local sewn boats, the kind called *madarte*. Both ports of trade export to Barygaza and Arabia pearls in quantity but inferior to the Indian; purple cloth; native clothing; wine; dates in quantity; gold; slaves".[732]

---

[732] *Periplus* 36, transl. Casson (1989: 73), Παραπλεύσαντι δὲ τοῦτο τὸ στόμα τοῦ κόλπου μετὰ δρόμους ἓξ ἕτερον ἐμπόριόν ἐστιν τῆς Περσίδος, ἡ λεγομένη Ὄμμανα. Ἐξαρτίζεται δὲ εἰς αὐτὴν συνήθως ἀπὸ μὲν Βαρυγάζων εἰς ἀμφότερα ταῦτα τῆς Περσίδος ἐμπόρια πλοῖα μεγάλα χαλκοῦ καὶ ξύλων σαγαλίνων καὶ δοκῶν καὶ κεράτων καὶ φαλάγγων σασαμίνων καὶ ἐβενίνων, εἰς δὲ τὴν Ὄμανα καὶ ἀπὸ Κανὴ λίβανος καὶ ἀπὸ Ὀμάνων εἰς τὴν Ἀραβίαν ἐντόπια ῥαπτὰ πλοιάρια, τὰ λεγόμενα μαδαράτε. Εἰσφέρεται δὲ ἀπὸ ἑκατέρων τῶν ἐμπορίων εἴς τε Βαρυγάζαν καὶ εἰς Ἀραβίαν πινικὸν πολὺ μὲν χεῖρον δὲ τοῦ Ἰνδικοῦ καὶ πορφύρα καὶ ἱματισμὸς ἐντόπιος καὶ οἶνος καὶ φοῖνιξ πολὺς καὶ χρυσὸς καὶ σώματα.

Indian, Parthian and Arabian Networks in the *Periplus*

Table 5: Indian, Arabian and Parthian maritime contacts in in the *Periplus*

From: \ To:	Adulis	Far-side ports	Rhapta	Muza	Kanê	Moscha	Socotra	Omana/Apologos	Barbarikon	Barygaza	Limyrikê	Coromandel
Far-side ports				aromatics, ivory, tortoise-shell, myrrh, cassia, frankincense, slaves, *makeir, duka, kankamon* (7, 8)	myrrh, cassia, frankincense, slaves, *makeir, duka, kankamon* (8)							
Rhapta				ivory, rhinoceros-horn, tortoise-shell, nautilus-shell (17)								
Muza			Spears, axes, knives, awls, glass stones, wine, grain (17)							"Trade" (21), "Arabian wine" (49)		
Kanê						"Some vessels are customarily sent to it from Kanê" (32)		"trade" (27), frankincense (36)	"trade" (27), frankincense (39)			
Moscha					frankincense (27)				Frankincense (32)	Frankincense (32)		
Socotra					tortoise shell, cinnabar (30-31)							
Persis					pearls, textiles, wine, dates, gold, slaves (36)					pearls, textiles, wine, dates, gold, slaves (36)		
Barygaza	iron, steel, textiles, lac dye (6)	grain, rice, ghee, sesame-oil, textiles, sugar (14)			textiles, grain, oil (32)	rice, grain, textiles, slaves (31)		copper, teak, sissoo, ebony (36)			"The voyage as far as Limyrikê…" (51) "Shipping" (54)	"Most vessels continue on to the Strand" (51)
Limyrikê					textiles, grain, oil (32)	rice, grain, textiles, slaves (31)						"vessels sailing from Limyrikê" (60)
Ganges											malabathron, nard, silk (56)	"local boats … to .. the Ganges region" (60)
Chrysê											tortoise shell (56)	"across to Chrysê" (60)

Such is the report in the *Periplus* of the trade of the Parthian ports of Omana and Apologos with Kanê in Hadramawt and Barygaza in Ariakê. We learn of Indian export of hardwood and copper and Arabian export of frankincense, paid for with textiles, pearls, wine, dates, slaves and gold by the Parthians. While the main subject matter in the *Periplus* is the trade between Egypt, Africa, India and Arabia, the unknown author frequently includes information on other trading networks, both in his descriptions of foreign ports of which he seemingly has firsthand knowledge, and in those of which he only knows by hearsay.[733]

Most connections between the ports of Arabia, Africa, India and Parthia have been discussed in the preceding geographical chapters. The information contained in the *Periplus* on these contacts is summarised with references in Table 5. These will necessarily be incomplete. To name but one instance, we have every reason to believe that merchants from Barygaza who apparently traded with Adulis in the Aksumite kingdom would also visit nearby Muza in Saba-Himyar, even though there is no mention of this in the *Periplus*. Similarly, archaeological finds from the Egyptian Red Sea port of Berenikê have opened the possibility that Indian merchants were settled at the port.[734] No mention of this can be found in the *Periplus* or in other Graeco-Roman sources. Only contacts that are explicitly mentioned in the text have been included here. Even considering the incomplete nature of the information, several aspects of this trade stand out:

The *Periplus* reveals three main maritime networks other than that originating in Egypt. An Arabian trade based in the ports of Muza and Kanê, covering the coast of Southern Arabia, the Red Sea, the Horn of Africa and the coast of East Africa, with extensions to the Persian Gulf and the west coast of India. Main exports were Arabian aromatics – myrrh and frankincense. Imports consisted of textiles, raw material and high value / prestige goods like wine and gold. In addition subsistence goods were imported to peripheral regions like Moscha and Socotra.

The next network is the geographically most extensive one attested in the *Periplus*. It originated in the kingdom of Ariakê and included ports across the whole western Indian Ocean from the Red Sea to the Horn of Africa to the Persian Gulf and past Cape Comorin to the east coast of India. The network was centered on the port of Barygaza, where maritime imports, with the exception of dates, are characterised by high value / low weight goods: aromatics, pearls, textiles, wine, gold and slaves. Exports, in contrast, represent the whole range of products in the Indian Ocean trade, from grain, oil and textiles to presumably high value goods like metal, hardwoods and slaves.

Ports of call for ships from the Tamil kingdoms of Southern India included peripheral regions under Arab control like Moscha and Socotra. Direct contacts with the primary ports of Hadramawt and Saba-Himyar seem likely, as does a trade in cinnamon between Southern India and the Far-side Ports, but none of these contacts are actually mentioned in the *Periplus* or in other sources. Furthermore, Tamil ships played a pivotal role as a link between the western Indian Ocean and the Bay of Bengal where direct contacts existed along the Indian east coast and across the Ocean to the Malay Peninsula.

A Parthian, network is implied in the *Periplus*, with connections from ports near the mouth of Euphrates and the Strait of Hormuz to Hadramawt and and Ariakê. The Persian Gulf trade constituted an important artery in the ancient east-west exchange, with overland connections from Parthia to Roman Syria via Vologesias, Hatra, Dura, Palmyra, Zeugma and Antioch. In the *Periplus*, the maritime leg of this route seems to be mostly on Indian carriers. Two second-century inscriptions from Palmyra, however, commemorate the successful return of merchants going to Skythia from the Gulf port of Spasinou Charax presumably on Palmyrene or Characene ships.[735] Sasanian glass is attested from a number of sites in East Arabia, and in one find from Yemen,[736] and Partho-Sasanian glazed ware has been found at Khor Rori, Qana and Adulis.[737] The sixth century *Christian Topography* of Cosmas contains references to Mesopotamian ecclesiastic ties to Socotra, Southern India and Sri Lanka and a lively Sasanian trade with the latter.[738]

The general pattern of the Indian, Arabian and Parthian networks resembles the trade originating in Egypt closely: ships went abroad carrying a range of goods adapted to local demand in their ports of call, in order to secure return cargoes, typically of one or a few key products for which there was a demand at home. Arguably, this stresses a general supply focus in the Indian Ocean trade. Besides profit, or rather in order to achieve profit, the main motive for going abroad seems to have been to secure certain foreign prestige goods for consumption at home. Accordingly, the export side of the trade was more flexible than the import side. Regions with far-flung maritime networks amil South India (Limyrikê), exported a mixture of subsistence goods, metals, tools, textiles, transit goods and prestige products in order to secure natural produce such as aromatics, tortoise shell and ivory from abroad. This echoes the continuing emphasis in the *Periplus* on which goods from Egypt that could be sold in different ports: a varied range of exports were exchanged for one or a few key local or transit goods.

---

[733] Cf. table 1, p. 15.
[734] Begley and Tomber 1999: 180f.
[735] Cantineau (1933: 187) and Inv. X. 96.
[736] Simpson 2007: 69ff.
[737] Simpson 2007: 75.
[738] Cosmas 3.65, 11.15-17.

Chapter 9: Separate societies, similar structures

In the preceding chapters, the polities of Aksum, Saba-Himyar, Hadramawt, Skythia, Ariakê, Chera, Pandya and Chola were discussed against the backdrop of the research strategy outlined in Chapter 2, but each region was treated separately, and, with some exceptions, the discussion was defined by the narrative of the *Periplus*. In this chapter the polities are compared according to the variables outlined in the research strategy: their spatial organisation, the strategies and attitudes of their rulers towards trade, key imports and exports in the monsoon trade and the potential role of trading diasporas. Similarities and differences are underlined with the hope of establishing the role of trade in the development of the states in question.

Spatial organisation

Aksum

Most maritime trade in the kingdom of Zoskalês in modern Ethiopia and Eritrea appears to have taken place from the port of Adulis, where the label *emporion nomimon*,[739] "legally limited port of trade", seems to signify some kind of legal protection over or regulation of trade or traders. Via the city, *polis*, of Koloê, overland trade routes led inland[740] where the capital, *mêtropolis*, of Aksum was situated in good agricultural areas[741] and at the junction of trade routes.[742] Aksum's main export, ivory, was available throughout the kingdom, although only rarely on the dry coastal plain.[743] The capital seems to have held some kind of coordinating role in the ivory trade.[744] The spatial-economic structure of Aksum as described in the *Periplus* can be expressed through Fig. 7, where A represents the political centre, B represents secondary centres, C, major outlets of maritime trade and D represents secondary coastal sites. The existence of more secondary inland centres seems likely and could perhaps be attested archaeologically, e.g. if archaeological sites such as Metara and Qohaito in the Eritrean highlands are contemporary with the description of the kingdom contained in the *Periplus*.

Aksum was a state in its initial stage of development. Neither dry farming nor larger scale irrigation was possible along most of the littoral. This limited major population concentrations to the highland regions of the kingdom. Otherwise, Aksum does not seem to have been geographically or ecologically seriously constrained by other polities or geographical features like deserts, mountains, rivers or lack of arable land in the first century, but its import of weapons and reports of raids on the port of Adulis indicate that the state was under military pressure and that its coastal presence had to be maintained by force.

Fig. 7: Aksum: spatial-economic organisation

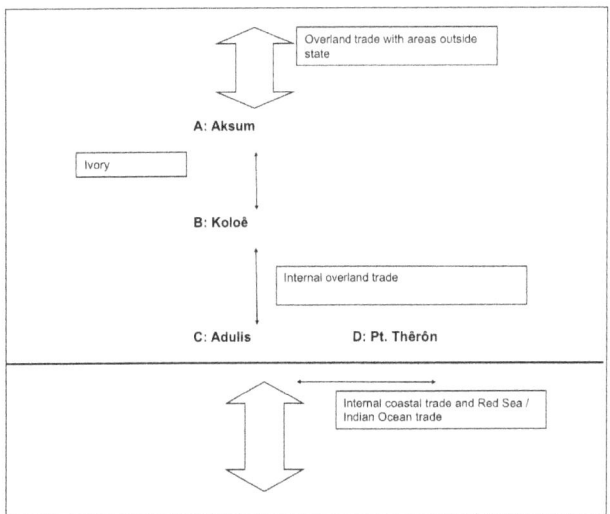

Saba-Himyar

The South Arabian kingdom of Saba-Himyar controlled three ports – Muza, Okêlis and Eudaimon Arabia. All long-distance maritime exchange with India, Egypt and the East African coast was conducted through Muza,[745] but Okêlis also had some maritime contacts across the Red Sea to the African side.[746] Eudaimôn Arabia had been an important port of trade in the past,[747] but was of no commercial significance at the time of the *Periplus*. The *Periplus* reports two inland political centres, the *polis* of Sauê and the *mêtropolis* of Saphar, the former being subordinate to the latter.[748] Himyar would later become an independent kingdom with their capital at Zafar, but it seems that they were still subordinate to the Sabaean capital of Marib at this time.[749] The key export from the kingdom of Saba-Himyar, myrrh, grew in the inland areas,[750] where centres of population were also situated, and could also be acquired through overland trade with Qatabanian areas to the east. As was the case with Aksum, the possibilities for agriculture near the coast were severely limited in Southern Arabia. Political centres and larger settlements were situated in inland areas separated from the coast by mountain ranges, here a combination of dry farming in the highlands and

---

[739] *Periplus* 4:1.20.
[740] *Periplus* 5.
[741] Butzer 1981: 474ff., 491f.
[742] *Periplus* 4.
[743] *Periplus* 4.
[744] *Periplus* 4.

[745] *Periplus* 21, 24.
[746] *Periplus* 25.
[747] *Periplus* 26.
[748] *Periplus* 22-23.
[749] De Maigret 2002: 236.
[750] Van Beek 1958: 143f.

irrigation on the desert fringe constituted a strong agricultural basis.[751] Unlike Aksum, the territory of Saba-Himyar was strictly confined by neighbouring states, deserts, mountains and limited access to agricultural land. Through Muza, Saba-Himyar had established an overseas presence on the East African coast,[752] apparently for the purpose of trade.

Hadramawt

The second South Arabian state with a coastal presence in the mid first century AD was Hadramawt. Its spatial organisation has many similarities to Saba-Himyar. The *mêtropolis* Shabwa,[753] was situated in inland areas where irrigation farming was possible,[754] and was separated from the coast and from other states by mountains and regions of arid desert. Hadramawt maintained three coastal settlements. The *emporion* of Kanê[755] was seemingly founded with the intention of participating in maritime trade[756] and for communication with coastal and overseas possessions. Syagros and Moscha Limên in the Dhofar region[757] were probably administrative and military strongholds maintained to control frankincense production. The island of Dioscuridês (Socotra) was also under Hadrami control and under the administration of a group of merchants.[758] Hadramawt had a stronger coastal presence than the other first century Indian Ocean states depicted in the *Periplus*. This seems to have been maintained only through considerable administrative effort and should be interpreted in light of the need to control the key Hadrami resource in the interregional exchange, frankincense, which has its main habitats in the Dhofar region and on Socotra,[759] far away from the Hadrami core population areas and accessible to outsiders approaching from the sea.

Skythia

Skythia, the Indo-Parthian kingdom on the Indus Plain, is only sketchily described in the *Periplus*. At the mouth of the Indus, the *emporion* of Barbarikon received the visiting ships, but cargoes were conveyed upstream for the king at the inland *mêtropolis* of Minnagar.[760] The Indian ports were not dominated by one key export to the same extent as Adulis and the Arabian ports. Most of the exports from the region had arrived from the other direction, down the Indus from Northern India, modern Afghanistan and over the passes to central Asia and eventually China.[761]

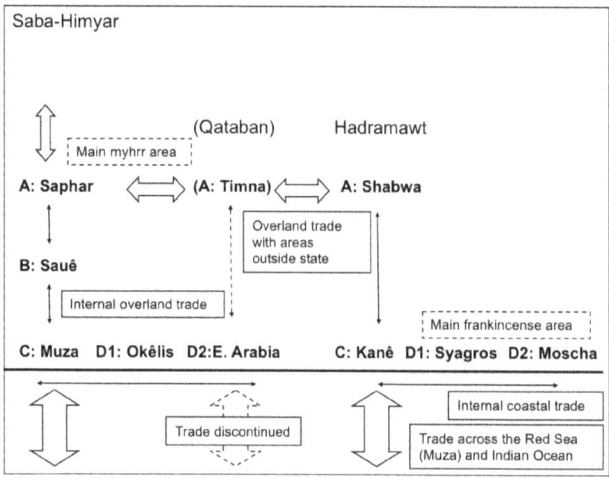

Fig. 8: Southern Arabia: spatial-economic organisation

Economically, the Skythian capital served as a mediator between overland and maritime trade with the king as a key actor, maintaining strict control with maritime exchange.[762] Minnagar was situated on the Indus Plain[763], which was also the agricultural basis of the polity. Neither of the Indian states faced the same challenges as the Arabian with regard to access to agricultural land, because large parts of their territories were well suited for dry farming. To the west, Skythia was separated from Parthia proper by mountain ranges and the arid Makran coast. The wastelands of Kutch and the Thar Desert constituted natural barriers to the east and southeast, while the landscape opened towards the northwest from where overland communication eastwards to the Ganges plain and across the mountains to Central Asia and Iran was possible.

Ariakê

The geographical situation of Ariakê is more complicated. The main port was the *emporion* of Barygaza on the Narmada River,[764] but there were also three other ports, Akabaru, Suppara and Kalliena, of which Kalliena is especially mentioned in the *Periplus* as a previous port of trade, and we learn that ships calling at these ports were brought under guard to Barygaza,[765] from where all maritime exchange was conducted. We also encounter two political centres, the previous royal residence, *basileia*, of Ozênê / Ujjain[766] and the *mêtropolis* of Minnagara,[767] not to be confused with the one in Skythia. Ozênê and Minnagara were probably both situated to the northeast, on the other side of the Vindhya Range and able to draw on agricultural resources from a large hinterland. Behind the mountains of the Western Ghats, the Satavahanas of the Deccan were cut off from

---

[751] Wilkinson 2002.
[752] *Periplus* 16-17.
[753] *Periplus* 27.
[754] Breton 1991: 419.
[755] *Periplus* 27.
[756] Sedov 1992: 125.
[757] *Periplus* 30, 32.
[758] *Periplus* 31.
[759] Van Beek 1958: 142; Groom 1981: 104f.
[760] *Periplus* 38-39.
[761] Cf. *Periplus* 64.

[762] *Periplus* 39.
[763] Cf. Casson 1989: 189.
[764] *Periplus* 49.
[765] *Periplus* 51.
[766] *Periplus* 48.
[767] *Periplus* 4.

their earlier coastal possessions, but were nevertheless carrying on overland trade with Barygaza from the cities of Paithana and Tagara.[768]

As at Barbarikon, many of the exports from Barygaza had arrived from considerable distance. Most of them came through the former royal centre at Ozênê,[769] which probably still had some administrative importance. From there, overland routes led to the Ganges, which offered connections northwards to Central Asia and eastwards to the Bay of Bengal.[770] The Ghats constituted a natural barrier towards the Satavahanas in the south, while the Narmada River facilitated inland transport from the port at Barygaza. In order to reach both the new and the old capital, goods would, however, have to be transported across the mountains of the Vindhya Range.

Fig. 9: Skythia and Ariakê: spatial-economic organisation

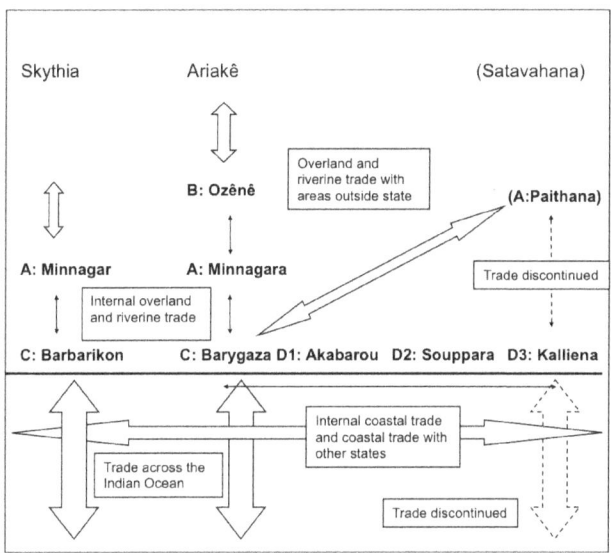

Chera, Pandya, Chola

Southern India constitutes yet a different ecological environment, with a humid coastal plain in the west, the tall mountains of the Southern Ghats rising sharply from the plain and the land then gradually sloping towards the east coast. The capitals of the three Tamil kingdoms, Chera, Pandya and Chola, being Karur, Madurai and Urayur, were situated in rice growing areas in inland river valleys.[771] Products in the maritime exchange were derived partly from the mountains and forests (spices, gems and ivory), from the coast (pearls), partly from the river valleys (textiles) and partly through transit commerce along the east coast of India and across the Bay of Bengal.

---

[768] *Periplus* 51.
[769] *Periplus* 48.
[770] *Periplus* 64.
[771] Champakalakshmi 1999: 26f.

The kingdoms of Southern India were relatively sheltered from their northern neighbours, the Satavahanas, by mountains and forests, but there were few major geographical barriers between the three kingdoms, which frequently waged war against each other. Control of coastal areas secured access to good harbours and important pearl fisheries and was one possible source of unrest.[772]

The Chera and Pandya kingdoms took direct part in the Indian Ocean exchange; and though both controlled a number of coastal sites, they concentrated their long-distance exchange on one port each, the Chera in Muziriz and the Pandya in Bakarê / Nelkynda,[773] both situated on the Malabar Coast with overland routes across the mountain passes to their respective capitals.

The Chola kingdom probably participated only indirectly in the commerce on the western Indian Ocean, but supplied the system with a number of commodities from the Satavahanas, from the Ganges region and from Southeast Asia. Kaveripattinam is attested as a centre of Chola commerce in Tamil literature[774] and must have played a role in the Indian Ocean exchange, but its role compared to other centres, among them the archaeologically attested site of Arikamedu, cannot be established.

Fig. 10: Tamil South India: spatial-economic organisation

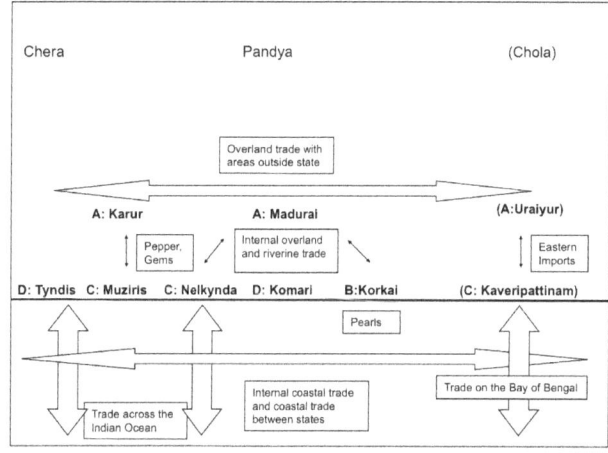

Conclusions: historical geography and infrastructure

To sum up the results relating to the first variable of the research strategy, all states on the Indian Ocean rim had their political centres in good agricultural areas inland. And they all participated in the monsoon exchange. Long-distance maritime commerce was in the main restricted to a single port in each kingdom. In some cases, these ports seem to have been established especially for

---

[772] Champakalakshmi 1999: 94.
[773] *Periplus* 54-56.
[774] *Pattinappalai*.

this purpose. In most cases, the actual commerce seems to have taken place at these ports, except in Skythia, where goods were taken upriver to the capital.

Trade routes and outlets of commerce were subject to change according to political conditions. Geographically convenient coastal outlets for hinterland products such as Eudaimôn Arabia in Saba-Himyar and Kalliena in Ariakê had been closed for trade at the time of the *Periplus*. Most products in the Indian Ocean exchange were inland products or transit goods that would be likely to pass through the political centre on the way to the coast. Important exceptions were the frankincense from Hadramawt and the pearls from Southern India, which were both coastal products. The presence of such important trade goods on the coast appears to have prompted increased administrative presence in these areas.

The economic layout of the Indian Ocean states thus seems to have great similarities. The inland situation of the political centre and other population centres underlines the agricultural nature of the subsistence economy of these states. Trade was not a sufficient economic basis for statehood alone. Still, the universal participation in maritime exchange points towards the activity being of considerable economic importance, as does the maintenance of coastal settlements with the outspoken purpose of trade. Long-distance trade was a way of satisfying material needs, but social and political ones rather than subsistence needs. The scarcity of good harbours and the inland origin of most of the goods traded made the control of the flow of goods through the political centre manageable.

Test case: areas outside state control

Polities along the coast of Africa southeast of modern Eritrea are described as ruled by chiefs (*tyrannoi*) and did not meet the levels of complexity and centralisation present in polities described as ruled by kings (*basileis*). This does not, of course, necessarily imply that they did not participate in maritime exchange, some of them did, but the patterns of trade appears to have been somewhat different. A comparison between the regions seems a relevant way of determining to what extent the presence of centralised polities influenced trade.

Areas outside state control are described as coastal polities only, not subject to, dependent on, or in contact with inland centres, as the kingdoms are. To the degree that centres existed, these were situated on the coast. In certain areas outside state control, mainly modern Somalia, the distribution of ports of trade seems to have been wider than in the states. In contrast to the states, all ports mentioned on this coast were also markets. It seems that the existence of ports of trade here was linked to the local availability of trade goods rather than to the centralisation of resources to certain spots as the case arguably was in state controlled areas. Inland centres that could have directed the flow of hinterland resources to the points of maritime exchange were seemingly lacking. In the case of the Far-side Ports in northern Somalia, little agricultural potential existed for such centres in the hinterland of the ports, except for areas between modern Berbera and Hargeysa,[775] that is, south of the Far-side port of Malaô.

The existence of state power thus seems to have had a considerable effect both on the organisation of trade and on the economic organisation of the areas taking part in maritime trade.

Trade and rulers – strategies and attitudes

While rulers of Indian Ocean kingdoms all took active measures to profit from maritime trade, they did so in different ways and to different extent. Rulers such as Zôskalês of Aksum,[776] the king of Skythia on the Indus[777] and the Chera king controlling the Malabar coast[778] seem to have taken direct interest and acted as mediators between maritime and overland exchange, the Arabian kings and the king of Ariakê are more impersonal in our sources, for we learn of royal officials and agents taking part in, restricting and / or facilitating commerce.[779] The *Periplus* reveals a range of strategies in order to profit from maritime trade. Here they are grouped under the headings "centralisation", "administration" and "expansion". A comparison with areas where societies were not organised as states is less relevant in this case, because the strategies presuppose central planning and capability to act accordingly.

Centralisation

The most obvious strategy of centralisation has already been introduced – confining long-distance, maritime exchange to one port in each kingdom. This policy, however, was pursued in different ways. In some cases, it could happen by rather harsh means. The city of Eudaimôn Arabia in Saba-Himyar is for instance described in the *Periplus* as a once thriving trading city, which by the mid-first century had been sacked and reduced to a watering station for passing ships.[780] Thus trade was moved to Muza, and the kingdom of Qataban was cut off from its previous coastal outlet. Dioscuridês had earlier been frequented by merchants from Saba-Himyar, Ariakê and Limyrikê (the Malabar coast), but these were now excluded form the island by the merchants who had leased the island from king of Hadramawt,[781] and Kanê had become the main outlet of Hadrami trade. Related methods seem to have been in use in Ariakê, where ships that strayed to ports south of Barygaza were brought there under guard.[782] In Limyrikê, Muziris and Nelkynda are described as the markets,

---

[775] Colonial Office 1952: 127f.; Central Intelligence Agency 2002.
[776] *Periplus* 5.
[777] *Periplus* 39.
[778] *Purananuru* 343.
[779] *Periplus* 32, 44, 52.
[780] *Periplus* 26.
[781] *Periplus* 31.
[782] *Periplus* 52.

Table 6: Terms denoting ports in the Periplus

Kingdom	Port	Label(s)	Reference
Aksum	Ptolemais Thêrôn	*mikron emporion* ("small port of trade")	3:1.12
Aksum (?)	Adulis	*emporion nomimon* ("legally limited port of trade")	4:13.20
Saba-Himyar	Muza	*emporion nomimon* ("legally limited port of trade")	21:7.19
Saba-Himyar	Okêlis	*kômê* ("village") / *hormos kai hydreuma* ("harbour and watering station")	25:8.19; 25:8.20
Saba-Himyar	Eudaimôn Arabia	*kômê* ("village")	26:8.23
Hadramawt	Kanê	*emporion* ("port of trade")	27:9.4
Hadramawt	Syagros	*limên* ("harbour")	30:10.1
Hadramawt	Moscha Limên	*limên* ("harbour") / *hormos apodedeigmenos* ("designated harbour")	32:10.29; 32:10.30
Skythia	Barbarikon	*emporion* ("port of trade")	38:13.2
Ariakê	Kammôni	*kômê* ("village")	43:14.25
Ariakê	Barygaza	*emporion* ("port of trade")	49:16.20
Dachinabadês (Partly under control of Ariakê)	Akabaru, Suppara, Kalliena, Sêmylla, Mandagora, Palaipatmai, Melizeigara, Byzantion, Toparon, Tyrannosboas	*emporia topika* ("local ports of trade")	52:17.52; 53:17.22-24
Limyrikê	Naura	*emporion* ("port of trade") (indirectly reported to be inactive)	53:17.27
Limyrikê / Kêprobotos (Chera)	Tyndis	*kômê* (village) / *emporion* ("port of trade") (indirectly reported to be inactive)	53:17.27; 54:17.29
Limyrikê / Kêprobotos (Chera)	Muziris	*emporion* ("port of trade")	55:18.12
Limyrikê / "Pandion's kingdom" (Pandya)	Nelkynda	*emporion* ("port of trade")	55:18.12
Limyrikê / "Pandion's kingdom" (Pandya)	Bakarê	*kômê* ("village")	55:18.8
Limyrikê / "Pandion's kingdom" (Pandya)	Balita	*hormos* ("harbour") / *kômê* ("village")	58:19.17
Limyrikê / "Pandion's kingdom" (Pandya)	Komar	*limên* ("harbour")	58:19.18
Limyrikê / "Pandion's kingdom" (Pandya)	Kolchoi[783]	*polis* ("city")	58:19.15

"which are now the active ones",[784] indicating that the others mentioned in the same paragraph, Nayra and Tyndis, were not active at the time.

To some extent, the centralisation seems to have been institutionalised. The author of the *Periplus* employed a number of terms to refer to the ports he described. The ports serving as maritime outlets and other ports in the same kingdoms are labelled as described in table 6.

While the *Periplus* is not consistent in its description of ports, the work acknowledges a division of work between settlements. All the maritime outlets of states are called *emporion* / "port of trade", two of them with the additional label *nomimon* / "regulated", indicating that the arrangement was institutionalised. Other ports called *emporion* have additional labels of "small" or "local", indicating that they were of secondary commercial importance, while in all kingdoms except Ariakê and Aksum, only the main ports qualify as *emporia* at all, other coastal sites being "villages" or "harbours" or "cities".

The centralisation of long-distance maritime exchange at certain ports does not indicate that no trade took place in other harbours. Indeed, regional coastal trade, the numerous references to "local" and "small" ports of trade and the cases of Moscha and Okêlis, where limited trade with India and Africa is mentioned, shows the opposite. Still, the weight of the evidence indicates that these ports were of limited importance in the monsoon exchange except as centres for the collection of resources.

---

[783] Kolchoi bears no such label in the translations. The passage ἐν ᾗ καὶ κολύμβησίς ἐστιν ὑπὸ τὸν βασιλέα Πανδίονα πινικοῦ καὶ πόλις ἡ λεγομένη Κόλχοι, (a region called the Seaboard) "under king Pandion, where diving for pearls goes on, and a city called Kolchoi" (*Periplus* 58:19.15-16) has been left out by all translators after Müller (1855: 299b) because it occurs outside its geographical context and closely resembles 59:19.22-23: ἐν ᾗ κολύμβησις τοῦ πινικοῦ ἐστίν (...) ὑπὸ τὸν βασιλέα Πανδίονά ἐστιν, (a region) "Where diving for pearls go on (...) under king Pandion." The first passage, however, provides an important piece of information that is not contained in section 59 and is lost by those following Müller here, namely that Kolchoi had the size or status of a *polis*.

[784] *Periplus* 53: "αἱ νῦν πράσσουσαι".

This leads to a second aspect of centralisation: the concentration of commodities for export through or under control of the political centre, for use in the monsoon trade. The *mêtropolis* of Aksum is described as a collection centre for ivory from the African interior.[785] The kings of Saba-Himyar had the opportunity to control the flow of myrrh, because it was mainly an inland commodity and all export was conducted from one harbour. The kings of Hadramawt made considerable efforts to concentrate all frankincense harvested at Kanê through the establishment of collection centres in the main frankincense producing areas.[786] In Skythia and Ariakê the political centres were conveniently situated between the areas from which most commodities originated and the commercial outlets on the coast. The same was true in the Tamil kingdoms except for the pearls and for transit goods brought from the east through coastal exchange.

Administration

Such coastal products led to the second strategy used by rulers in order to profit from trade. As all the Indian Ocean states had extensive, but sparsely populated coastlines, coastal-, maritime- and transit products must have constituted special problems for the rulers in terms of controlling production and trade. This seems to have been solved by increased administrative and military presence.

The island of Socotra with its abundance of frankincense was, for instance, placed under guard.[787] The Hadrami government not only established outposts for the gathering of frankincense on the Dhofar Coast,[788] far away from the central areas of the kingdom; if we can trust the *Periplus* on this point, the actual work was carried out by slaves and convicts.[789] Correspondingly, on the Indian side, pearls in the Pandian kingdom were gathered by condemned criminals.[790]

Trade was also subject to administrative control. At Moscha in Hadramawt, we learn that the little trade that did take place passed through the hands of government agents.[791] In Aksum it seems that king Zôskalês, who is described as "tight with his possessions and always striving for more"[792] took a rather personal interest in trade, while in Skythia, trade took place under royal surveillance at the capital.[793]

Administrative means could also be used to facilitate trade. The term *emporion nomimon* – "legally limited port of trade" for Adulis[794] and Muza[795] certainly implies administrative presence and control of trade, even if we do not know in exactly what manner. At Adulis, the government hold on the coastal region seems to have been so weak that trade outside the *emporion nomimon* was impossible,[796] and we can assume that the term signified at the very least a place where the lives and property of visiting traders were protected.

The best examples of rulers providing the infrastructure for trade are, however, from India, where at Barygaza, pilots met the ships approaching from the sea and escorted them to the port.[797] This had the function of providing safety and guidance for visiting ships on a coastline that is described as highly dangerous and with few good navigational aids,[798] but it also made certain that the traders did not call at the wrong ports, so that rulers would not lose income from trade. Although not stated explicitly, it seems that a similar arrangement was to be found at Nelkynda in the Pandian Kingdom, where cargoes bought by visiting merchants had to be brought down by rafts to the ships waiting at the roadstead of Bakarê.[799]

The most manifest and almost universal administrative measure taken by rulers on the Indian Ocean rim was their interest in a number of commodities imported especially for them. Except for the Tamil ports, about which nothing is said, and Barbarikon where *all* goods are reported to be for the king,[800] all lists of exports from Egypt to ports in the Indian Ocean states contain special sections of goods imported for the rulers.[801]

The lists imply that there was no royal monopoly on trade except perhaps at Barbarikon. If there had been royal monopolies on foreign trade, no special lists of imports for the king would have been needed. Goods outside this list must also have been available to other actors.

Rather, the lists point towards a separate sphere of exchange where rulers secured certain key imports. What we see are not monopolies on trade, but on the possession of certain kinds of commodities. The significance of these imports are discussed below, here it suffices to show that rulers went beyond taxing transactions, collecting dues and receiving gifts from traders, but were active participants in the trade, although in most cases almost certainly through their representatives. This was possible because rulers would also be major suppliers of important exports. Except for textiles, which demanded considerable processing, almost all exports from African, Arabian and Indian coasts were natural produce. As we

---

[785] *Periplus* 4.
[786] Cf, ch. 4, pp. 31ff.
[787] *Periplus* 31.
[788] *Periplus* 30, 32.
[789] *Periplus* 29.
[790] *Periplus* 59.
[791] *Periplus* 32.
[792] *Periplus* 5:2.20-21, (Ζωσκάλης), ἀκριβὴς μὲν τοῦ βίου καὶ τοῦ πλείονος ἐξεχόμενος.
[793] *Periplus* 39.

[794] *Periplus* 4:13.20.
[795] *Periplus* 21:7.19.
[796] Cf. ch. 5, pp. 35f.
[797] *Periplus* 44.
[798] *Periplus* 43-46.
[799] *Periplus* 55.
[800] *Periplus* 39.
[801] Adulis: *Periplus* 6; Muza: *Periplus* 24; Kane: *Periplus* 28; Barygaza (as a thing of the past): *Periplus* 49.

have seen, rulers did to some extent seek to control the production of certain of these products, but maintaining monopolies on products that could be harvested or hunted over huge areas must have been difficult and expensive. Through market, harbour and road dues, production on royal estates, taxation and land rent in kind, rulers would, however, potentially end up with far larger volumes of these products than they needed for their own consumption. This would arguably make the king the most important single supplier of important exports, even if private merchants, guilds, religious communities or local noblemen were also involved in the trade.

Expansion

In some cases, the desire to profit from maritime trade seems to have prompted territorial expansion. Of prime importance was access to the coast and control over ports, which might in part explain the struggle for control of coastal areas attested in Aksum,[802] Southern Arabia,[803] Ariakê,[804] and Tamil South India.[805] Arabian states, however, also expanded far beyond their geographical core areas, seemingly in order to control frankincense production and to trade.

Hadramawt established military strongholds and settlements in the Dhofar region, most importantly the colony of Moscha Limên / Khor Rori / Sumhuram in modern Oman.[806] A less direct solution seems to have been chosen at Socotra, which was farmed out to a group of merchants.[807] Saba-Himyar maintained permanent settlements on the coast of East Africa; here the king got his share by farming out rights of taxation to merchants.[808] All these Arabian settlements overseas seem to have been maintained for commercial reasons, either for production, which seems likely at Khor Rori, or for trade as must have been the case in East Africa, with its substantial local population and a diverse trade with the Arabian port of Muza.[809] These settlements all imported foodstuffs,[810] something which makes it unlikely that they were established as a result of population pressure or lack of agricultural land at home, the explanation usually given for similar processes of territorial expansion in the Mediterranean.

To sum up, states and rulers around the Indian Ocean in the first century AD employed a range of strategies in the course of their effort to profit from trade. Some are found in most states, e.g. the direct state participation in trade, others were only used in single states, e.g. the royal monopoly possibly maintained in Skythia and the establishing of colonies to control commodities in Hadramawt. Different situations would call for different solutions. Even in their diversity they show that all rulers were keen to profit from trade and that this desire affected their policy. Above, the strategies are grouped under the headings "centralisation", "administration" and "expansion"; they could all have carried the common heading "control". The kingdoms on the Indian Ocean rim show no fear of or scepticism about trade in our, albeit biased, source material. Quite the opposite, they show an eagerness to take part in maritime trade that alone should be sufficient to establish the importance of trade for these polities. This places them in contrast to the mainstream picture of Greek city states and the Roman Empire, where it has been argued that strong ideological reservations against commercial activities existed within the elites.[811]

Key resources – imports and exports

Why would rulers engage in trade? "Satisfaction of material wants is the key concept", Moses Finley wrote in his seminal *Ancient Economy*, dismissing the notion of state policy being influenced by economic motives in the ancient world.[812] By material wants he meant primarily the supply of food. In contrast to this, our sources indicate that rulers around the Indian Ocean understood such "material wants" to go far beyond what was needed for everyday consumption. The political importance of trade seems to a large extent to have been centred on the supply of certain key products for consumption.[813] Royal imports are clearly identified at most ports, but other imports are also of potential interest. A brief summary of some of these goods shows that different rulers had different ideas about which products were important.

Imports

At Adulis, royal imports included precious-metal tableware and heavy cloaks. Wine and drinking vessels were among other imports that would have been fit for ruler consumption.[814]

At Muza, the king got horses and mules, precious-metal tableware, copperware and expensive textiles. Other

---

[802] Cf. ch. 5, pp. 35f.
[803] Cf. ch. 4, pp. 22f. 31f.
[804] *Periplus* 52.
[805] Champakalakshmi 1999: 94.
[806] Cf. ch. 5, pp. 29ff.
[807] *Periplus* 31.
[808] *Periplus* 16.
[809] *Periplus* 17.
[810] *Periplus* 17, 31, 32.

[811] Polanyi, Arensberg, and Pearson 1957; Finley 1992.
[812] Finley 1992: 160.
[813] Cf. Frankenstein and Rowlands (1978) and Wells (1980), who have argued that control of imported luxuries and especially wine played a pivotal role in the development and maintenance of centralised political structures in early Iron Age central Europe. Dietler (1990) argued that the control and redistribution of imported wine was politically more important than other kinds of luxuries in the political economy of early Iron Age France. These authors all based their conclusions on the distribution of archaeological material and stressed the importance of control of imports from the Mediterranean world (Frankenstein and Rowlands 1978: 76; Wells 1980: 92ff.; Dietler 1990: 387f.) While sufficient archaeological data is lacking for the Indian Ocean Rim, the pattern reflected in the *Periplus*, with a political centre coordinating, restricting and controlling maritime trade, seems structurally to resemble that found in the central European pre-state societies studied in the mentioned works. Cf. also Qviller 2004: chs. 1-7, on the political and social importance of communal drinking in archaic societies.
[814] *Periplus* 6.

imports included money and wine, the latter even though Arabia produced its own wine at the time.[815]

At Kanê, the king wanted silverware, money, horses, statues and good quality clothing. Among Kanê's other imports was also wine.[816]

At Barbarikon, all import was under royal supervision,[817] but this did not necessarily mean that they were all reserved for his consumption; a fair share was probably resold on the local market or re-exported from Skythia by the riverine and overland routes attested by the goods available for export at Barbarikon.[818] Goods of potential special interest to a ruler include glassware, silverware, money, wine and a range of textiles.

At Barygaza the list of royal imports includes silverware, slave musicians and slave girls, fine wine, expensive clothing and choice unguents. Wine is also among the goods on the list of general imports, as is money.[819] At this port the list refers to a situation predating the *Periplus*.

The description of the Tamil ports[820] contains no special list for the king, and unlike other ports, drinking vessels or tableware do not figure among the imports to them. Tamil poems, however, mention golden drinking vessels, gold and wine as imports brought to their kings from the *Yavanas* – "westerners",[821] while wine, money and textiles *are* among the goods included on the list in the *Periplus*, but not especially for the king.

The Roman money imported at most ports was not necessarily in demand for its monetary value, but had an obvious appeal to any ruler wanting to fill his coffers. Coins offered a combination of durability, recyclable quality, high value and low weight that made them attractive objects of accumulation, redistribution or further exchange. Other royal imports fall into two broad categories – goods well suited for the conspicuous consumption connected with court life, and more everyday goods for the needs of the royal household and perhaps the army. Expensive tableware was a near universal import, and is everywhere included on the list for the king rather than among the general imports. Whether this is a result of the king wanting to keep these commodities for himself or of his supreme purchasing power compared to other actors is hard to say. In either case, expensive tableware represented durable high status imports that could easily be employed in royal displays of wealth and splendour and could also be used in re-distributive and reciprocal settings in order to form and strengthen ties to allies, friends and retainers.

Wine was also imported at all ports of trade, but is nowhere mentioned exclusively on the list of goods for the king. Tamil poets lauded their rulers for enjoying imported wine,[822] and the political importance of the commodity is also likely elsewhere. The import of tableware and drinking vessels seems to indicate that communal dining was an important aspect of political life in these states. To eating belonged drinking, and the *symposium*, or drinking party, seems to have been an almost universal institution in patrimonial societies like these, where personal ties and loyalties took precedence over bureaucratic structures.[823]

Textiles are also included in all lists of royal imports, but their price, quality and probably also function differ. Expensive textiles could fill much of the function that drinking vessels did – as shows of splendour and lavish gifts. Plainer varieties could, however, be of equal or greater economic importance to a royal household. Servants, slaves and soldiers needed to be dressed, and textiles in larger quantities could also be employed in trade and gift-exchange with local communities or nearby populations outside the main state structure, e.g. the *Nomades*,[824] *Barbaroi*[825] and *Ichtyophagoi*[826] mentioned in or near African and Arabian states. While slave musicians, slave girls and statues must have been imported for court life and displays of wealth, the horses imported by Arabian kings could serve dual puposes. In Southern Arabia where suitable pastures and agricultural land were scarce resources, horses would serve as excellent tokens of prestige, but also fulfil military functions. Mules were, on the other hand, vital to the infrastructure of a mountainous country, where wheeled and waterborne transport was usually impossible.

Exports

The access to certain imports might have been the prime motivation for rulers to participate in the monsoon exchange. Above, the importance of control over certain key exports was discussed as a prime motivation for ruler policy towards trade and production. Rulers sought to control the export trade by limiting the number of ports where trade took place, and in some cases they seem to have taken direct interest in commodity harvesting and production. In this way a surplus extracted by rulers by means of taxation or production of local products demanded by foreign traders, could be converted into imports of potential political importance. What exports a state could offer was, however, limited by its natural environment, and the diverse ecology of the Indian Ocean rim must itself have furthered maritime exchange.

From Aksum, ivory was probably the main export. Saba-Himyar was the only state exporting myrrh. Hadramawt was known to the Greeks by its dominant export as "The

---

[815] *Periplus* 24.
[816] *Periplus* 28.
[817] *Periplus* 39.
[818] *Periplus* 39 and ch. 6, pp. 50f.
[819] *Periplus* 48 and 49.
[820] *Periplus* 56.
[821] *Purananuru* 56.

[822] *Purananuru* 56.
[823] Dietler 1990: 359ff.; Qviller 2004: esp. 49ff.
[824] *Periplus* 27:9.2.
[825] *Periplus* 2:1.6, 4:2.4.
[826] *Periplus* 2:1.7, 4:2.15, 20:7.7, 27:9.3, 33:11.16.

frankincense-bearing land". These regions yielded products that were highly sought after in the Mediterranean world and in the other states bordering the Indian Ocean, with only limited competition from other areas. Aromatics were also available in the Far-side Ports, but the lack of centralised polities in this region must not only have limited the total commercial output, but also divided it between a number of outlets, making the available volume at each port smaller. Egyptian traders could buy ivory at Rhapta[827] and in Southern India,[828] but Aksum was much closer to the ports of Roman Egypt and the ivory from Rhapta was allegedly of inferior quality to the Aksumite.[829]

For the Indian ports, the picture is slightly different. They not only served as outlets for indigenous products, but also constituted the link between the monsoon network on the western Indian Ocean and routes further eastwards to China and Southeast Asia. Pepper must have been a key export from the ports on the Malabar Coast and pearls from the Pandian kingdom, but here a range of products acquired through coastal and trans-oceanic exchange was also available. The most desirable ports of call in the monsoon trade were in other words those which had something special to offer. This could be a commodity that was hard to come by in other ports or it could be a link to other trading systems.

Test case: areas outside state control

Regions not organised as states also participated in the monsoon exchange. In this context, the Far-side Ports in northern Somalia and the East African coast are the most relevant areas. At Socotra there is no trace of a local elite: all trade appears to have been with the foreign diaspora, while the indigenous population, if there was any, seemingly did not take part. The *Periplus* gives a short list of earlier imports to the island from India and from Muza. It seems to consist of commodities needed by resident foreigners settled there for trade, not agriculture and for a limited time only, rather than by a sustainable local population: rice, grain, cotton cloth and slaves.[830]

The most striking difference between areas under state control and those outside is that the descriptions of ports in the latter regions do not contain lists of special imports for rulers. While this might seem evident, areas not organised as states also had rulers, who could and probably would be interested in revenue from trade. There are at least two possible reasons as to why no such special sphere of exchange can be found at these ports. Firstly, the lack of state organisation implies the lack of an apparatus that could enforce any claims of monopoly on trade or on certain kinds of imports. It would also be impossible to achieve any degree of centralisation of resources through taxation or otherwise, that would enable the local ruler to dominate the supply of exports.

Secondly, the lack of control over larger territorial areas not only allowed a number of ports to participate in the trade, reducing the potential for ruler control and revenue, but this must also have made it more difficult to secure and centralise resources from the hinterland, as inland populations would have a larger choice of where and to whom they would sell their products.

Nevertheless, there were few differences between the articles imported in state and non-state areas. The Far-side Ports also imported drinking vessels, wine, textiles and Roman money.[831] We learn that grain and wine was imported to the ports of East Africa "as an expenditure for the good will of the Barbaroi",[832] providing a hint that imported goods filled a role in the political and social life of these regions.

The concept of key exports was not limited to states. The Far-side Ports on the coast of northern Somalia also offered a commodity that according to the *Periplus* was not only attractive, but also unique to the area, namely cassia,[833] probably acquired through trade with Southern India or Southeast Asia.[834]

The existence of such key exports, which were all of special interest to Mediterranean markets, seems to indicate that outside demand was pivotal in establishing trade. Rulers, however, responded actively to the opportunities offered by this foreign demand.

To sum up, the impetus for rulers to participate in trade seems to have been to acquire imported products which could be employed in the political processes at home, either for conspicuous consumption, forging alliances, further trade or the needs of the royal household or the army. To acquire a number of specific prestige goods from the outside, rulers mobilised whatever resources available to them in order to meet the demands of foreign traders. State organisation was necessary in order to succeed in reserving resources for exclusive ruler use and in order to centralise the necessary amounts of exports to secure the attractive imports. State organisation was not, however, needed to facilitate trade itself, nor to secure the supply of exports for the visiting traders. In other words, participation in trade was both attractive and useful for the Indian Ocean states represented by their rulers. From the trader's point of view, the better security and more certain availability of exports offered at ports in established kingdoms might have been attractive, but it was not necessary: trade was more important to the state than the state to trade.

Trading diasporas

Drawing on the work of Abner Cohen, Philip Curtin pointed to the universal or near universal presence of

---

[827] *Periplus* 17.
[828] *Periplus* 56.
[829] *Periplus* 17.
[830] *Periplus* 31.

[831] *Periplus* 8, 10.
[832] *Periplus* 17:6.17, δαπάνης χάριν εἰς φιλανθρωπίαν τῶν Βαρβάρων.
[833] *Periplus* 8, 9, 10, 12, 13.
[834] Cf. ch. 5, pp. 40ff

trading diaspora – settlements of merchants on foreign ground, as facilitators of foreign trade in the pre-modern world.[835] Such communities could overcome the challenges of security, language, culture, credit and transfer inherent to cross-cultural trade in the ancient period. The patterns of the monsoon wind would mean that traders and sailors would have to reside in their foreign ports of call for several months before they could return home. Some of them would marry abroad; some would settle permanently in order to carry on trade or to work as craftsmen. Survivors from shipwrecks would occasionally stay at the port where their rescuers brought them, and slave trade meant that people ended up far from their places of origin. Throughout history, a common way of organising long-distance commerce has been to have a resident agent, whether a freedman, slave, relative or friend at the foreign port of call to see to it that a cargo was at hand when the ships arrived.[836] In fact we can be fairly certain that all the ports involved in the monsoon trade would have a population with resident elements from most of the other participating regions. While such communities remain hard to trace archaeologically, the *Periplus* and other literary sources give an impression of the distribution and variety of the Indian Ocean diasporas.

At Adulis we learned that there was a market for "a little Roman money for the resident foreigners".[837] The use of Roman money by a group of foreigners settled at the coast of the Aksumite kingdom indicates that they were maintaining an economy parallell from that of their host society, and that they wanted to keep their economic ties to their home culture. That Greek influence was felt at Adulis and that it carried substantial prestige is underlined by the Aksumite king, Zôskalês, being educated in the language.[838]

At Socotra the *Periplus* reports people of Greek, Arab and Indian origin who "sail out there to trade".[839] This population of mixed settlers were the only inhabitants of Socotra known to the author of the *Periplus*. If there was an indigenous population, it seems to have been unable to absorb the visitors, who must have retained their cultural identity, which they apparently still held on to when Cosmas sailed past the island in the sixth century.[840] The foreign presence at Socotra thus qualifies as a true trading settlement abroad, although one which over time turned into a permanent settlement, as the report of Cosmas also indicates.

At Rhapta and on the East African coast, Arab merchants had also settled in order to trade. We learn that they intermarried with the local population and that they spoke the native language. Still they retained their ties with their home port, Muza, and exercised political power over the region in the name of their king.[841]

This is a non-exhaustive list. Other examples include the fourth century map *Tabula Peutingeriana*, placing a *templum Augusti* at Muziris,[842] traces of the resident Indian community might have been found at the Roman Red Sea port of Berenikê,[843] and Roman soldiers are attested to have been stationed at the Farasan Island in the southern Red Sea ca 143–144 AD.[844] Although foreigners must have been settled all around the Indian Ocean, the existence of the strong trading diasporas described by the *Periplus* at Rhapta and Socotra seems to be linked to the absence or weakness of local political power and to the nature of the local economy. In these places foreign traders arguably filled a vacuum by providing a way to carry on trade without a local political infrastructure.

On the evidence of the *Periplus,* the trading diasporas, although universally present, appear not to have had any great influence on how the states and rulers related to maritime trade. Their significance seems to have been critical only in areas outside state control or with weak state control. With regard to the research strategy outlined in Chapter 2,[845] the trading diaspora must thus be seen as insignificant in the development of maritime trade compared to state institutions.

Separate states, similar structures: conclusions

The above comparison between the states on the Indian Ocean rim aimed to assess the importance of trade for state existence and development. The first variable, "spatial organisation", revealed remarkable similarities in the geographical and economic organisation of the Indian Ocean states and significant differences between state and non-state areas that participated in the monsoon trade. The variable proves to be a good indication both of the influence of maritime trade on state organisation and of the importance of state structures for the volume and organisation of trade.

The next variable, "trade and rulers – strategies and attitudes", proved useful to reveal the eagerness of rulers and states to participate in trade and to profit from it. While this was a universal trait, rulers developed a range of strategies adapted to local conditions in order to achieve one overall aim: to secure their share of attractive foreign imports offered by the maritime network by offering a surplus of attractive local commodities in return.

The third variable, "key resources", sheds light on the motives of rulers for participating in maritime exchange.

---

[835] Curtin 1996; Cohen 1971.
[836] Dem. 34.8, represents perhaps the most famous instance from the ancient world.
[837] *Periplus* 6:2.32, δηνάριον ὀλίγον πρὸς τοὺς ἐπιδημοῦντας.
[838] *Periplus* 5.
[839] *Periplus* 30:10.9-10, ...τῶν πρὸς ἐργασίαν ἐκπλεόντων.
[840] Cosmas 3.65.

[841] *Periplus* 16.
[842] *Tab. Peut.* seg. 12.
[843] Sidebotham and Wendrich 1999: 452f.
[844] Phillips, C., F. Villeneuve, and W. Facey. 2004
[845] Pp. 10ff.

Imported commodities served potential purposes of conspicuous consumption, redistribution, accumulation and further exchange. Export commodities were in most cases limited to one or a few key resources, mainly natural produce. The variable reveals an overall picture of the Indian Ocean network as a system where states imported a range of manufactured and semi-manufactured goods, many of them in the prestige sphere, and selected carefully in order to meet local demand; while exports, with the important exception of textiles, consisted mainly of local raw produce and transit goods demanded by the visiting merchants.

The significance of a fourth variable, the "trading diaspora", was also considered; but while the presence of foreign merchants must have been a universal feature in ports participating in the monsoon exchange, the political and economic significance of foreign diasporas seems to have been limited to areas outside state control.

Together, these variables seem to lend firm support to the assumption that trade was of significant importance for the development and existence of the Indian Ocean states. One critical problem, however, remains before final conclusions can be drawn. Several of the Indian Ocean states were already firmly established by the time of the *Periplus*, and the firsthand knowledge of the author of the *Periplus* is limited to the Roman segment of the Indian Ocean trade. Are the conclusions drawn from that source valid outside the empirical and chronological setting provided by the source itself? This will be addressed in the last chapter.

Chapter 10: Complex societies and maritime trade in the *Periplus*

The comparison between eight Indian Ocean kingdoms in the previous chapter aimed to show how maritime trade was significant for the Indian Ocean states of the mid-first century AD. While the discussion was based primarily on the interaction of these societies with the trade originating in Roman Egypt, it was argued in chapter 8, that the different long-distance networks in the region resembled each other closely.

Although the *Periplus* sketches the situation in the first century AD. the co-existence and structural resemblance of parallel networks highlight the potential of the monsoon trade as an agent of change over time. At the time of the *Periplus,* the significance of maritime exchange in processes of societal change seems perhaps best reflected in the African and Arabian cases.

In modern Ethiopia / Eritrea, the Aksumite kingdom emerges in this very period. When it does, it structurally resembles the other Indian Ocean polities in the *Periplus* in economic matters, with an inland centre co-ordinating the supply of export commodities and restricting trade to one coastal market.[846] This strengthens the notion that control with maritime commerce was a significant factor in the formation of the first complex society in this region in centuries.

In Southern Arabia, the period ca 50 BC–50 AD was marked by several changes to established commercial and political patterns. The overland routes through the Hejaz appear to have lost importance to maritime trade on the Red Sea.[847] At the same time, polities with coastal access, Hadramawt and Himyar, gained importance at the expense of the inland states of Saba and Qataban. Hadramawt invested heavily in control with its main commodity – frankincense. This was achieved by excluding others from trade with Socotra and investing in a commercial harbour at Kanê and the fortified colony of Moscha / Khor Rori in the prime frankincense producing region of Dhofar.[848]

In Southern India, the Chera, Pandya and Chola kingdoms developed parallel with the monsoon trade. Prestige products acquired by way of maritime trade seem to have played an instrumental role in the stratification of societies where rulers lacked stable systems of taxation or tribute from agricultural land.[849] Control with coastal settlements which provided access to the maritime network thus became an important asset in the competition between South Indian rulers[850] that lead to the establishment of the three-state structure of early historic South India.

The northwestern polities of Skythia and Ariakê took active part in the monsoon trade and particularly Ariakê had already developed extensive maritime contacts by the time of the *Periplus*. By that time, the states of Skythia and Ariakê resembled the other Indian Ocean states in the way they related to maritime trade, and the development of Skythia and Ariakê might well have been closely linked to maritime trade with Arabia, Africa, Southern India and Persia as well as to overland connections with Central Asia, the Deccan and the Ganges Plain. Again, control with long distance commerce seems to have been considered an important asset for rulers wishing to attain and retain political power.

In his *Maritime Trade and Early State Development in Southeast Asia* (1985), Kenneth Hall concluded that maritime trade had been instrumental in the formation of the first Southeast Asian states. Drawing on the work of Bennett Bronson,[851] he divided these states into two categories: island states with river systems flowing from interior highlands to the coast, where the areas of denser population was to be found, and mainland states centred on extremely fertile river plains.[852] Economically, the former was dominated by a combined political and commercial centre on the mouth of a river, which pulled secondary and third-rank centres upriver into a riverine exchange system by coercive means.[853] The rice-plain states on the other hand were characterised by a hierarchy of markets, connecting local village clusters via intermediate centres with the port, royal centre or capital at the top level.[854]

The kingdoms described in the *Periplus* were different from the states of Southeast Asia studied by Bronson and Hall: importantly, the western Indian Ocean has few major rivers, restricted opportunities for agriculture near the coast and one large island only with climate and soil suitable for agriculture – Sri Lanka. Outside the area of South India and Sri Lanka, staple crops were wheat and millet, rather than the rice cultivated in Southeast Asia. Hall's models would not stand a transfer to the setting of the *Periplus*, neither were they intended to. Nevertheless, they offer a valuable contrast to the states of Africa, Arabia, western and southern India.

In Chapter 2 (p. 8), the notion of applying the terminology of the *Periplus* itself in order to draw a line between states and other societies was introduced. The author of the *Periplus* uses a fairly consistent set of terms

---

[846] Cf. ch. 5, pp. 38f.
[847] Cf. ch. 4, pp. 18f.
[848] Seland 2005a: 272ff.; ch. 4, pp. 29f.
[849] Champakalakshmi 1999: 29, 97f.
[850] Champakalakshmi 1999: 94.

[851] Bronson 1978.
[852] Hall 1985: 3f.
[853] Hall 1985: 13ff.
[854] Hall 1985: 15ff.

not only to denote port sites (cf. table 6, p. 75), but also other population centres in the areas he describes. These not only reveal hierarchies of centres within the different regions, but also facilitate comparison between societies. As significant similarities between the polities existed with regard to most variables outlined in the research strategy, the source that describes them all should also be the best point of departure for a more analytical description of the typical Indian Ocean state inspired by Bronson and Hall's model for the early Southeast Asian state..

Places of royal residence are generally called *mêtropoleis* in the *Periplus*, literally "mother-cities" or rather "capitals" in this context. Other important inland centres are called *poleis*, "cities". Coastal settlements serving as centres of trade are invariably called *emporia*, in some cases with an additional epithet like "regulated", *nomimos*, or "lawful", *enthesmos*. Other ports where trade took place also carry the heading *emporion*, but when they occur within areas under state control they carry labels like "local", *topikon* or "small", *mikron*. Coastal settlements from which little or no long-distance exchange took place are simply called villages, *kômai*, and harbours, *hormoi* or *limenes*. The labelling of such centres in the *Periplus* in the polities touched by this survey is summarised in the table below:

The list is not complete, as it does not include areas outside the kingdoms discussed in this study. Furthermore, the *Periplus* describes Indian Ocean societies from a maritime perspective and has no knowledge of minor inland settlements and probably only little knowledge of important inland centres except for the capitals. The hierarchy is also not consistent in all aspects. Kalliena in Ariakê is e.g. called both a "city" and a "local port of trade".[856] An anonymous polis mentioned above the "small port of trade" of Hôraia west of Skythia, probably in Parthian areas, was at least from time to time a seat of royal power without being called a *mêtropolis*.[857] In the kingdoms of Pandya and Chera we only learn that the kings dwelled in the interior.[858] Several polities are described without any intermediate *polis* level between the *mêtropolis* and the coastal settlements.

The *Periplus*, however, is a practical and descriptive handbook, not a treatise on the ancient model state and cannot be expected to be complete or consistent. As long as that is kept in mind, the model provides a useful tool, which allows us to compare the states around the Indian Ocean and to some extent fill in the blank spaces from other sources. For instance, Tamil sources mention Karur and Madurai as the cities of royal residence in the Chera and Pandya realm and they can fill in the blank *mêtropolis* spaces in those states. In Aksum, the two large

Table 7: Terms denoting centres in the *Periplus*

Rank	Term	Aksum	Himyar	Hadramawt	Skythia	Ariakê	Chera	Pandya
A	*mêtropolis*	Aksum	Saphar	Saubatha	Minnagar	Minnagara	(Karur)	(Madurai)
B	*Polis*	Koloê (Qohaito) (Metara)	Sauê			Ozênê Kalliena		Kolchoi
C	*Emporion*	Adulis,	Muza	Kanê	Barbarikon	Barygaza	Muziris	Nelkynda
D	*kômê, hormos, limên, mikron emporion, topikon emporion*	Pt.Theron	Okêlis, Eudaimôn Arabia	Syagros, Moscha		Akabaru, Suppara, Kalliena	Tyndis	Bakarê Balita

The *Periplus* hence draws a picture of a model kingdom with a four-level hierarchy. The king ruled from a capital / *mêtropolis* (A). There were large centres of secondary political importance called cities / *poleis* (B). All maritime trade took place from an appointed port of trade / *emporion* (C) on the coast,[855] but minor coastal settlements and markets also existed (D).

inland settlements of Matara and Qohaito could both represent the Koloê of the *Periplus* and arguably fit into the *polis* slot under Aksum in the chart above.

This hierarchy of centres described in the *Periplus* lays the foundation for a descriptive model of commercial aspects of the first century Indian Ocean state. A model facilitates the comparison with other polities and other periods, it gives a framework for the interpretation of a fragmentary source material and it provides a picture of how polities reacted to the common agent of change represented by the monsoon trade.

---

[855] The term "port of trade" creates a clear cut distinction between the royal outlets of trade in the monsoon network and other coastal settlements found in each state. No acceptance of Karl Polanyi's port of trade model is signified by this. Polanyi believed the typical port of trade to be politically and institutionally semi-independent of the larger polities it served (1963: 30ff.) While the *emporion nomimon* term used for some ports described in the *Periplus* does seem to imply an institutional framework outside the legal structure of the respective states, none of the ports seem to have been independent of the political authority of surrounding states, just the opposite, authorities seem to have taken a keen interest in the affairs of the port cities.

[856] *Periplus* 52.
[857] *Periplus* 37.
[858] *Periplus* 55.

Fig. 11: The Indian Ocean state and the monsoon trade

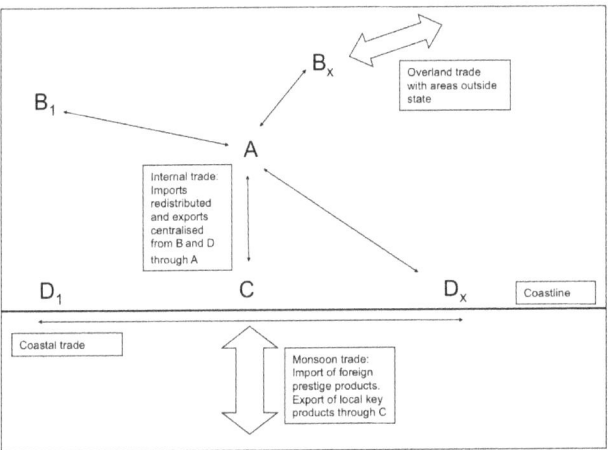

By the mid-first century parallel structures appear to have existed in all the Indian Ocean kingdoms described in the *Periplus*: from an inland centre (A), the political elite controlled the flow of export commodities from peripheral regions with secondary centre(s) (B_x) and (D_x). Typically these export commodities were inland products, either from mountainous or forested regions within the centre's area of political dominance or acquired through overland trade with areas outside the state. In some cases, most prominently frankincense in Hadramawt and pearls in the Pandian kingdom, coastal or marine products constituted important exports. This would prompt a heavier administrative presence on the coast and a more direct involvement in the harvesting of the commodity than with inland commodities, which would have to pass through the political centre on their way to the coast anyway.

Most maritime, long-distance exchange would take place from one and only one *emporion* / port of trade (C) in each state. C also took part in coastal exchange, but had little economic importance apart from its role in the monsoon trade. Except for the presence of drinking water and the existence of a good harbour, C's special position was founded on its supply of trade goods from the interior, an administrative presence from A and the port's offer of security and services to visiting traders. In other words, while D was cut of from direct involvement in the monsoon trade, C's role in the exchange was dependent on the policy of A. The model provides a graphical expression of ruler effort to benefit from trade as well as trade influence on state structure.

The hierarchy reflects variables of rank and function, rather than of size. While it is likely that a capital would be larger than a city and a city larger than a village, the important difference was the former being the seat of the ruler. The port of trade is of greater commercial importance than the harbour or even the local or small market, but the *Periplus* gives us no information as to size. The *polis* is probably larger than the port of trade, but in most cases we know little of the political relation between the two and between each of them and the capital. Rather than an A – B – C – D hierarchy with the former controlling the latter, we have a model with *one* political centre, A, which relates to a number of centres, B, C and D with different functions. The model is flexible as to the number of centres B, D and even A, but cannot accommodate several ports of trade (C) if it is not attestable that they played different roles in the system.

Concluding remarks

The stated purpose of this study is to investigate the relationship between the parallel processes of the developing monsoon trade and the emergence or reorganisation of complex societies on the Indian Ocean rim, using the first century Greek merchant's guide *Periplus Maris Erythraei* as the point of departure.

In Chapter 2 it was argued that in order to understand the economic and thus the political importance of trade in an empirical setting devoid of statistical material, the best option was to study the importance of trade to the representatives of the state – its rulers.

This is an attempt at history on a system or "global" level, showing how mutual interaction and common variables affected the development of separate societies. To some extent any such attempt will remain selective and superficial, as detail is lost in the attempt to sketch the big picture. The importance of maritime exchange to the rulers of each of the states on the Indian Ocean rim is, however, visible through the range of policies they employed in order to profit from trade. Two problems remain, however; firstly which role trade played compared to other social and economic variables like religion, agriculture, irrigation etc., secondly the critical question of whether the importance of trade for the existence of these states as we encounter them in the *Periplus* reports anything about its importance for their formation.

The first of these issues has been addressed indirectly in this chapter and the answer is expressed in the model of the Indian Ocean state introduced above: The main clue to the importance of trade compared to other variables lies in the similar influence trade seems to have had on the spatial organisation of these states, which allows the construction of a model valid for all of them. While the role of trade compared to other factors can never be established beyond doubt, the similar manner in which all the states in the survey organised their productive, commercial and administrative activities in order to participate in the monsoon exchange, points toward trade being among the significant variables influencing the political and economic organisation of the Indian Ocean kingdoms.

The second of these questions cannot be answered satisfactorily within the scope of this work. In areas like Southern Arabia and Northwestern India, statecraft had long traditions before the first century AD. Nevertheless, it seems plausible that the monsoon trade had contributed to the formation of the polities we encounter in the region at that time: in modern Ethiopia / Eritrea, Aksum emerged as the first centralised polity in centuries. The *Periplus* is contemporary with the start of an Aksumite archaeological record, and its description is that of a state and a king already deeply involved in long distance trade. In Arabia, Himyar and Hadramawt with their control of ports, coasts and key trade commodities gradually came to marginalise Saba and Qataban, caravan kingdoms and the dominant powers in the region before the apparent shift from overland towards maritime trade between South Arabia and the Mediterranean. Other factors surely also contributed to their rise to power, but income from maritime trade stands out as an asset Himyar and Hadramawt held in the internal power struggle, which their rivals did not share. In Northwestern India, Sakas and Indo-Parthians established states on the foundation of earlier Hellenistic and Hindu polities. Trade was hardly important for their conquest, but might have contributed to their success at turning the conquest into permanent states. In Southern India, three dynasties emerged among scores to divide the rule of the Tamil country between them. Warfare again played an important role, but control of coastal sites and the establishment of regional exchange systems and long-distance maritime trade seem to have been instrumental in the process. The resemblance between the different commercial networks on the Indian Ocean also also hints at the importance of maritime trade for rulers prior to the first century.

In the end it comes down to the old question of the chicken or the egg, but for once perhaps the question can be answered: trade might have meant nothing without food supply, manpower, religion and tradition to a societies experiencing the increased specialisation and stratification characterising statehood. Still, gold, silver, wine, slaves, weapons, ivory, silk, aromatics and spices were powerful assets in the hands of rulers who knew how to apply them, and this study has tried to demonstrate that only the rulers and societies which knew how to profit from maritime trade succeeded in establishing and maintaining political power along the coasts of the Indian Ocean in the first century AD.

Bibliography

Sources

Acts of Judas Thomas the Apostle, ed. / transl. Klijn, A.F.J. 1962. *The Acts of Thomas: Introduction – text – commentary*. Supplements to Novum Testamentum, vol 5. Leiden: Brill.

Ahananuru, (excerpts), transl. Iyengar, P.T. 1982. *History of the Tamils from the earliest times to 600 A.D.* New Delhi: Asian Educational Services. Original edition 1929.

Arrian, *Indika*, ed. / transl. Brunt, P.A. 1976. *Anabasis Alexandri – Arrian with an English Translation*. Loeb Classical Library, vol. 269. Cambridge Mass. / London: Harvard University Press.

Arthasastra, ed. / transl. Kangle, R.P. 1988. *The Kautiliya Arthasastra*. 2nd ed. Delhi: Motilal Banarsidass. Original edition Bombay 1965.

Cosmas, ed. / transl. Wolska-Conus, W. 1968. *Cosmas Indicopleustes: Topographie Chrétienne*. Sources Chretiennes, vols. 141, 159, 197. Paris: Cerf.

CPG398 = *Codex Palatinus Graecus* 398. Universitätsbibliothek Heidelberg, Handschriftsammlung. Also available from http://digi.ub.uni-heidelberg.de/cpgraec398 (accessed 01.15.2010).

Dem. = Demosthenes, *Orationes*, ed. / transl. Murray, A.T. 1994. *Demosthenes, Orations XXVII–XL*. Loeb Classical Library, vol. 318. Cambridge, Mass. / London: Harvard University Press. Original edition 1936.

Digesta, ed. / transl. Watson, A., and Krueger, P. 1985. *The Digest of Justinian*. Philadelphia: University of Pennsylvania Press.

Dioscorides, ed. Wellmann, M. 1907. *Dioscorides: De materia medica libri quinque*. Berolini (Berlin): Weidmann.

Gawlikowski = Gawlikowski, M. 1994. "Palmyra as a Trading Centre". *Iraq* 56: 27–33. No. 24 originally published in Cantineau, J. 1933. "Tadmorea". *Syria* 14:187.

Inv. = Cantineau, J. 1930–1949. *Inventaire des inscriptions de Palmyre*. Publications de Musee national syrien de Damas. Beyrouth: Musee national.

Isidore, ed. / transl. Schoff, W.H. 1989. *Isidorus, Characenus. Parthian stations : an account of the overland trade route between the Levant and India in the first century B.C.* Chicago: Ares. Original edition London 1914.

Josephus, *bell.* = *De Bello Judaico*, ed. / transl. Thackeray, H.S.J. 1976. *Josephus: The Jewish War, books 1–3*. Loeb Classical Library, vol. 203. Cambridge, Mass. / London: Harvard University Press. Original edition 1927.

Kings in *The Holy Bible: containing the Old and New Testaments*. Cambridge: Cambridge University Press.

KR, ed. / transl. Avanzini, A., ed. 2002. *Khor Rori Report I* Arabia Antica, vol. 1. Pisa: Edizioni Plus.

Maduraikanchi, ed. / transl. Chelliah, J.V. 1962. *Pattupattu: Ten Tamil Idylls*. Tirunleveli / Madras: South India Saiva Siddhanta Works Publishing Society.

Mark (*Gospel of*) in *The Holy Bible: containing the Old and New testaments*. Cambridge: Cambridge University Press.

Mullaipattu, ed. / transl. Chelliah, J.V. 1962. *Pattupattu: Ten Tamil Idylls*. Tirunleveli / Madras: South India Saiva Siddhanta Works Publishing Society.

Narrinai, transl. Subramanian, A.V. 1989. *Narrinai (an Anthology of Amour)*. Thanjavur: Department of Tamil Development-Culture, Government of Tamil-Nadu.

Palladius, ed. / transl. Weerakkody, D.P.M. 1997. *Taprobanê – Ancient Sri Lanka as known to Greeks and Romans*. Turnhout: Brepols.

Patirruppattu (excerpts), transl. Zvelebil, K.V. 1956. "The Yavanas in Old Tamil Literature". Pages 401–409 in *Charisteria Orientalia praecipue ad Persiam pertinentia*, edited by F. Tauer, V. Kubickova, I. Hrbek. Praha: Ceskoslovenska Akademie Ved.

Periplus, ed. / transl. Casson, L. 1989. *The Periplus Maris Erythraei*. Princeton: Princeton University Press.

Also referred to in the following editions when stated:

Fabricius, B. 1883. *Der Periplus des Erythräischen Meeres – von einem Unbekannten – Griechisch und Deutsch mit kritischen und Erklärenden Anmerkungen nebst vollständigem Wörterverzeichnisse*. Leipzig: Von Veit & Comp.

Frisk, H., ed. 1927. "Le Périple de la Mer Érythrée – Suivi d'une étyde sur la tradition et la langue". *Göteborgs Högskolas Årsskrift* 33 (1):1–145.

Huntingford, G.W.B. 1980. *The Periplus of the Erythraean Sea – by an unknown author ; with some extracts from Agatharkides "On the Erythraean Sea"*. Works issued by the Hakluyt Society. Second series, vol 151. London: Hakluyt Society.

Müller, C.C.M. 1855. "Anonymi (Arrian ut fertur) Periplus Maris Eythraei" Pages

257–305 in *Geographi Græci Minores*. Paris: Ambrosio Firmin Didot.

Schoff, W.H. 1995. *The Periplus of the Erythraean Sea – Travel and trade in the Indian Ocean by a merchant of the first century*. Delhi: Munshiram Manoharlal. Original edition Philadelphia 1912.

Vincent, W. 1998. *The commerce and navigation of the ancients in the Indian Ocean*. New Delhi: Asian Educational Services. Original edition 1807.

Pliny, ed. / transl. Rackham, H et al. 1997–2001. *Natural history: in ten volumes / Pliny ; with an English translation by H. Rackham, W.H.S. Jones, D.E. Eichholz*. Loeb Classical Library. Cambridge, Mass. / London: Harvard University Press. Original edition 1938–1963.

Also referred to in the following edition when stated:

    Mayhoff, C. 1906–1909. *C. Plini Secundi Naturalis Historiae, Vol. 1–2*. Lipsiae [Leipzig]: B.G. Teubner.

P. Vindob. G40822, ed. / transl. Thür, G. 1987. "Hypotheken Urkunde eines Seedarlehens für eine Reise nach Muziris und Apographe für die Tetarte in Alexandria (zu P. Vindob. G. 40. 8222)". *Tyche* 2: 229–245.

Pattinappalai, ed. / transl. Chelliah, J.V. 1962. *Pattupattu: Ten Tamil Idylls*. Tirunleveli / Madras: South India Saiva Siddhanta Works Publishing Society.

Polybius, ed. / transl. Paton, W.R. 1922. *Polybius: The Histories*. Cambridge, Mass.: Harvard University Press.

Porunararrupatai, ed. / transl. Chelliah, J.V. 1962. *Pattupattu: Ten Tamil Idylls*. Tirunleveli / Madras: South India Saiva Siddhanta Works Publishing Society.

Ptolemaeus / Ptolemy, ed. Nobbe, C.F.A., 1843–1845. *Claudii Ptolemaei Geographia*. 3 vols. Lipsiae [Leipzig]: Carolus Tauchnitus.

Purananuru, transl. Hart, G.L., and Heifetz, H. 1999. *The four hundred Songs of War and Wisdom*. New York: Colombia University Press.

RES 4337, ed. / transl. Avanzini, A. 2004. *Corpus of South Arabian Inscriptions I–III: Qatabanic, Marginal Qatabanic, Awsanite Inscriptions*. Arabia Antica, vol II. Pisa: Edizioni Plus.

Also referred to in the following edition when stated:

    Beeston, A.F.L. 1959. *The Mercantile Code of Qataban*. Qahtan: Studies in Old South Arabian Epigraphy I. London: Luzac & Co. With addenda from Beeston, A.F.L. 1971. *The Labakh Texts (with Addenda to 'the Mercantile Code of Qataban')*. Qahtan: Studies in Old South Arabian Epigraphy II. London: Luzac & Co.

Res Gestae, ed. / transl. Shipley, F.W. 1924. *Velleius Paterculus, Compendium of Roman History, Res Gestae Divi Augusti*. Loeb Classical Library, vol 152. London: Heinemann.

Silappadikaram, transl. Parthasarathy, R. 1992. *The Cilappatikaram – an epic of South India*. Translations from the Asian Classics. New York: Columbia University Press.

Strabo, ed. / transl. Jones, H.L. 2001. *The Geography of Strabo with an English Translation*. Loeb Classical Library. Cambridge, Mass. / London: Harvard University Press. Original edition 1917–1932.

Suetonius *Aug*. ed. / transl. Rolfe, J.C. 1913. *Suetonius*. Loeb Classical Library, London: Heinemann.

Tab. Peut. = *Tabula Peutingeriana*, Weber, E. 1976. *Tabula Peutingeriana: Codex Vindobonensis 324 : vollständige Faksimile-Ausgabe im Originalformat*. Graz: Akademische Druck- u. Verlagsanstalt.

Zosimus, transl. Veh, O., and S. Rebenich. 1990. *Zosimos: Neue Geschichte*. Bibliothek der Griechischen Literatur, vol. 31. Stuttgart.

Secondary literature

Albright, F.P. 1980. "Sumhurâm". Pages 61–66 in *Mischellanées d'ancient arabe* XI, edited by Jamme, A. Washington DC: Author's edition.

———. 1982. *The American Archaeological Expedition in Dhofar, Oman*. Publications of the American Foundation for the Study of Man (AFSM), vol. VI. Washington DC: AFSM.

Alvares, F. 1961. *The Prester John of the Indies : a true relation of the lands of the Prester John being the narrative of the Portuguese Embassy to Ethiopia in 1520*. Works issued by the Hakluyt Society. Second series, vol. 114–115. Cambridge: The University Press.

Anfray, F. 1974. "Deux villes Axoumites; Adoulis et Matara". Pages 745–766 in *IV Congresso Internationale di Studi Etiopici*, vol. 1. Roma: Accademia Nazionale dei Lincei.

Avanzini, A. 2000. "Excavations and restoration of the complex of Khor Rori, mid's interim report (1999–2000)". *Egitto e Vicino Oriente* 22–23: 189–228.

———, ed. 2002. *Khor Rori Report I*. Arabia Antica, vol. 1. Pisa: Edizioni Plus.

———, ed. 2004. *Corpus of South Arabian Inscriptions I–III: Qatabanic, Marginal Qatabanic, Awsanite Inscriptions*. Arabia Antica, vol. 2. Pisa: Edizioni Plus.

Avanzini, A. and A.V. Sedov. 2005. "The stratigraphy of Sumhuram: new evidence". *Proceedings of the Seminar for Arabian Studies* 35: 11–17.

Avanzini, A., V. Buffa, A. Lombardi, R. Orazi, A.V. Sedov, and V. Castellani. 2001. "Excavations and restoration of the complex of Khor Rori, interim report (october 2000 – april 2001)". *Egitto e Vicino Oriente* 24: 5–63.

Avanzini, A., C. Benvenuti, V. Buffa, A. Lombardi, R. Orazi, and A.V. Sedov. 2002. "Excavations and restoration of the complex of Khor Rori, interim report (october 2001 – april 2002)". *Egitto e Vicino Oriente* 25: 5–50.

Bagrow, L. 1945. "The Origin of Ptolemy's Geographia". *Geografiska Annaler* 27: 318–387.

Bard, K.A., R. Fattovich, A. Manzo, and C. Perlingieri. 1997. "Archaeological Investigations at Bieta Giyorgis (Axum), Ethiopia, 1993–1995 field seasons". *Journal of Field Archaeology* 24 (4): 387–403.

Bauer, W. 1988. *Griechisch-deutsches Wörterbuch zu den Schriften des Neuen Testaments und der frühchristlichen Literatur*. Berlin and New York: Walter De Gruyter.

Beeston, A.F.L. 1959. *The Mercantile Code of Qataban*. Qahtan: Studies in Old South Arabian Epigraphy, vol 1. London: Luzac & Co.

———. 1972. "Kingship in Ancient South Arabia". *Journal of the Economic and Social History of the Orient* 15: 256–258.

———. 1976. "The Settlement at Khor Rori". *Jounal of Oman Studies* 2: 39–42.

———. 1978. "Kataban". Pages 746–748 in Encyclopaedia of Islam, New Edition, vol IV edited by E. van Donzel, B. Lewis and Ch. Pellat. Leiden: Brill.

Begley, V. 1983. "Arikamedu Reconsidered". *American Journal of Archaeology* 80 (2): 461–481.

———. 1988. "Rouletted Ware at Arikamedu: A New Approach". *American Journal of Archaeology* 92 (3): 427–440.

———. 1993. "New Investigations at the Port of Arikamedu". *Journal of Roman Archaeology* 6: 93–108.

Begley, V., and R. Tomber. 1999. "Indian Pottery Sherds". Pages 161–182 in *Berenike 1997. Report of the 1997 Excavations at Berenike and the Survey of the Egyptian Eastern Desert, including Excavations at Shenshef*, edited by S.E. Sidebotham and W.Z. Wendrich. Leiden: Research School CNWS.

Begley, V., and R.D. De Puma, eds. 1991. *Rome and India, the Ancient Sea Trade*. Madison, Wisconsin: University of Wisconsin Press.

Begley, V., P.J. Francis, I. Mahadevan, K.V. Raman, S.E. Sidebotham, K.W. Slane, and E.L. Will. 1996. *The Ancient Port of Arikamedu*. Mémoires Archeologiques, vol. 22. Pondicherry / Paris: École Francaise d'Extrême–Orient.

Bent, T.J. 1895. "Exploration of the Frankincense Country, Southern Arabia". *Geographical Journal* 6 (2): 109–133.

Beyhl, F.E. 1998. "Anmerkungen zum Drachenblut und zu den Namen der Insel Soqotra". *Zeitschrift für die deutsche morgenländische Gesellschaft* 148: 35–82.

Blue, L., J. Cooper, R. Thomas and J. Wainwright, eds. 2009. *Connected Hinterlands: Proceedings of Red Sea Project IV held at the University of Southampton September 2008*. Society of Arabian Studies Monographs no. 8. Oxford: BAR Publishing.

Bolin, S. 1926. *Fynden av romerska mynt i det fria Germanien : studier i romersk och äldre germansk historia*. Lund: C.W. Lindström.

———. 1958. *State and currency in the Roman Empire to 300 A.D*. Stockholm: Almqvist & Wiksell/Geber.

Bopearachchi, O., and W. Pieper. 1998. *Ancient Indian coins*. Indicopleustoi, vol. 2. Tournhout: Brepols.

Botting, D. 1958. *Island of the Dragon's Blood*. London: Hodder and Stoughton.

Boussac, M.-F., and J.-F. Salles, eds. 1995. *Athens, Aden, Arikamedu: Essays on the interrelations between India, Arabia and the Eastern*

Mediterranean. Delhi: Manohar. Reprint of *Topoi*, vol. 3(2), 1993: 387–623.
———, eds. 2005. *A Gateway from the Eastern Mediterranean to India: The Red Sea in Antiquity*. New Delhi: Manohar.
Bowen, R.L. 1958. "Ancient Trade Routes in South Arabia". Pages 31–42 in *Archaeological Discoveries in South Arabia*, edited by R.L. Bowen and F.P. Albright. Baltimore: John Hopkins Press.
Bowersock, G.W. 1971. "A report on Arabia Provincia". *Journal of Roman Studies* 61: 219–242.
Breton, J.-F. 1991. "Conclusion: Shabwa et les Capitales Sud-Arabiques (Ier – IVer Siécle de Notre Ère)". *Syria* 68: 419–431.
Breton, J.-F., and S. Munro-Hay. 2002. "New Himyaritic Coins from Aksum (Ethiopia)". *Arabian Archaeology and Epigraphy* 13: 256–58.
Bronson, B. 1978. "Exchange at the Upstream and Downstream Ends: Notes Toward a Functional Model of the Coastal State in Southeast Asia". Pages 39–52 in *Economic Exchange and Social Interaction in Southeast Asia: Perspectives from Prehistory, History and Ethnography*, edited by K.L. Hutterer. Ann Arbor: University of Michigan, Center for South and Southeast Asian Studies.
Brown, L. 1982. *The Indian Christians of St Thomas: An Account of the Ancient Syrian Church of Malabar*. Cambridge: Cambridge University Press. Original edition 1956.
Burnett, A. 1998. "Roman Coins from India and Sri Lanka". Pages 179–189 in *Origin, Evolution and Circulation of Foreign Coins in the Indian Ocean*, edited by O. Bopearachchi and D.P.M. Weerakkody. New Delhi: Manohar-
Burstein, S.M. 1989. *Agatharchides of Cnidus on the Erythraean Sea*. Works issued by the Hakluyt Society. Second series, vol. 172. London: Hakluyt Society.
Butzer, K.W. 1981. "Rise and Fall of Axum; A geo-archaeological Interpretation". *American Antiquity* 46 (3): 471–495.
Bücher, K. 1979. "Die Entstehung der Volkswirtschaft". In *The Bücher-Meyer Controversy*, edited by M. Finley. New York: Arno Press. Original edition Tübingen 1906.
Cantineau, J. 1933. "Tadmorea". *Syria* 14: 169–202.
Cappers, R.T. 2006. *Roman Foodprints at Berenike: archaeological evidence of subsistence and trade in the Eastern Desert of Egypt*. Los Angeles: Cotsen Institute of Archaeology.
Cartledge, P. 2002. *The Greeks, a Portrait of Self & Others*. Oxford: Oxford University Press. Original edition 1993.
Casal, J.M. 1949. *Fouilles de Virampatnam-Arikamedu*. Paris: Imprimerie Nationale.
Casson, L. 1984a. "Cinnamon and Cassia in the Ancient World". Pages 225–246 in *Ancient Trade and Society*, edited by L. Casson. Detroit: Wayne State University Press.
———. 1984b. "Sakas Versus Andhras in the Periplus Maris Eythraei". Pages 211–224 in *Ancient Trade and Society*, edited by L. Casson. Detroit: Wayne State University Press.
———. 1989. *The Periplus Maris Erythraei*. Princeton: Princeton University Press.
———. 1993. "Ptolemy II and the Hunting of African Elephants". *Transactions of the American Philological Association* 123: 247–260.
Central Intelligence Agency. 2002. *Agricultural land use and natural resources, Somalia Summary Map*. Washington DC: Central Intelligence Agency.
Chakrabarti, D.K. 2001. *India: An Archaeological History – Palaeolithic Beginnings to Early Historic Foundations*. New Delhi: Oxford University Press.
Chami, F.A. 1999. "Roman Beads from the Rufiji Delta, Tanzania: First Incontrovertible Archaeological Link with the Periplus". *Current Anthropology* 40 (2): 237–41.
Champakalakshmi, R. 1999. *Trade, Ideology and Urbanization South India 300 BC to AD 1300*. New Delhi: Oxford University Press. Original edition 1996.
Chelliah, J.V. 1962. *Pattupattu: Ten Tamil Idylls*. Tirunleveli and Madras: South India Saiva Siddhanta Works Publishing Society.
Cherian, P.J., V. Selvakumar and K.P. Shajan. 2007. "The Muziris Heritage Project Excavations at Pattanam – 2007." *Journal of Indian Ocean Archaeology* 4: 1–10.
Cherian, P.J., G.V. Ravi Prashad, K. Dutta, D.K. Ray, V. Selvakumar, K.P. Shajan. 2009. "Chronology of Pattanam: a multi-cultural port site on the Malabar coast". *Current Science* 97 (2): 236–240.
Childe, G. 1950. "The Urban Revolution". *The Town Planning Review* 21: 2–17.
Chittick, N. 1979. "Early Ports in the Horn of Africa". *The International Journal of Nautical Archaeology and Underwater Exploration* 8 (4): 273–277.
Claessen, H.J.M., and P. Skalnik, eds. 1978. *The Early State*. New Babylon: Studies in the Social Sciences, vol. 32. The Hague: Mouton.
Cohen, A. 1971. "Cultural strategies in the organisation of trading diasporas". Pages 266–284 in *The Development of Indigenous Trade and Markets in West Africa*, edited by C. Meillassoux. London: Oxford University Press.
Cohen, R., and E.R. Service, eds. 1978. *Origins of the State*. Philadelphia: Institute for the Study of Human Issues.
Coleman-Norton, P.R. 1926. "The Authorship of the Epistola de Indicis Gentibus et de Bragmanibus". *Classical Philology* 21 (2): 154–160.

Colonial Office. 1952. *An Economic survey of the colonial territories 1951, Volume II, The East African Territories*. London: HMSO.

Comfort, H. 1960. "Some Imported Pottery at Khor Rori". *Bulletin of the American Schools of Oriental Research* 160: 15–20.

Cook, S. 1966. "The Obsolete "Anti-Market" Mentality: A Critique of the Substantive Approach to Economic Anthropology". *American Anthropologist,* New Series 68 (2): 323–345.

Costa, P.M. 2002. "The South Arabian Coast and the Ancient Trade Routes in light of recent exploration and a discussion of the written sources". Pages 19–27 in *Studies on Arabia in Honour of Professor G.Rex Smith*, edited by L. Healy and V. Porter. Oxford: Oxford University Press.

Crowfoot, J.W. 1911. "Some Red Sea Ports in the Anglo-Egyptian Sudan". *The Geographical Journal* 37 (5): 523–550.

Curtin, P.D. 1996. *Cross Cultural Trade in World History*. Cambridge: Cambridge University Press. Original edition 1984.

De Maigret, A. 2002. *Arabia Felix: An Exploration of the Archaeological History of Yemen*. Translated by R. Thompson. London: Stacy International. Original edition Rome 1996.

De Romanis, F. 1996. *Cassia, Cinnamono, Ossidiana*. Roma: Bretschneider.

De Romanis, F. 1997a. "Romanukharattha and Taprobane: Relations between Rome and Sri Lanka in the First Century AD". Pages 161–237 in *Crossings: Early Mediterranean Contacts with India*, edited by F. De Romanis and A. Tchernia. New Delhi: Manohar.

———. 1997b. "Rome and the Nótia of India: Relations between Rome and Southern India from 30 BC to the Flavian Period". Pages 80–160 in *Crossings: Early Mediterranean Contacts with India*, edited by F. De Romanis and A. Tchernia. New Delhi: Manohar.

De Romanis, F., and A. Tchernia, eds. 1997. *Crossings: Early Mediterranean Contacts with India*. New Delhi: Manohar.

Derret, J.D.M. 1962. "The Theban Scholasticus and Malabar in c. 355–60". *Journal of the American Oriental Society* 82 (1): 21–31.

Deshpande, M.N. 1994. "The Archaeological Site of Ter (Tagara)". Pages 175–177 in *Ancient Rome and India: commercial and cultural contacts between the Roman world and India*, edited by R.M. Cimino. Rome / New Delhi: Istituto Italiano per il Medio ed Estremo Oriente / Italian Embassy Cultural Centre.

Detienne, M. 1977. *The gardens of Adonis: spices in Greek mythology. European philosophy and the human sciences*. Hassocks: Harvester Press.

Dietler, M. 1990. "Driven by drink: The Role of Drinking in the Political Economy and the Case of Early Iron Age France". *Journal of Anthropological Archaeology* 9 (4): 352–406.

Dihle, A. 1965. *Umstrittene Daten – Untersuchungen zum Auftreten der Griechen am Roten Meer*. Wissenschaftliche Abhandlungen der Arbeitsgemeinschaft für Forschung des Landes Nordrhein-Westfalen. Köln und Oplanden: Westdeutscher Verlag.

———. 1984. *Antike und Orient – Gesammelte Aufsätze*. Heidelberg: Heidelberger Akademie der Wissenschaften.

Doe, B. 1961. "Husn al-Ghurab and the site of Qana". *Le Museon: revue d'etudes orientales* 74 (1–2): 191–198.

———. 1971. *Southern Arabia*. London: Thames and Hudson.

———. 1996. "The Coastal Population of Socotra". Pages 133–144 in *Society and Trade in South Arabia / R.B. Serjeant*, edited by R.G. Smith. Aldershot: Variorum.

Drake-Brockman, R.E. 1912. *British Somaliland*. London: Hurst & Blackett.

Engels, F. 1970. *Familiens, privateiendommens og statens opprinnelse*. Translated by Holm, H. 2 ed. Oslo: Forlaget Ny Dag. Original edition Hottingen-Zürich 1884: "Der Ursprung der Familie, des Privateigentums und des Staats".

Fabricius, B. 1883. *Der Periplus des Erythräischen Meeres – von einem Unbekannten – Griechisch und Deutsch mit kritischen und Erklärenden Anmerkungen nebst vollständigem Wörterverzeichnisse*. Leipzig: Von Veit & Comp.

Facey, W. 2004. "The Red Sea: the wind regime and location of ports". Pages 7–17 in *Trade and Travel in the Red Sea Region: Proceedings of the Red Sea Project I. Held in the British Museum October 2002*, edited by P. Lunde and A. Porter. Oxford: BAR Publishing.

Fattovich, R. 1997. "Archaeology and Historical Dynamics: the Case of Bieta Giyorgis (Aksum), Ethiopia". *Annali dell'Istituto Universitario Orientale di Napoli* 57 (1–2): 48–79.

———. 2003. *The development of Urbanism in the northern Horn of Africa in ancient and medieval times*. e-text available from http://www.arkeologi.uu.se/afr/projects/BOOK/fattovich.htm (accessed 01.18.2005).

———. 2004. "The 'Pre–Aksumite' State in Northern Ethiopia and Eritrea Reconsidered". Pages 71–77 in *Trade and Travel in the Red Sea Region: Proceedings of the Red Sea Project I. Held in the British Museum October 2002* 1269, edited by P. Lunde and A. Porter. Oxford: BAR Publishing.

Ferguson, J. 1978. "China and Rome". Pages 581–601 in *Aufstieg und Niedergang der Römischen Welt*, vol. II.9.2, edited by H. Temporini and W. Haase. Berlin: Walter de Gruyter.

Finley, M. 1992. *The Ancient Economy*. Reprint of the 2nd ed. London: Penguin Books. Original edition 1985 (Hogarth Press), 1st ed. 1973, Chatto & Windus.

Finneran, N. 2007. *The Archaeology of Ethiopia*. London: Routledge.

Firth, R. 1972. "Methodological Issues in Economic Anthropology". *Man* 7 (3): 467–475.

Flannery, K.V. 1998. "The Ground Plans of Archaic States". Pages 15–58 in *Archaic States*, edited by G.M. Feinman and J. Marcus. Santa Fe: School of American Research Press.

Foreign Office. 1969. *Vol. XVI. British Possessions, II: The Congo – 97. British Somaliland and Sokotra*. Peace Handbooks. New York: Greenwood Press. Original edition London 1920.

Frankenstein, S., and M.J. Rowlands. 1978. "The internal structure and regional context of Early Iron Age Society in south-western Germany". *Bulletin of the Archaeological Institute (University of London)* 15: 73–112.

Frezouls, E. 1984. "Quelques enseignements du Périple de la mer Érythrée". *Ktema* 9: 305–325.

Fried, M.H. 1967. *The Evolution of Political Society*. New York: Random House.

Frisk, H. 1927. "Le Périple de la Mer Érythrée – Suivi d'une étyde sur la tradition et la langue". *Göteborgs Högskolas Årsskrift* 33 (1): 1–145.

Fussman, G. 1991. "Le Periple et l'historie politique del'Inde". *Journal Asiatique* 279 (1991): 31–38.

Gawlikowski, M. 1994. "Palmyra as a Trading Centre". *Iraq* 56: 27–33.

Gerini, G.E. 1974. *Researches on Ptolemy's Geography of Eastern Asia*. 2 ed. New Delhi: Oriental Books Reprint Corporation. Original edition London 1909.

Giangrande, G. 1975. "On the text of the Periplus Maris Erythraei". *Mnemosyne* 28: 293–296.

Gokhale, B.K. 1987. "Bharukaccha / Barygaza". Pages 67–80 in *India and the Ancient World – History, Trade and Culture before 650 AD*, edited by G. Pollet. Leuven: Departement Oriëntalistik.

Groom, N. 1981. *Frankincense and Myrrh – a Study of the Arabian Incense Trade*. London: Longman.

———. 1995. "The Periplus, Pliny and Arabia". *Arabian Archaeology and Epigraphy* 6: 180–195.

Gupta, S. 2002. "The Archaeo–Historical Idea of the Indian Ocean". *Man and Environment* 27 (1): 2–24.

———. 2007. "Chapter 5: Frankincense in the 'Triangular Indo–Arabian–Roman Aromatics Trade". Pages 112–121 in *Food for the Gods: New Light on the Ancient Incense Trade,* edited by D. Peacock, D. Williams and S. James. Oxford: Oxbow.

Gupta, S.P., S. Gupta, T. Garge, R. Pandey, A. Geetali and Sonali Gupta. "On the Fast Track of The Periplus: Excavations at Kamrej–2003". *Journal of Indian Ocean Archaeology* 1: 34–92.

Gurukkal, R., and C.R. Whittaker. 2001. "In Search of Muziris". *Journal of Roman Archaeology* 2001: 334–351.

Hall, K. 1985. *Maritime Trade and State Development in early Southeast Asia*. Honolulu: University of Hawaii Press.

———. 1999. "Coinage, trade and economy in early South India and its Southeast Asian neighbours". *Indian Economic and Social History Review* 36 (4): 432–459.

Hiebert, F. and P. Cambon. 2008 (eds.) *Afghanistan. Hidden Treasures from the National Museum, Kabul*. Washington: National Geographic.

Hopkins, K. 2002. "Rome, Taxes, Rents and Trade". Pages 190–230 in. *The Ancient Economy.* Edited by W. Scheidel and S. Von Reden. Edinburgh: Edinburgh University Press.

Horton, M. 1990. "The Periplus and East Africa". Review of L. Casson, the Periplus of the Erythraean Sea. *Azania* 25: 95–99.

Huntingford, G.W.B. 1980. *The Periplus of the Erythraean Sea – by an unknown author; with some extracts from Agatharkhides "On the Erythraean Sea"*. Works issued by the Hakluyt Society. Second series, vol. 151. London: Hakluyt Society.

Hydrographer of the Navy. 1967. *Red Sea and Gulf of Aden Pilot*. 11th ed. London: Hydrographer of the Navy.

Ingrams, H. 1945. "From Cana to Sabbatha". *Journal of the Royal Asiatic Society*: 169–185.

Iyengar, P.T. 1982. *History of the Tamils from the earliest times to 600 A.D.* New Delhi: Asian Educational Services. Original edition 1929.

Jameson, S. 1968. "Chronology of the Campaigns of Aelius Gallus and C. Petronius". *Journal of Roman Studies* 58 (1–2): 71–84.

Jones, H.L. 2001. *The Geography of Strabo with an English Translation*. Loeb Classical Library. Cambridge, Mass. / London: Harvard University Press. Original edition 1917–1932.

Kangle, R.P. 1988. *The Kautiliya Arthasastra*. 2nd ed. 3 vols. Delhi: Motilal Banarsidass. Original edition Bombay 1972 (1965).

Karttunen, K. 1989. *India in Early Greek Literature*. Helsinki, Finnish Oriental Society.

Kervan, M. 1999. "Multiple Ports at the Mouth of the River Indus: Barbarike, Deb, Daybul, Lahori Bandal, Diul Sinde". Pages 70–153 in *Archaeology of Seafaring*, edited by H.P. Ray. Delhi: Pragati Publications.

Kirwan, L.P. 1972. "The Christian Topography and the Kingdom of Aksum". *Geographical Journal* 138: 166–177.

Kitchen, K.A. 1994. *Documentation for Ancient Arabia. Part I: Chronological Framework & Historical Sources*. Liverpool: Liverpool University Press.

———. 2000. *Documentation for Ancient Arabia. Part II: Bibliographical Catalogue of Texts.* Liverpool: Liverpool University Press.

Kobishchanow, Y.M. 1965. "On the Problem of Sea Voyages of Ancient Africans in the Indian Ocean". *Journal of African History* 6 (2): 137–141.

Kobishchanow, Y.M., and J. Michels. 1979. *Axum*. Translated by Kapitanoff, L. T. London: Pennsylvania State University Press. Original edition Moscow 1968.

Lowie, R.H. 1962. *The Origin of the State*. New York: Russel & Russel. Original edition 1927.

Lidell, H.S., R. Scott H.S. Jones. 1996. *A Greek-English Lexicon*. Oxford: Clarendon Press. Reprint of the 1940 9th edition.

Lunde, P. & Porter, A. eds. 2004. *Trade and Travel in the Red Sea Region. Proceedings of the Red Sea Project I*. Oxford: BAR Publishing.

Mac Dowall, D.W. 1998. "The Evidence of the Gazetteer of Roman Artefacts in India". Pages 78–95 in *Tradition and Archaeology - Early Maritime Contacts in the Indian Ocean*, edited by H.P. Ray and J.-F. Salles. New Delhi: Manohar. Original edition 1996.

———. 2004. "Foreign Coins Found in India in View of the Monetary Systems Operating in the Countries of Their Origin". Pages 9–14 in *Foreign Coins found in the Indian sub-continent*, edited by A. Jha and D.W. Mac Dowall. Nasik: Indian Institute of Research in Numismatic Studies.

Maloney, C. 1975. "Archaeology in South India: Accomplishments and Prospects". Pages 1–40 in *Essays on South India*, vol. 15, edited by B.Stein. Honolulu: University of Hawaii.

Marcus, J., and G.M. Feinman, eds. 1998. *Archaic states*. School of American Research advanced seminar series. Santa Fe, N.M.: School of American Research Press.

Master, D.M. 2001. "State Formation Theory and the Kingdom of Ancient Israel". *Journal of Near Eastern Studies* 60 (2): 117–131.

Mathew, G. 1975. "The Dating and the Significance of the Periplus Maris Erythraei". Pages 147–163 in *East Africa and the Orient: Cultural syntheses in pre-colonial times*, edited by N. Chittick and R. Rotberg. New York / London: Africana Publishing Company.

Mayhoff, C. 1906. *C. Plini Secundi Naturalis Historiae, Vol. 1: Libri I–VI*. Lipsiae (Leipzig): B.G. Teubner.

Mehendale, S. 2008. "Begram: at the Heart of the Silk Roads". Pages 131–143 in *Afghanistan. Hidden Treasures from the National Museum, Kabul*, edited by F. Hiebert and P. Cambon. Washington: National Geographic.

Meyboom, P.G.P. 1995. *The Nile Mosaic of Palestrina*. Leiden: Brill.

Meyer, J.C. 2007. "Roman Coins as a Source for Roman Trading Activities in the Indian Ocean". Pages 59–68 in *Definite Places, Translocal Exchange: The Indian Ocean in the Ancient Period*, edited by E.H. Seland. Oxford: BAR Publishing.

Michels, J.W. 2005. *Changing Settlement Patterns in the Aksum-Yeha Region of Ethiopia: 700 BC – AD 850*. Oxford: BAR Publishing.

Miller, J.I. 1998. *The Spice Trade of the Roman Empire*. Oxford: Oxford University Press. Original edition 1969.

Mitchiner, M. 1976. "Greeks, Sakas and their Contemporaries in Central and Southern India." *Indo-Greek and Indo-Scythian Coinage*, vol. 9. London: Hawkins Publications.

———. 2004. "The Interpretation of Foreign Coins Found in Southernmost India." Pages 15–24 in *Foreign Coins found in the Indian sub-continent*, edited by A. Jha and D.W. Mac Dowall. Nasik: Indian Institute of Research in Numismatic Studies.

Mommsen, T. 1904. *Römische Geschichte – fünfter Band: die Provinzen von Caesar bis Diocletian*. Berlin: Weidmannsche Buchhandlung. Original edition 1885.

Mordtmann, J.H. 1890. "Anzeige, Glaser's Skizze der Geschichte Arabiens". *Zeitschrift für die deutsche morgenländische Gesellschaft* 44: 173–195.

Morrison, H.M. 1989. "The Glass". Pages 188–209 in *Excavations at Aksum: an account of research at the ancient Ethiopian capital directed in 1972–4 by the late Dr Neville Chittick*, edited by S. Munro-Hay and D.W. Phillipson. London: The British Institute in Eastern Africa.

Munro-Hay, S. 1982. "The foreign trade of the Aksumite port of Adulis". *Azania* 27: 107–125.

———. 1991. *Aksum – An African civilisation of late antiquity*. Edinburgh: Edinburgh University Press.

———. 2003. *Coinage of Arabia Felix – The Pre-Islamic Coinage of the Yemen*". Nomismata, vol. 5. Milano: Edizioni Ennerre.

Munro-Hay, S. and D.W. Phillipson eds., 1989. *Excavations at Aksum: an account of research at the ancient Ethiopian capital directed in 1972–4 by the late Dr Neville Chittick*. Memoirs of the British Institute in Eastern Africa, vol. 10. London: The British Institute in Eastern Africa.

Müller, C.C.M. 1855. *Geographi Græci Minores*. 2 vols. Paris: Ambrosio Firmin Didot.

Naval Intelligence Division. 1946. *Western Arabia and the Red Sea*. Geographical Handbook Series B.R. 527. [London]: Naval Intelligence Division.

Naumkin, V.V., and A.V. Sedov. 1995. "Monuments of Socotra". Pages 193–250 in *Athens, Aden, Arikamedu: essays on the interrelations between India, Arabia and the Eastern Mediterranean*, edited by M.-F. Boussac and J.-F. Salles. New Delhi: Manohar. Reprint of *Topoi* 3(2), 1993: 569–623.

Niebuhr, C. 1774. *Reisebeschreibung nach Arabien und andern umliegenden Ländern*. 2 vols. Kopenhagen: Nicolaus Möller.

Olivelle, Patrick, ed. 2006. *Between the empires : society in India 300 BCE to 400 CE*. Oxford: Oxford University Press

Palmer, J.A.B. 1947. "Periplus Maris Erythraei: The Indian Evidence as to the Date". *Classical Quarterly* 41 (3/4): 136–140.

Paribeni, R. 1907. "Richereche nel luogo dell'antica Adulis". *Monumenti Antichi, Reale* 18: 438–572.

Parker, G. 2002. "Ex Oriente Luxuria: Indian Commodities and Roman Experience". *Journal of the Economic and Social History of the Orient* 45 (1): 40–95.

Parker, G. 2004. "Topographies of Taste: Indian Textiles and Mediterranean Contexts." *Ars Orientalis* 34: 19–37.

Parker, G. 2008. *The Making of Roman India*. Cambridg: Cambridge University Press.

Peacock, D., L. Blue, Y. Gebreyesus, and D. Habtemichael. 2004. *The Eritreo-British Project at Adulis, Interim Report 2004*. Asmara and Southampton: Author's Edition.

Peacock, D. and L. Blue, eds. 2006. *Myos Hormos – Quseir al-Qadim. Roman and Islamic Ports on the Red Sea. Volume 1: Survey and Excavations 1999–2003*. Oxford: Oxbow.

Peacock, D., D. Williams, and S. James, eds. 2007. *Food for the Gods: New Light on the Ancient Incense Trade*. Oxford: Oxbow.

Peacock, D., D. Williams and S. James. 2007. "Chapter 3: Basalt as Ships' Ballast and the Roman Incense Trade". Pages 29–70 in *Food for the Gods: New Light on the Ancient Incense Trade*, edited by D. Peacock, D. Williams and S. James. Oxford: Oxbow.

Peacock, D. and L. Blue, eds. 2007. *The Ancient Red Sea Port of Adulis, Eritrea. Report of the Eritro–British Expedition, 2004–2005*. Oxford: Oxbow.

Phillips, C., F. Villeneuve, and W. Facey. 2004. "A Latin inscription from South Arabia". *Proceedings of the Seminar for Arabian Studies* 34: 239–250.

Phillipson, D.W. 1998. *Ancient Ethiopia: Aksum, its antecedents and successors*. London: British Museum Press.

Pirenne, J. 1975. "The inscence port of Moscha (Khor Rori) in Dhofar". *Journal of Oman Studies* 1: 81–96.

Polanyi, K. 1963. "Ports of trade in early societies". *Journal of economic history* 23 (1): 30–45.

Polanyi, K., C.M. Arensberg, and H.W. Pearson, eds. 1957. *Trade and markets in early Empires*. New York: Free Press.

Potter, D. S. 2004. *The Roman Empire at Bay. AD 180–395*. London and New York: Routledge.

Puskas, I. 1987. "Trade Contacts between India and the Ancient World". Pages 141–156 in *India and the Ancient World – History, Trade and Culture before 650 AD*, edited by G. Pollet. Leuven: Departement Oriëntalistik.

Qviller, B. 2004. *Bottles and Battles : the rise and fall of the dionysian mode of cultural production : a study in political anthropology and institutions in Greece and Western Europe*. Oslo: Hermes Publishing.

Rackham, H. ed.. 1997–2001. *Natural history: in ten volumes / Pliny ; with an English translation by H. Rackham, W. H. S. Jones, D. E. Eichholz*. 10 vols. Loeb Classical Library. Cambridge, Mass.: Harvard University Press. Original edition 1938–1963.

Rajan, K. 1996. "Early Maritime Activities of the Tamils". Pages 97–108 in *Tradition and Archaeology – Early Maritime Contacts on the Indian Ocean*, edited by H.P. Ray and J.-F. Salles. New Delhi: Manohar.

Raschke, M.G. 1978. "New Studies in Roman Commerce with the East". Pages 604–1361 in *Aufstieg und Niedergang der Römischen Welt,* vol. II.9.2, edited by H. Temporini and W. Haase. Berlin: Walter De Gruyter.

Raunig, W. 2004. "Adulis To Aksum: charting the course of antiquity's most important trade route in Eastern Africa". Pages 87–91 in *Trade and Travel in the Red Sea Region: Proceedings of the Red Sea Project I. Held in the British Museum October 2002*, edited by P. Lunde and A. Porter. Oxford: BAR Publishing.

Ray, H.P. 1986. *Monastery and Guild: Commerce under the Satavahanas*. Delhi: Oxford University Press.

———. 1987. "Early Historical Urbanization: The Case of the Western Deccan". *World Archaeology* 19 (1): 94–104.

———. 1995. "A Resurvey of Roman Contacts with the East". Pages 97–114 in *Athens, Aden, Arikamedu: Essays on the interrelations between India, Arabia and the Eastern Mediterranean*, edited by M.-F. Boussac and J.-F. Salles. New Dehli: Manohar. Reprint of *Topoi* 3 (2),1993: 479–492.

———. 1998. *The Winds of Change – Buddhism and the Maritime Links of early South Asia*. Delhi: Oxford University Press. Original edition 1994.

———. 2003. *The Archaeology of Seafaring in Ancient South Asia*. Cambridge: Cambridge University Press.

———. 2007. *Colonial Archaeology in South Asia (1944–48): The Legacy of Sir Mortimer Wheeler*. Oxford University Press, New Delhi.

———, ed. 1999. *Archaeology of Seafaring: The Indian Ocean in the Ancient Period*. Delhi: Pragati Publications.

Ray, H.P., and J.-F. Salles, eds. 1998. *Tradition and Archaeology – Early Maritime Contacts in the Indian Ocean*. New Delhi: Manohar. Original edition 1996.

Reade, J., ed. 1996. *The Indian Ocean in antiquity – Papers from a conference held at the British Museum 4.–8. July 1988*. London: Kegan Paul International.

Redmount, C.A. 1995. "The Wadi Tumilat and the "Canal of the Pharaohs"". *Journal of Near Eastern Studies* 54 (2): 127–135.

Renfrew, C. 1986. "Introduction: Peer polity interaction and socio-political change". Pages 1–18 in J. Cherry and C. Renfrew 1986. *Peer polity interaction and socio-political change*. Cambridge: Cambridge University Press.

Retsö, J. 2000. "Where and what was Arabia Felix?". *Proceedings of the Seminar for Arabian Studies* 30: 189–192.

Robin, C. 1984. "La civilisation de l'Arabie meridionale avant l'Islam". Pages 195–224 in *L'Arabie du Sud – Histoire et Civilisation: Tome I – Le peuple yemenite et ses racines*, edited by J. Chelhod, J. Paris: Maisonneuve & Larosse.

———. 1997. "The Date of the Periplus of The Erythraean Sea in Light of South Arabian Evidence". Pages 41–65 in *Crossings: Early Mediterranean Contacts with India*, edited by De Romanis, F. and A. Tchernia. New Delhi: Manohar. Original edition *Journal Asiatique* 279, 1991 (1–2): 1–30.

Rodbertus, K. 1865. "Zur Geschichte der römischen Tributsteuern". Pages 341-427 in *Jahrbücher für Nationalökonomie und Statistik*, vol. IV, edited by B. Hildebrand.

Romm, J.S. 1994. *The Edges of the Earth in Ancient Thought*. Princeton: Princeton University Press. Original edition 1992.

Saller, R. 2002. "Framing the Debate over Growth in the Ancient Economy". Pages 251–279 in *The Ancient Economy*, edited by W. Scheidel and S. Von Reden Edinburgh: Edinburgh University Press.

Salles, J.-F. 1995. "The Periplus of the Erythraean Sea and the Arab-Persian Gulf". Pages 115–146 in *Athens, Aden, Arikamedu. Essays on the interrelations between India, Arabia and the Eastern Mediterranean*. Edited by M.-F. Boussac and J.-F. Salles.New Delhi: Manohar / Centre de Sciences Humaines.

———. 1996. "Achaemenid and Hellenistic Trade in the Indian Ocean". Pages 251–267 in *The Indian Ocean in antiquity – Papers from a conference held at the British Museum 4.–8. July 1988*, edited by J. Reade. London: Kegan Paul International.

Sarma, A. 1978. "The Paleoecology of Coastal Tamilnadu, South India: Chronology of Raised Beaches". *Proceedings of the American Philosophical Society* 122 (6): 411–426.

Sastri, K.A.N. 1976. *A history of South India from prehistoric times to the fall of Vijayanagar*. 4 ed. Madras: Oxford University Press. Original edition 1955.

Schiltz, V. 2008. "Tillya Tepe, the Hill og Gold: a Nomad Necropolis". Pages 219–231 in *Afghanistan. Hidden Treasures from the National Museum, Kabul*, edited by F. Hiebert and P. Cambon. Washington: National Geographic.

Schippmann, K. 2001. *Ancient South Arabia: From the Queen of Sheba to the Advent of Islam*. Translated by A. Brown. Princeton, NJ: Markus Wiener. Original edition Darmstadt 2001: "Geschichte der alt-südarabischen Reiche".

Schoff, W.H. 1920. "Cinnamon, Cassia and Somaliland". *Journal of the American Oriental Society* 40: 260–270.

———. 1995. *The Periplus of the Erythraean Sea – Travel and trade in the Indian Ocean by a merchant of the first century*. Delhi: Munshiram Manoharlal. Original edition Philadelphia 1912.

Scullard, H.H. 1974. *The Elephant in the Greek and Roman World*. London, Thames and Hudson.

Sedov, A.V. 1992. "New Archaeological and Epigraphical Material from Qana". *Arabian Archaeology and Epigraphy* 3: 110–137.

———. 1996. "On the Origin of Agricultural Settlements in Hadramawt". Pages 67–86 in *Arabia Antiqua: Early Origins of South Arabian States*, edited by C.J. Robin and I. Gajda. Roma: Istituto Italiano per il Medio ed Estremo Oriente.

———. 1998. "Qana' (Yemen) and the Indian Ocean: the archaeological evidence". Pages 11–35 in *Tradition and Archaeology – Early Maritime Contacts in the Indian Ocean*, edited by H.P. Ray and J.-F.Salles. New Delhi: Manohar. Original edition 1996.

———. 2007. "The Port of Qana' and the Incense trade" Pages 71–111 in *Food for the Gods: New Light on the Ancient Incense Trade,* edited by D. Peacock, D. Williams and S. James,. Oxford, Oxbow.

Sedov, A.V. and C. Benvenuti. 2002. "The Pottery of Sumhuram: General Typology". Pages 177–248 in *Khor Rori Report I*, edited by A. Avanzini. Pisa: Edizioni Plus.

Selaisse, H.S. 1972. *Ancient and Medieval Ethiopian History*. Addis Ababa: Haile Selaisse I University.

Seland, E.H. 2005a. "Ancient South Arabia: trade and strategies of state control as seen in the Periplus Maris Erythraei". *Proceedings of the Seminar for Arabian Studies* 35: 271–280.

———. 2005b. "The *Periplus'* report of a Roman Attack on Aden – an unintended result of successful propaganda?" *Symbolae Osloenses* 80: 60–67.

———. 2007. "Ports, Ptolemy, Periplus and Poetry – Romans in Tamil South India and on the Bay of Bengal". Pages 69–82 in *Definite Places, Translocal Exchange: The Indian Ocean in the Ancient Period*, edited by E.H. Seland. Oxford: BAR Publishing.

———. 2007, ed. *The Indian Ocean in the Ancient Period: Defintie Places, Translocal Exchange*. Oxford, BAR Publishing.

———. 2008. "The Indian ships at Moscha and the Indo–Arabian trading circuit" *Proceedings of the Seminar for Arabian Studies* 38: 283–288.

Service, E.R. 1975. *Origins of the State and Civilization – The Process of Cultural Evolution*. New York: W.W. Norton & Co.

Shinnie, P.L. 1960. "Socotra". *Antiquity* 34: 100–110.

Shipley, F.W. 1924. *Velleius Paterculus, Compendium of Roman History, Res Gestae Divi Augusti*. Loeb Classical Library, vol. 152. London: Heinemann.

Sidebotham, S.E. 1986. *Roman economic policy in the Erythra Thalassa: 30 B.C.–A.D. 217*. Mnemosyne Supplementum, vol. 91. Leiden: Brill.

Sidebotham, S.E., and W.Z. Wendrich. 1995. *Berenike 1994: Preliminary Report of the 1994 Excavations at Berenike (Egyptian Red Sea Coast) and the Survey of the Eastern Desert*. Leiden: Research School CNWS.

———. 1999. *Berenike 1997: Report of the 1997 excavations at Berenike and the survey of the Egyptian Eastern Desert, including Excavations at Shenshef*. Leiden: Research School CNWS.

———. 2000. *Berenike 1998: Report of the 1998 Excavations at Berenike and the Survey of the Egyptian Eastern Desert, including Excavations in Wadi Kalalat*. Leiden: Research School CNWS.

Simpson, St J. 2007. "From San Marco to South Arabia: Observations on Sasanian Cut Glass. Pages 59–88 in *Facts and Artefacts Art in the Islamic World. Festschrift for Jens Kröger on his 65th Birthday,* edited by A. Hagedorn and A. Shalem. Leiden and Boston: Brill.

Singer, C. 2007. "Chapter 2: The Incense Kingdoms of Yemen: An Outline History of the South Arabian Incense Trade". Pages 4–27 in *Food for the Gods: New Light on the Ancient Incense Trade,* edited by D. Peacock, D. Williams and S. James. Oxford: Oxbow.

Smith, V.A. 1914. *The Early History of India: From 600 B.C. to the Muhammadan Conquest including the invasion of Alexander the Great*. 3 ed. Oxford: Clarendon Press.

Starkey, J., ed. 2005. *People of the Red Sea. Proceedings of the Red Sea Project II*. Society for Arabian Studies Monographs No. 3. Oxford: BAR Publishing.

Starkey, J., P. Starkey & T. Wilkinson, eds. 2007. "Natural Resources and Cultural Connections of the Red Sea. Proceedings of the Red Sea Project III". Society for Arabian Studies Monographs No. 5. Oxford: BAR Publishing.

Tarn, W.W. 1985. *The Greeks in Bactria & India*. Chicago: Ares Publishers. Third edition. Original edition Cambridge 1938.

Tchernia, A. 1997. "Winds and Coins: From the Supposed Discovery of the Monsoon to the Denarii of Tiberius". Pages 256–276 in *Crossings: Early Mediterranean Contacts with India,* edited by F. D. Romanis and A. Tchernia. New Delhi, Manohar.

Tomber, R. 2007. "Rome and Mesopotamia – importers into India in the first milennium AD." *Antiquity* 81: 972–988.

———. 2008. *Indo-Roman Trade, From Pots to Pepper*. London: Duckworth.

Trautmann, T.R. 1971. *Kautilya and the Arthasastra – a statistical investigation of the authorship and evolution of the text*. Leiden: Brill.

Turner, P.J. 1989. *Roman Coins from India*. Special Publications, vol. 22. London: Royal Numismatic Society.

Valle, P. della. 1665. *The travels of Sig. Pietro della Valle, a noble Roman, into East-India and Arabia Deserta*. Whitehall: Will. Morice.

———. 1958. "Frankincense and Myrrh in Ancient South Arabia". *Journal of the American Oriental Society* 78 (3): 141–152.

Vansina, J. 1997. "Slender Evidence, Weighty Consequenses: On One Word in the "Periplus Maris Erythraei"". *History in Africa* 24: 393–397.

Van Beek, G. 1958. "Frankincense and Myrrh in Ancient South Arabia." *Journal of the American Oriental Society* 78(3): 141-152.

Veblen, T. 1957. *The Theory of the Leisure Class*. London: George Allen & Unwin. Original edition 1925.

Vickers, M. 1994. "Nabatea, India, Gaul and Carthage: Reflections on Hellenistic and Roman gold vessels and red-glass pottery". *American Journal of Archaeology* 98 (2): 231–248.

Vincent, W. 1998. *The commerce and navigation of the ancients in the Indian Ocean*. New Delhi: Asian Educational Services. Original edition 1807.

Warmington, E.H. 1995. *The Commerce Between the Roman Empire and India*. Reprint of the 2nd. ed. New Dehli: Munshiram Manoharlal. Original edition London 1928.

Weber, M. 1964. *Wirtschaft und Gesellschaft*. Tübingen: J.C.B. Mohr. Original edition 1922.

———. 1992. "Politik als Beruf". Pages 157–252 in *Max Weber Gesamtausgabe* I / 17, edited by W.J. Mommsen and W. Schluchter. Tübingen: J.C.B. Mohr. Original edition 1919.

———. 2006. "Agrarverhältnisse im Altertum (3. Fassung). Pages 320–747 in *Max Weber Gesamtausgabe* I / 6, edited by J. Deninger. Tübingen: J.C.B. Mohr. Original edition 1908.

Weerakkody, D.P.M. 1997. *Taprobanê – Ancient Sri Lanka as known to Greeks and Romans*. Indicopleustoi, vol. 1. Turnhout: Brepols.

Wellesley, K. 1954. "The fable of a Roman attack on Aden". *La Parola del passanto: rivista di studi antichi* 9: 401–405.

Wells, P.S. 1980. *Culture contact and culture change : Early Iron Age central Europe and the Mediterranean world*. Cambridge: Cambridge University Press.

Wendrich, W.Z., R.S. Tomber, S.E. Sidebotham, J.A. Harrel, R.T.J. Cappers, and R.S. Bagnall. 2003. "Berenike Crossroads: The Integration of Information". *Journal of the Economic and Social History of the Orient* 46 (1): 46–87.

Wenig, S. 2003. "Enno Littmanns Deutsche Aksum Expedition 1906 und die German Archaeological Mission to Eritrea (G.A.M.E.) 90 Jahre später" *Nürnberger Blätter zur Archaelogie* 18: 79–98.

Wheeler, M. 1955. *Rome Beyond the Imperial Frontiers*. 2nd ed. Middlesex: Penguin Books. Original edition 1954.

Wheeler, M., A. Gosh, and K. Deva. 1946. "Arikamedu: An Indo-Roman trading-station on the east coast of India". *Ancient India* 2: 17–38.

Whittaker, C. R. 1998. "'To reach out to India and pursue the dawn': The Roman View of India" *Studies in History* 14 (1): 1–20.

Wilding, R.F. 1989. "The Pottery". Pages 235–316 in *Excavations at Aksum*, edited by S. Munro-Hay and D.W. Phillips. London: The British Institute in Eastern Africa.

Wilkens, B. 2002. "The Consumption of Animal Products at Sumhuram". Pages 271–322 in *Khor Rori Report I*, edited by A. Avanzini. Pisa: Edizioni Plus.

Wilkinson, T.J. 2002. "Agriculture and the Countryside". Pages 102–109 in *Queen of Sheba*, edited by Simpson, St J. London: British Museum Press.

Wissmann, H.v. 1976. "Die Geschichte des Sabäerreiches und der Feldzug des Aelius Gallus". Pages 308–544 in *Aufstieg und Niedergang der Römischen Welt*, vol. II.9.1, edited by H. Temporini, H. and W. Haase. Berlin: Walter de Gruyter.

———. 1977. "Das Weihrauchland Sa'kalan, Samarum und Moscha". *Sitzungsberichte der Österreichische Akademie der Wissenschaften. Hist.–Phil. Klasse*, vol. 324. Wien: Akademie der Wissenschaften.

Wittfogel, K.A. 1959. *Oriental Despotism – a comparative study of total power*. New Haven: Yale University Press. Original edition 1957.

Wright, H.T., and G.A. Johnson. 1975. "Population, Exchange, and Early State Formation in Southwestern Iran". *American Anthropologist*, New Series 77 (2): 267–289.

Young, G.K. 2001. *Rome's Eastern Trade: International commerce and imperial policy, 31 BC – AD 305*. London / New York: Routledge.

Zvelebil, K.V. 1956. "The Yavanas in Old Tamil Literature". Pages 401–409 in *Charisteria Orientalia praecipue ad Persiam pertinentia*, edited by F. Tauer, V. Kubickova and I Hrbek. Praha: Ceskoslovenska Akademie Ved.

———. 1973. *The Smile of Murugan: On Tamil literature of South India*. Leiden: Brill.

———. 1975. *Tamil Literature*. Handbuch der Orientalistik, vol.2 (2). Leiden: Brill

———. 1995. *Lexicon of Tamil Literature*. Handbuch der Orientalistik, vol. 2 (9). Leiden: Brill

www.ingramcontent.com/pod-product-compliance
Lightning Source LLC
Chambersburg PA
CBHW041708290426
44108CB00027B/2893